Ireland on the World Stage

Ireland on the World Stage

Edited by
William Crotty and David E. Schmitt

Routledge
Taylor & Francis Group
LONDON AND NEW YORK

First published 2002 by Pearson Education Limited

2 Park Square, Milton Park, Abingdon, Oxon OX14 4RN
711 Third Avenue, New York, NY 10017, USA

Routledge is an imprint of the Taylor & Francis Group, an informa business

First issued in hardback 2017

ISBN 13: 978-0-582-42357-2 (pbk)
ISBN 13: 978-1-138-45906-9 (hbk)

British Library Cataloguing-in-Publication Data

A catalogue record for this book is available from the British Library

Library of Congress Cataloging-in-Publication Data

A catalog record for this book is available from the Library of Congress

Set in 10/12pt Times by 35

Contents

Contributors

John Bradley, PhD (Trinity College Dublin) is a Research Professor and a Senior Economist at the Economic and Social Research Institute (ESRI) in Dublin. He has published extensively on the economics of the island of Ireland, with a particular focus on North–South interactions. His 1996 report, *An Island Economy: Exploring Long Term Consequences of Peace and Reconciliation in the Island of Ireland*, was prepared for the Forum on Peace and Reconciliation. He has also researched the economic implications of structural funds and the single market within the EU periphery (Greece, Ireland, Portugal, Spain and East Germany). He currently directs an EU ACE-Phare project on the study of the transition of a range of Central and Eastern European Economies to EU membership. He is the author and co-author of a number of articles and reports on international trade, labour markets, the EU and comparative economic development.

William Crotty, PhD (University of North Carolina, Chapel Hill), Thomas P. O'Neill Chair in Public Life, Director of the Center for the Study of Democracy and Professor of Political Science at Northeastern University. Research interests include political representation, political parties, democratisation, electoral change and comparative election procedures and policy. He is the author and editor of a number of books, has served as president of several professional organisations and was the recipient of the Lifetime Achievement Award of the political parties' section of the American Political Science Association and the Hubert H. Humphrey Award of the Policy Studies Association. He is the co-editor and co-author with David Schmitt of *Ireland and the Politics of Change*.

Richard B. Finnegan is Professor and Chair of the Political Science Department and Director of Irish Studies at Stonehill College in Easton, MA. He holds his **BA** from Stonehill College and his **MA** from Boston College. His **PhD** is from Florida State University and he also holds an **EdM** from Harvard University. He has been a Visiting Professor at Boston University and a Visiting Scholar at Harvard University. He is the author of *Ireland: The Challenge of Conflict and Change* (Westview Press, 1983); *Aspirations and Real-ities: A Documentary History of Economic*

Development Policy in Ireland since 1922 (with James L. Wiles; Greenwood Press, 1993); *A Guide to Irish Government Publications: 1972–1992* (with James L. Wiles; Irish Academic Press, 1995); *Ireland: Historical Echoes, Contemporary Politics* (with Edward McCarron; Westview Press, 2000); and *Irish Women and Public Policy: A Documentary History since 1922* (with James L. Wiles; Irish Academic Press, forthcoming, 2002).

John Fitz Gerald is a Research Professor at the Economic and Social Research Institute (ESRI) in Dublin. He has published extensively on the macro-economics of the Irish economy. His work in recent years has focused on the impact on Ireland of EU integration, economic and monetary union (EMU) and of the EU Structural Funds.

Adrian Guelke, PhD (London School of Economics). Professor of Comparative Politics and Director of the Centre for the Study of Ethnic Conflict, Queens University Belfast. Formerly Jan Smuts Professor of International Relations at the University of Witwaterstrand, Johannesburg. Research interests include international relations and the politics of deeply divided societies (particularly South Africa and Northern Ireland). He edited *The South African Journal of International Affairs* between 1995 and 1998. Books include *Northern Ireland: The International Perspective* (Gill and Macmillan, 1988); *New Perspectives on the Northern Ireland Conflict* (editor; Avebury, 1994); *The Age of Terrorism and the International Political System* (I.B. Tauris, 1995); *The Police, Public Order and the State* (with John Brewer, Ian Hume, Edward Moxon-Browne and Rick Wolford; Macmillan, 2nd edition 1996); and *South Africa in Transition: The Misunderstood Miracle* (I.B. Tauris, 1999). He has had articles published in a wide range of journals, including *International Affairs*, *Comparative Politics*, and *Nationalism and Ethnic Politics*.

Niamh Hardiman, Politics Department, University College Dublin; **BA**, **MA** (National University of Ireland), **DPhil** (Oxford). Research interests include Irish politics, political attitudes and political culture, comparative political economy, including issues such as states and markets, welfare states, labour movements and wage regulation. She is the author of *Pay, Politics and Economic Performance* (Clarendon Press, 1988), and various journal articles and contributions to edited volumes. She is currently working on a book about the political economy of the Irish state.

Brigid Laffan, BCS (Limerick), **PhD** (Dublin), Jean Monnet Professor of European Politics, Department of Politics and Director, Dublin European Institute, University College Dublin. Visiting Professor, College of Europe, Brugge; Director, European Studies MA; Council Member, Institute of Foreign Affairs, Dublin; adviser in EU enlargement to Foreign Affairs Committee, Oireachtas. Research interests include governance in the EU, constitution building in the EU, finances and the EU, and Ireland and European integration. Select publications include *Integration and Co-operation in Europe* (Routledge, 1992); *Constitution-building in the European Union* (contributing editor; Institute of European Affairs, 1996); 'The politics of identity and political order in Europe', *Journal of Common Market Studies* (1996); and *The Finances of the European Union* (Macmillan, 1997).

Eunan O'Halpin is Professor of Contemporary Irish History at Trinity College, Dublin. His most recent works are *Defending Ireland: The Irish State and Its Enemies since 1922* (Oxford University Press, 1999); *Ireland and the Council of Europe: From Isolation Towards Integration* (with Michael Kennedy; Council of Europe, 2000); and *Documents on Irish foreign policy, Volume II: 1923–1926* (edited with R. Fanning, M. Kennedy and D. Keogh; Royal Irish Academy, 2000).

Joseph Ruane is statutory lecturer at University College Cork. He has published extensively on Irish development and on the Northern Irish conflict. His current research is concerned with the impact of globalisation on Ireland, and in Europe. His books include *The Dynamics of Conflict in Northern Ireland: Power, Conflict and Emancipation* (with Jennifer Todd, Cambridge University Press, 1996) and *After the Good Friday Agreement: Analysing Political Change in Northern Ireland* (contributing co-editor, UCD Press, 1999). He is currently preparing a new revised edition of *Dynamics of Conflict.*

David E. Schmitt, PhD (University of Texas, Austin), Edward W. Brooke Professor of Political Science at Northeastern University. Research interests include the political systems of the Republic of Ireland, Northern Ireland and Canada. He is the author of numerous articles and books dealing with political development, ethnic conflict and public administration as well as Northern Ireland and the Republic, including *The Irony of Irish Democracy* (1973). He is co-editor (with W. Crotty) of *Ireland and the Politics of Change* (1998).

Jennifer Todd is statutory lecturer at University College Dublin. She is the author and co-author of numerous articles and books on political ideologies and on the Northern Ireland conflict, including *The Dynamics of Conflict in Northern Ireland* (Cambridge University Press, 1996), *After the Good Friday Agreement* (UCD Press, 1999) and 'The politics of transition', *Political Studies* (forthcoming, 2001–2, with Joseph Ruane). Her current research is on globalisation in comparative and Irish contexts and she is working as contributing co-editor on a comparative volume on the impact of globalisation on Britain, France and Spain.

Ben Tonra, PhD (University of Dublin), is Deputy Director of the Dublin European Institute based at University College Dublin (UCD) where he also lectures and conducts research on European foreign, security and defence policy, Irish foreign policy and European integration. Formerly a lecturer at the Department of International Politics, University of Wales, Aberystwyth, at the Department of Political Science, Trinity College Dublin (TCD), and Research Associate at the Center for Strategic and International Studies (CSIS), Washington DC. His published work includes *The Europeanisation of National Foreign Policies: Ireland, Denmark and The Netherlands in the European Union* (Ashgate, 2001) and *Amsterdam: What the*

Treaty Means (Institute of European Affairs, 1997) as well as more than two dozen journal articles and book chapters covering aspects of Irish and EU foreign and security policy.

Eilís Ward is a graduate of University College Galway, Northeastern University Boston and completed her **PhD** at Trinity College, Dublin. She is a lecturer in the University of Limerick. Her research interests are Irish and European foreign policy, human rights, and women and politics. She has worked for the International Foundation for Election Systems in Central Asia and served in East Timor as a District Electoral Officer with the United Nations. She is contributing co-editor of Galligan, Wilson and Ward, *Contesting Politics, Women, in Ireland North and South* (Westview and PSAI Press, 1998) and has published several articles on aspects of Irish foreign policy and EU policy towards East Timor.

Preface

This book was conceived in a sense both to meet our curiosity about developments in Ireland as they related to the international arena and to fill what we believed to be a gap in the literature on Ireland. The intention was to develop a volume with a far-ranging series of analyses examining a series of problem areas relating to Ireland's international presence. The focus was to be on Ireland in the contemporary period, its role in the international community, its distinctive foreign policy, and its successful economic development and trade and fiscal relationships, both on a regional basis within the European Union and more broadly within a globalised world economic and political system. The forces that shape Ireland's approach to the international community, the history behind these, and, to a lesser degree, the social and cultural changes within the society that have both resulted from, and contributed to, the developments underway were all to be topics of concern.

The volume is intended to a degree to be a companion piece to our earlier *Ireland and the Politics of Change* (1998), which focused primarily on the transformations underway in Irish society, their causes, and their consequences. In one respect at least we have been successful in this regard. As with the first volume, we have been able to work with an outstanding group of scholars, each an established expert in their particular areas. For this, we are most appreciative.

Each of the chapters by the authors focuses on a specific aspect of Ireland's international role and on a particular set of issues. Each develops a number of conceptual themes and comparative approaches of relevance to understanding the forces at work in the area and each includes an introduction to the background of the issues discussed in order to establish a context for understanding the contemporary dimensions of the problems and relationships being explored. The major focus is on the contemporary period and the distinguishing aspects of Ireland's place in the international arena. The objective is to present a multi-faceted series of perspectives by the most knowledgeable of observers intended to enrich our understanding of Ireland's role in, and contribution to, an increasingly globalised community of nations.

In addition to our co-authors, as editors we would like to express our thanks to a number of people who contributed to the publication of this book. These include:

Emma Mitchell, Pat Root and Verina Pettigrew of Pearson Education; three reviewers whose analyses were of particular help: Professor Michael Cox, University of Aberdeen, Todd Landman, Deputy Director, Human Rights Centre, University of Essex, and Dr Jonathan Tonge, University of Salford; Teresa M. Evans, Press and Public Affairs Officer, British Consulate-General, Boston; Janet Louise-Joseph, Barbara McIntosh-Chin and James Rossi, all of Northeastern University; Alvin C. Zises, who established the Edward W. Brooke Chair in Political Science at Northeastern in 1975; Maise, Tom and Helen Crotty; Kitty, Paudy, Eimear and Una Daly; Suzanne Crotty; Marian and Neal Flavin. We especially thank William Crotty's wife, Mary Hauch Crotty, and David Schmitt's sister Virginia Backus, to whom we have dedicated this book.

Publisher's Acknowledgements

We are grateful to the following for permission to reproduce copyright material:

Tables 1.4, 1.5 and 1.6 adapted from OECD Economic Outlook: December, No. 64, Volume 1998, Issue 2. Copyright OECD, 1998.

Whilst every effort has been made to trace the owners of copyright material, in a few cases this has proved impossible and we take this opportunity to offer our apologies to any copyright holders whose rights we may have unwittingly infringed.

To Mary Crotty and Virginia Backus

Chapter 1

Introduction: the Irish way in world affairs

William Crotty

Introduction

Ireland as a world power? Not quite! But Ireland as an international success story, yes. From a small (estimated population 3.6 million) and backward country, traditionally one of the 'poor cousins' on the fringes of Europe and historically wedded economically and, pre-independence, by force to the needs and colonial ambitions of Great Britain, Ireland has emerged in recent decades as a country reborn – prosperous, self-confident, and a player of consequence on the international scene. Marked by a newly evolving social culture and a demand for more of the fruits of prosperity, it is a nation that through careful planning, discipline, and a skilful use of the resources at its disposal has taken an aggressive approach to international trade and finance, self-consciously positioning itself to benefit from the regional interdependence and globalised marketplace now in place. The strategies being followed are not without risk, but the successes to date far outdistance the trouble spots that remain in its society and the potential problems of future years are (as of now) seemingly far off.

It is a story worth telling in its own right; the case of a country redirecting its priorities and marshalling its energies to break from a traditional past and competitively challenge, with a high degree of success eventually, for a place in the economic developments of its age. There are few success stories like it.

This is not to say that Ireland has suddenly emerged as a Super Power (in itself a small group of one). But the country has transformed itself from an impoverished, isolationist, rural and sectarian nation largely bypassed by the Industrial Revolution into a more cosmopolitan, wealthier and economically competitive force in Europe and also, if to a lesser extent, in the newly globalised economy.

The primarily domestic and internal aspects (along with considerations of its relationship to Northern Ireland and England) of the changes underway are developed in our earlier *Ireland and the Politics of Change* (1998). In the studies in this volume, we and our co-authors explore the nature of the changes that have taken place in Ireland's international relations and the ramifications these have for the society. The present volume is in many respects a companion piece to the earlier one, this time with the focus on Ireland's external presence and the place the country has carved for itself in the international arena.

Ireland prior to the contemporary era

From its founding in 1922 until the late 1950s (and a transfer of power and the beginning of a new political age), Ireland was a nation content to go its own way, shielding itself from the political currents and upheavals of the day. Its focus was on asserting its own nationhood, and its distinctive cultural and societal values, freed of the obligations of world citizenship and removed from the struggles that were to engulf Europe (Brown 1985; Lee 1995; Kennedy 1996).

In large part, this was a conditioned response to centuries of suppression and oppression by its ruler and more powerful neighbour, Great Britain. After Independence, its political life had been shaped by the bitter and divisive civil war that followed (Garvin 1996). The intense and emotional divisions revolved around the Anglo-Irish Treaty of 1922 that divided Ireland North and South and led to the Civil War (Garvin 1981). This conflict was to form the basis for the structural divisions of the two major political parties, Fianna Fáil and Fine Gael, ones that have continued to this day.

The dominant political presence of the post-independence decades was Eamon de Valera, a founder of Fianna Fáil in 1926 and its leader until 1959. His contributions to the evolving state were legendary: President of the Executive Council, 1932–37; Taoiseach (Prime Minister), 1937–48, 1951–54 and 1957–59; and President of the Republic, 1959–75. De Valera was to put his stamp on the newly independent Ireland. He was responsible for removing all official traces of association with Great Britain and for framing the Irish Constitution that codified not only government structures and powers and the assumptions underlying its laws but also spelled out the values and ambitions he held for the newly evolving developing state. The 'Age of de Valera' was noted for its emphasis on a 'rural economy and rural virtues'; its sectarianism (the special position of the Catholic Church was acknowledged in the 1937 Constitution and the people were overwhelmingly Catholic in religion) (Berger 1973; Whyte 1980; MacGréil 1991; Drudy and Lynch 1993; Fahey 1994; Hornsby-Smith 1994; Hornsby-Smith and Whelan 1994; Inglis 1998); its antipathy toward England, resulting in long-term economic battles particularly notable during the 1930s; its social solidarity and cultural traditionalism; a subordinate position for women in society with an emphasis on their roles as homemakers and mothers (Whelan and Fahey 1994; Galligan 1998a and b, 1993); and its independence and neutrality in world affairs (as an example of the latter, Ireland remained neutral in World War II despite intense lobbying by both the United States and Great Britain) (Sloan 1997a and b; Fanning 1998; Fitz Gerald 1998). Ireland during these years was an inward-looking nation, one that chose to build on its cultural strengths, qualities that had contributed to its cohesiveness and shaped its world views and social institutions during the centuries of British domination. In effect, this can be seen as a healing period when the patterns of social conduct, the forms of government, its perception of the ways in which the world operated and the qualities that would come to distinguish the new state were put into place. A major consequence of this inward-looking nation-building, as indicated, was a withdrawal from world politics, a reluctance to engage in international trade and a form of ardent isolationism that closed the nation to external concerns (Fisk 1985; Dwyer 1988; Keogh 1988).

All of this was to change, and change dramatically, with de Valera's stepping down as Taoiseach and the choice of his long-time associate and deputy, Sean Lemass, to succeed him. Lemass' career lines and political résumé was strikingly similar to de Valera's: a founding member of Fianna Fáil in 1926 and its leader from 1959 to 1966; a veteran of the War of Independence and the Civil War; Vice-President of the Executive Council (Deputy Head of Government) when de Valera served as Taoiseach from 1937 on; and the holder of ministerial portfolios virtually non-stop in Fianna Fáil governments beginning in 1932. While his political pedigree resembled de Valera's, his political and, most importantly, economic objectives did not. Lemass was a proponent of free trade and an advocate of systematic government planning to develop in the Irish economy an ability to compete internationally. He saw this approach as an antidote to the poverty and social backwardness of the country whose leadership he had inherited, the avenue to a more prosperous and economically more rewarding future for its citizens. His government introduced the first of what were to be a series of national plans to establish the nation's priorities; mobilise its resources; foster a consensus among government, business and the trade unions as to wage restraints (best exemplified by the 1987 business–labour agreement to curtail labour costs in return for job growth); and provide marking points for the transition to an internationally competitive economy. It bears repeated emphasis that the fundamental changes instituted and the prosperity that followed in time were the consequences of deliberate, reasoned choice made by successive governments committed to strengthening the economy and forcing Ireland to compete in the international marketplace (Goldthorpe and Whelan 1994; Kennedy, Giblin and McHugh 1994; Burke 1995; Girvin 1997; Murphy 1997).

There was nothing accidental or providential about the course chosen or any ambiguity as to who set the priorities or what they were to be (Munck 1993; Ó Gráda 1995, 1997; O'Hagan 1995). The role of government in instituting the transformation from the Old Ireland to the New Ireland is a distinguishing feature of what has occurred (Shirlow 1995; Sweeney 1998; Crotty 2001). It is a potential reference point for countries wishing to follow the same course that has served the Irish so well. Yet it is an approach that makes certain assumptions and builds on a distinctive set of national advantages (see below). It should be noted also that there are competing models of government intervention in the economy (Korea, Taiwan, Malaysia and, on a different scale, Japan as examples) that despite their difficulties might be more applicable in some cases.

The Lemass' government of the 1950s and early 1960s then and the earliest of the national plans thus set the course for Ireland's economic development and a refashioning of its international relationships. While highly successful, the ride has been anything but trouble-free, however. My colleague David E. Schmitt writes:

> Progress from the late 1950s through the 1990s . . . was by no means smooth. The country sustained a serious recession as well as inflation during the late 1970s to early 1980s. Indeed, through 1985 Ireland had low income and consumption growth as well as high unemployment and national debt compared with other EC [European Community] members . . . basic structural and international factors limiting the effectiveness of economic planning were the oil crises of the 1970s and inflationary pressures resulting in part from Ireland's close economic linkage to Britain . . . as Ireland modernized economically later than the small, open economies of states such as Norway, Sweden, Switzerland, and Austria, the government had to oversee fundamental changes . . . the limited policy and class differentiation among the major political parties as well as a relatively weak and fragmented labor movement provided less coherence to efforts aimed at developing a national pay and wage policy during the 1970s and early 1980s . . . These attributes contributed to labor unrest and inflation. (2000: 788–9)

The 1980s provided some of the most serious of the setbacks encountered (Goldthorpe and Whelan 1994; Jacobsen 1994; Guiomard 1995; Haughton 1998; Tansey 1998). The manner in which these were handled established the contours for economic policy up through the ensuing decade and into the new century and are credited with realising the prosperity Ireland has come to enjoy.

Richard Rapaport explains:

> If a new economic paradigm is being born in Ireland, it is the result of a long-shot wager made by government planners in the dark days of the '80s when Ireland's unemployment reached a high of 18%, the national debt was a staggering 125% of the country's gross national product, and 1,000 people a week were emigrating. During one dismal year in the early '80s recruiters from Sweden poached an entire graduating IT [Information Technology] class from the University of Limerick for overseas jobs. (1999: 115)

Today 'Ireland's economy has been growing faster than any other in the Western world' and the problems that have emerged are mainly those associated with affluence (Hoge 2000).

Rapaport reviews how this has all come about:

> Ireland's high tech gamble went like this: Tempt multinational technology manufacturers with tax incentives and the promise of getting educated workers with little history of labor unrest. This was the first step of a three-generation IT development plan. This plan also called for an educational system that would rapidly respond to industry needs and a new communications infrastructure to transfer a country referred to as 'an offshore island of an offshore island' into the technology 'middleman' between the United States and Europe.
>
> By the early 90's, technology's most important multinationals were on board, including Microsoft, Apple, Sun, Hewlett-Packard, and Intel. They came to Ireland because of the tax breaks and a bright, eager, competitive-wage, English-speaking workforce. Some, such as Intel, IBM, and Dell, liked what they found and stayed. Others, such as Seagate, split for cheaper climes due to disappointing marketing results. But the effect of those first multinationals was to create a legion of skilled workers.
>
> They also spawned indigenous hardware and software suppliers, as well as a generation of Irish executives knowledgeable in the ways of American high-tech . . . they were the models for the next generation . . . who found niches in e-commerce,

> financial services, Web development, communications infrastructure support, and other fields, and built Ireland's leading digital enterprises. (1999: 115–16)

Rapaport writing in *Forbes ASAP* notes that an '$8 billion technology sector . . . is driving Europe's hottest high tech environment' and concludes that 'Ireland is rich' (1999: 114–15). His bullishness appears justified.

It may be that Ireland will provide a road map of consequence for other small nations wishing to benefit from the new international economic order. It would not be easy and would necessitate a country and its citizenry willing to develop the leadership, discipline, communal priorities and social and political teamwork necessary to reverse generations of economic stagnation and, more often than not, political and social disorder. There can not be too many post-Communist nations and developing countries with the level of resolve and official foresight evidenced by the Irish and with its distinctive natural advantages (in a country once referred to as 'resource poor'). Ireland had much to capitalise on and did so with skill and vision.

Whether Ireland can serve as a model for others beginning the long climb towards economic respectability is yet to be seen. Few emerging countries would have implicit advantages similar to Ireland's – an English-speaking and well-educated population (with an educational system intentionally redesigned to attune itself better to the demands of information age technology); a democratic culture and a strong social cohesive solidarity; positioning at the doorsteps of Europe with access to its markets; European Union (EU) membership with subsidies provided to upgrade its economic competitiveness; free of external threats to its independence and relieved of the need to invest in a large military and defence presence; and culturally and emotionally, and more recently economically, tied to the United States, the world's one remaining Super Power and its largest economy. In relation to the last point, 40 per cent of the overseas companies located and doing business in Ireland in the mid-1990s were from the United States (compared to Germany with 18 per cent and Britain with 16 per cent, the runners-up). Few to any other developing nations are likely to enjoy such advantages, although again it should be stressed it took government initiative to harness and focus these in the manner necessary to achieve the goals desired. Ireland's economic success has driven its international role and is the primary force shaping its contemporary presence in an increasingly globalised world economic and political order.

Indicators of social and economic development and international trade

Various gauges can be explored to illustrate the changes that have taken place in Irish society and in Ireland's world position (Organization for Economic Cooperation and Development, OECD 1998a, b, 1997; United Nations 1998a, b, c; World Bank 2000a, b, c, 1997). First, in terms of demographic change, the developments are significant (Whelan 1994; Whelan and Fahey 1994; Breen and Whelan 1996;

Table 1.1 Demographic change in Ireland: selected indicators

Indicator	Year				
	1950	**1960**	**1970**	**1980**	**1990**
Life expectancy[1]	–	69.6	71.4	72.5	74.6
Birth rate[2]	21.3	21.4	21.9	21.8	15.1
Infant mortality[3]	45.3	29.3	19.5	11.1	8.2
Age 65 and over[4]	10.7	11.2	11.2	10.7	11.4
Females in labour force[5]	–	25.6	25.8	28.7	31.6

Notes:
1 In years.
2 Annual live births/1,000 population.
3 Deaths before age 1/1,000 population.
4 Age 65 and over as percentage of population.
5 In percentages.
Sources: Lane *et al.* (1997): Table 1.7, p. 14; Table 1.9, p. 16; Table 1.9, p. 16; Table 1.6, p. 13; and Table 3.2, p. 37; and the sources cited therein.

Fahey 1998; Hardiman and Whelan 1998; Westarp and Boss 1998). Table 1.1 shows life expectancy to be up; the birth rate, historically high, has fallen; infant mortality is down substantially (and lower than comparative figures for the United States); the ageing of the population has increased somewhat, and is now significantly above levels for the 1960s and 1970s; and the female participation in the labour force, discouraged in more traditional times and while still behind most other advanced democratic countries (42.8 per cent in the United Kingdom, 44.5 per cent in the United States), to have increased to about one-third.

Employing a comparative measure used by the United Nations, the 'Human Development Index', comprising the dimensions of longevity, adult literacy and mean years of formal education and income (per capita purchasing power parity in dollars), Ireland again demonstrates impressive gains between 1960 and 1992 (Table 1.2). It continues to rank behind other advanced industrial nations such as the United States, Canada, Australia and France. Of significance, however, change is evident and it is in the right direction.

In relation to economic development, Table 1.3 illustrates the redistribution in sector employment for the decades between 1950 and 1990. As much as anything else, these figures tell the story of the shifts in the Irish economy (Breen *et al.* 1990; Whelan *et al.* 1994). The changes are pronounced. Employment in industry has remained stable. The transformation that has taken place has been in agricultural employment, down to 12 per cent of the labour force entering the 1990s, and services, the bedrock of the new economy, approaching two-thirds of those employed.

Measures of each sector's proportionate contribution to the total GDP (Gross Domestic Product) tell much the same story. Most pronouncedly, agriculture has become considerably less important and services considerably more important, the latter approaching 60 per cent of the total GDP by the early 1990s. Industry also

Table 1.2 Human Development Index: selected countries, 1960–92[1]

Country	Year			
	1960	1970	1980	1992
Ireland	0.710	0.829	0.862	0.892
United Kingdom	0.857	0.873	0.892	0.919
United States	0.865	0.887	0.911	0.932
Australia	0.850	0.862	0.890	0.926
France	0.853	0.871	0.895	0.927

Note:
1 Includes measures of longevity, literacy/formal education, and income per capita, each weighted equally.
Source: Lane *et al.* (1997): Table 2.12, p. 33.

Table 1.3 Sector impact on the Irish economy

Sector	Year				
	1950	1960	1970	1980	1990
Sector employment on the Irish economy, 1950–90					
Agriculture	39.6	35.2	25.4	15.6	12.4
Industry	24.3	25.4	31.3	35.0	24.4
Services	36.1	39.4	43.2	49.4	62.8
Sector contribution to the GDP (Gross Domestic Product)					
Agriculture	29.0	–	14.4	13.3	9.0
Industry	25.0	–	31.4	34.2	33.4
Services	46.0	–	54.2	52.5	57.6

Note:
1 Measured in terms of employment in civilian population and presented as percentages. The data are from the International Labour Organization
Sources: Lane *et al.* (1997): Tables 3.3, 3.4 and 3.5, pp. 38–39 and the sources cited therein.

had become significant, although not comparative to services, with a little under one-third of the GDP.

Ireland's role in the technological trade is a prime example of the change underway. Ireland has become a player in the technology game. By the late 1990s, technology contributed an estimated 20 per cent to the country's GDP and Ireland ranked second only to the United States in software exports, accounting for 40 per cent of the packaged software sold in Europe (Rapaport 1999: 114).

Other indicators reinforce the economic restructuring underway. As examples, the GDP was up in the 1990s (compared to the 1980s) as were measures of consumption,

Table 1.4 Irish economic indicators 1: GDP, consumption, capital formation, goods and services, exports/imports, savings and government expenditures

Measure	Year							
	1971–81	**1982**	**1985**	**1988**	**1990**	**1995**	**1997**	**2000[1]**
Real GDP[2]	4.7	2.3	3.1	5.2	8.5	11.1	9.8	6.5
Real private[2] consumer expenditures	4.0	−7.1	4.6	4.5	1.4	4.1	6.3	5.1
Real total gross[2] fixed capital formation	5.9	−3.4	−7.7	5.2	13.4	10.9	10.9	7.8
Real export of[2] goods and services	7.1	5.5	6.6	9.0	8.7	19.6	23.6	7.8
Real imports of food and services[2]	6.2	−3.1	3.2	4.9	5.1	15.8	15.6	9.4
Gross national saving[3]	18.2 (1979)	16.1	15.0	16.7	21.1	21.8	23.7	–
General government total outlays[3]	–	52.2	51.0	45.2	39.0	37.6	34.7	32.1

Notes:
1 Based on estimates and projections.
2 Percentage change from previous period.
3 As percentage of total GDP.
Source: OECD, *OECD Economic Outlook* (Paris: Organization for Economic Cooperation and Development, December 1998c), pp. 191, 193, 195, 199, 200, 206, 217, 218.

capital formation, the import and export of goods and services, and national savings, while government expenditures decreased by 20 per cent compared to the early 1980s (Table 1.4). In addition, interest rates (long-term and short-term) were down; the trade balance had shifted markedly in Ireland's favour; and the account balance (as a percentage of GDP) was positive, a significant improvement over the 1981–90 period (Table 1.5). The government's debt decreased by over one-half and Ireland was projected to have the lowest public debt of the 15 OECD countries as analysed under Maastricht Treaty definitions (Table 1.6).

Ireland has done well. This point is not in question. It is how well the country has done that attracts particular attention. In the mid-1990s Ireland ranked tenth among 50 countries ranked in terms of international competitiveness and internal investment strategies (McCarter 1997: 213). By the end of the decade, it would seem the picture was even brighter. In 1999 alone (the last year for which complete data were available):

> Ireland's economy grew a staggering 11 per cent . . . four times the EU average. All the numbers . . . up: consumer spending up 9 per cent over the year, retail spending up 14 per cent, industrial investment up 25 per cent just in the last year's third quarter . . . [and] Union leaders . . . [were demanding] fresh price controls so that the 50,000 new homes built . . . [in 2000] can be bought by workers. (Nyhan 2000: E4)

Table 1.5 Irish economic indicators 2: interest rates, exports/imports, and trade balances, 1981–2000

Indicator	Year					
	1981	**1985**	**1990**	**1995**	**1997**	**2000**[1]
Long-term[2] interest rates	17.3	12.6	10.0	8.3	6.5	4.4
Short-term[2] interest rates	15.2	11.9	11.3	6.2	6.1	3.1
Export volumes[3]	0.8	6.5	8.5	20.1	13.8	9.9
Import volumes[3]	2.1	3.3	6.8	14.4	14.4	9.4
Trade balance[4]	−2.2	0.6	4.0	13.5	18.7	28.8
Current account balance as percentage of GDP[2]	−13.7	−3.8	−0.8	2.7	2.8	2.0

Notes:
1 In percentages.
2 Based on estimates and proportions.
3 Total goods with percentage change from previous period.
4 In billions of dollars.
Source: OECD, *OECD Economic Outlook* (Paris: Organization for Economic Cooperation and Development, December 1998c), pp. 227, 228, 230, 231, 238.

Table 1.6 Maastricht definition of general government gross public debt: selected countries, 1992–2000[1]

Indicator	Year			
	1992	**1995**	**1997**	**2000**[2]
Ireland	98.8	82.3	65.2	40.6
United Kingdom	41.1	53.1	52.3	48.8
Belgium	129.0	130.8	121.9	47.8
France	39.7	52.5	57.8	59.8
Germany	44.1	58.3	61.5	59.7
Netherlands	79.6	78.6	70.9	64.8
Spain	48.3	66.0	61.6	54.8
Sweden	67.1	78.0	76.9	65.7

Notes:
1 Calculated as percentage of nominal GDP.
2 Based on estimates and projections.
Source: OECD, *OECD Economic Outlook* (Paris: Organization for Economic Cooperation and Development, December 1998c), p. 251.

Ireland's most pressing concern, it would seem, might well be too much prosperity too soon, with the attendant problems associated with a too rapid growth: urban sprawl; crime; drugs; an inflation of living and housing costs, among other items; traffic congestion; the immigration of unskilled workers looking for jobs (a new experience for the Irish); and over-burdened social and governmental agencies (see below). Whatever the potential costs, most observers believe the economic and trade boom is solidly grounded and that it should continue.

The OECD sees things in much the same light: a cooling off of the economy may be in order but a continued strong performance is projected:

> There is little reason to expect much of a slowdown in domestic demand. With tight labor markets and continuing employment increases, disposable income gains should remain sufficiently robust to make any easing in private consumption growth quite gradual. Capital formation . . . is projected to continue to grow at a vigorous albeit moderate rate, led by expected robust growth in public infrastructure outlays and still-rapid increases in inward direct investment . . . the pace of such capital inflows may decelerate in view of global financial tensions and particular problems in certain sectors of special interest to Ireland. This could hold export growth to rates which are slow only in relation to the explosive gains recorded in recent years . . . the cooling-off in net exports could rein output growth back towards rates of around 6½ per cent . . . the labor market . . . could yield some further acceleration in wages. Overheating will . . . be restrained by the moderating effects of currency appreciation on traded goods prices [*sic*]. (1998b: 93)

Economic performance in Ireland has been impressive and should continue to be so. It is based on an open economy, free tax incentives to attract multinationals, access to Europe and the EU, agreements to control wages, a strong relationship with the United States, forward-looking government policies and a skilled and motivated work force. A once predominantly rural and underdeveloped country, Ireland has basically skipped the Industrial Age and willed itself into the New Age, in the process becoming a player of consequence in Europe and, to a lesser extent, elsewhere in the world marketplace and one of the clear beneficiaries of the new global order. The economy has been the engine that has fuelled Ireland's changing role in the international community.

Foreign policy and foreign aid

Irish foreign policy is not built on a defensive posture mandated by security needs or an inherent vulnerability in an uncertain world. Ireland has no natural enemies in today's world. In addition, it has an umbrella association with the EU and the goodwill and security provided by its close relationship with the United States (Keatinge 1973, 1998; Dempsey 1998). Consequently, and driven by internal considerations of economic development, as well as by principles long associated with its national character, the policy is one of outreach, marked by the need to promote its Information Age, high-tech international trade, important for its domestic economic health, and to maximise values it considers important in its relationships with other countries. The primary focus of the latter is realised in relation to aid targeted on a selective basis to developing nations.

Thus economics, while the defining force in establishing present-day Ireland's international policy objectives, is far from providing the total picture of Ireland's often distinctive approach to foreign affairs. Qualities historically evolved from the nation's long struggle against colonial imperialism and the abuses it fostered in combination with Ireland's geopolitical positioning on the doorstep of Europe have made their contributions.

An empathy for the underdog, an anti-militarism and a dedication to promoting peace, a sensitivity to exploitation and a commitment to sharing in an effort to reduce inequalities have all helped shape the nation's national persona and its perspective on relations with other nations. At the same time, the country has not been unaware – in fact, it has been quick to capitalise on – the opportunities implicit in developing regional economic and political alliances.

Ireland has been an active member of the EU and has benefited substantially from the association (Anderson and Goodman 1995; Sommers 1995).

The significance of regional alliances, and specifically the EU, is developed by Brigid Laffan and Rory O'Donnell:

> The contemporary international system is characterised by an increasing interconnectedness and interdependence which is driven by capital flows, technology, investment patterns, growing linkages between societies and more rapid dissemination of ideas . . . The European Union (EU) represents the world's most extensive and intensive form of regionalism. No other system of regional cooperation is so heavily rooted in a dense pattern of co-operative institutions which has produced a loosely coupled albeit patchy form of European governance. Membership of the European Union alters the external environment of the traditional nation state and the internal dynamic of public policy-making. For Ireland, membership of the EU is different in character and in its consequences to participation in all other international organisations. It is bound up with the decision to open the economy in the search of prosperity for welfare. (1998: 156)

Subsidies from the EU have actively advanced Ireland's rush to modernisation (Walsh 1995). The Irish have done well for themselves in this regard. At the same time, they have used the subsidies to maximise effect. Successive Irish governments have strategically targeted roads, harbours, and transportation generally; education, with a special emphasis on the skills needed by multinationals in international trade and information services; agricultural improvement; and technological advancement. An intelligent use of the resources available; a willingness to aggressively seek out whatever supports that may be available; state planning; a cooperative and reinforcing association among government, business and labour to control wages (an approach that may be fraying under the pressures of inflation); and, more often than not, progressive political leadership have combined to pay off handsomely for Ireland.

One consequence of all of this has been a Europeanisation of Irish society, particularly noticeable among the more affluent, better educated and younger segments of the adult population. It can be seen in the closer affinity for continental lifestyles and social values, an international frame of reference in approaching decisions, and an evolving conception of citizenship that sees itself as more cosmopolitan and more European and, in the process, less parochial, sectarian and nationalistic than it might have been. There appears less concern with problems such as those presented by Northern Ireland and substantially less economic interaction with, and reliance on, Great Britain (Gillespie 1996; Sloan 1997). In many respects, and especially in Dublin and the urban centres that have profited most handsomely from the globalised economy, the Old Ireland seems almost a thing of the past, not quite forgotten but more and more a distant memory.

Ireland's decision to associate with the European Economic Community in 1973 (later to evolve into the EU) has been referred to as 'probably the most important and far-reaching development in . . . foreign policy since independence' (quoted in Tonra 1999: 155). It has led to economic development, political cooperation and a common approach to foreign and security policy, as well as more recently the Euro and the EU efforts to standardise fiscal policy (Dooge and Barrington 1999). Ben Tonra presents a model of the potential impact of the EU on Ireland (and other countries) when he writes:

> . . . the key dynamic in integration and within EU decision-making is not just one of the bargains and balancing expressed 'interests' but also one of the evolving beliefs and norms or, in other words, polity-forming . . . one would expect to see a process of transformation in which the self regard and beliefs of the policy actors evolve over time and have an impact upon the construction of the 'interests' that they pursue . . . one might even talk in terms of the 'fusion' of national political systems around a European core. (1999: 152)

Europeanisation has influenced then both Irish foreign policy and Irish culture, with the probability implicit in Tonra's analysis that more rather than less is to come, with the state and its citizenry conforming in greater degree to a regional European model of economic interaction, societal values and consensual foreign policy objectives (Coakley 1993; Kearney 1997, Laffan 1997).

Beyond the EU, Ireland's priorities in contributing to the United Nations fairly represent its foreign policy priorities: peacekeeping, disarmament, development cooperation and human rights (Rees 1998: 277). In relation to foreign aid and development, Ireland's objectives have changed little over recent decades. In reviewing 25 years of Irish foreign aid, Helen O'Neil stresses its 'strong humanitarian motivation' and quotes a 1997 Department of Foreign Affairs' report as to its goals:

> To contribute to the development needs of poor countries in partnership with the governments and people of those countries and in line with their priorities; support a process of self-reliant, sustainable, poverty-reducing and equitable growth and development, in particular in the least-developed countries; advance the concept of sustainable development in all its aspects including material well-being, human rights, fundamental freedoms, gender equality, protection of the environment, support for civil society and processes, as well as mechanisms to prevent, resolve and recover from conflict; ensure rapid and effective response to humanitarian emergencies; maintain coherence in all aspects of Ireland's relations with developing countries; and promote

> active participation in multilateral institutions concerned with development. (quoted in O'Neil 1999: 300)

The overall objectives according to the report are 'international peace, security, and a just and stable global economic system' (quoted in O'Neil 1999: 300). This represents both an ambitious policy agenda and a fair summation of the Irish position in foreign affairs, a combination of a concern with justice and a recognition of the need for a stable and predictable international political and economic environment.

The major beneficiaries of direct aid (42 per cent of the total budgeted in 1998) serve to reflect Ireland's stated concerns. These were: Lesotho, Tanzania, Zambia, Uganda, Ethiopia and Mozambique (O'Neil 1999: 294). Peacekeeping operations, in cooperation with United Nations, witnessed an Irish military presence in Lebanon, Cyprus, Iraq–Kuwait, Western Sahara, Macedonia, Croatia, Syria–Israel and Afghanistan (Rees 1999: 277).

The amount of Irish aid in absolute terms is not large. In 1999 it was estimated to be 0.34 per cent of the GNP (80 million Irish punts), below both the targets set by the United Nations (0.7 per cent) and the EU (0.4 per cent), but 'well over one hundred times the original amount' allocated by the government a quarter of a century earlier and substantial enough to place Ireland in the upper half of donor nations (O'Neil 1999: 298).

As there has been since independence, there is the continuing attention given to the Northern Ireland question (D'Arcy and Dickson 1995; Ruane and Todd 1996, 1998; Cox 1998; Guelke 1998). The government's policies in this regard are firmly established. Under both Taoiseaches John Bruton of Fine Gael and Bertie Ahearn of Fianna Fáil there has been a close working relationship with the British, and currently between Ahearn and British Prime Minister Tony Blair, to realise the objectives of the Good Friday Agreement of 10 April 1998 (Mitchell 1999a, b). It is a cooperative relationship that has survived the uncertainties and setbacks of succeeding years. The Good Friday Agreement provides the direction and the framework as to the objectives both nations are intent on pursuing (The Agreement 1998; McSweeney 1998).

On another level, Ireland's historic commitment to neutrality, anti-militarism and non-violence in international affairs may well be tested by the broader objectives of regional associations, the EU and NATO in particular, with which it has had working relationships. If so, it provides one more example of the country being drawn into an international arena it once shunned and a further challenge to national values, however the associations are presented or justified, that once appeared immutable. There is a price to pay, along with benefits to be gained, from international cooperation.

The limits of prosperity

There are limits, of course, to the newfound wealth (as briefly indicated above). Some of the problems are obvious, others more potential than actual at present. The difficulties – real or potential – are multi-faceted. Some are structural, that is built into the nature of Irish society and the culture at the time the development boom took off; some are economic, as for example the threat of inflation, possibly both significant and long-term, in an economy expanding as fast in Ireland in recent years as it has; some involve social tensions, products of affluent new lifestyles and the accompanying social ills that could serve to divide a people and present challenges that the nation has had little experience in dealing with; and some involve the uncertainties of a world economic order, the boom and bust cycles which Ireland is both vulnerable to and over which it has little control.

Ireland, as with other countries, although possibly more so given its commitment to an open economy and its heavy dependence on international trade and finance, can be subjected to the vagaries of capital flows; multinational relocations in the search for constantly cheaper labour, better tax deals and greater profits; oil and other unanticipated, and unplanned for, international crises; the collapse of industries or 'readjustments' in the economies of large countries or major trading blocs (fates that befell the Asian Tigers); the potential weakness of the Euro; deadlock, or something approaching it, in EU decision-making; and so on. The list of *potential* problems is virtually unlimited. Ireland's recent history, especially during the 1980s, suggests that setbacks of undetermined severity can be expected.

Inflation is of more immediate concern and Ireland's ability to cope with it more in question than in the past. According to one observer: 'With membership in the Euro Zone, Ireland cannot raise interest rates by itself; that has to be done by the new European central bank . . . the government's only braking power can come from raising taxes – which is never easy anywhere' (Nyhan 2000: E4). The full implications of EU membership, which it can be said has been a considerable plus for Ireland to date, have yet to become totally clear. Included in the economic resuscita-tion of Ireland, subsidies are being scaled back and soon will be eliminated and the country will move from being a recipient of such favours to becoming a donor to the common policy to help the less well-off EU members. The ultimate con-sequences of the regionalisation of fiscal and economic policy, as well as military, security and, to a greater extent than before, foreign policy, have yet to take full shape. To varying degrees, Ireland's (and other nations') independence in these areas will have to be subordinated to some extent to efforts to promote a common front. The questions are to what degree and with what consequences for Ireland (Schmitt 2000).

The structural problems embedded in the society are well established. Some individuals and groups benefit enormously from the newfound prosperity, others lag behind or are excluded entirely. The dividing lines are clear: the better trained and more technologically skilled are the success stories of the information age (Nolan and Callan 1994; Curtin *et al.* 1996; Hardiman 2000). Older, less-educated, poorer, and rural populations have received considerably less, constituting pockets of the under-rewarded; many are under-employed or unemployed in a booming economy. The society has found the conditions faced by the groups difficult to address in any meaningful manner. Successive governments have evidenced an awareness of the problems and they voice a need for remedial action. There are questions as to the intensity of the commitment and the priority to be given to such conditions. Niamh Hardiman writes:

> There is evidence of a widespread concern in Irish society at the scale of social inequalities, and a growing awareness of the ways in which poverty, unemployment, and poor educational attainment may combine to create severe social deprivation. To deal effectively with these issues would require radical changes to 'normal' policy priorities, beginning with targeted tax reforms, and would undoubtedly require considerable increases in targeted spending . . . despite widespread agreement on the importance of these issues, very little progress [has been made] . . . in tackling them systematically. The fruits of growth . . . [have been] shared very unevenly, and Ireland continues to be a society riven by serious social inequalities. (1998: 142)

As Hardiman indicates, the types of major programmes needed to address the inequalities are not likely to be put in place 'since the interests of the most disadvantaged are treated as residual concerns, not core issues' (1998: 142).

The tension between the haves and the have-nots translate into problems of social stratification and class politics, issues of a type the Irish are not familiar with and ones that could strain their historic commitment to social equity and fairness. The lifestyles and priorities of the newer urban elite also present a challenge to the national culture and its values (one example being in relation to religion and the role of the Catholic Church) that introduces additional pressures into the society. The Europeanisation of citizenship is far removed from traditional conceptions of what it meant to be Irish.

Ireland is facing another challenge also, one directly related to its economic success and its position in the EU. It is one that has been faced by Germany, France, the Scandinavian countries, England, and in fact most of the EU nations, but it is one that is new and unsettling to the Irish. Immigration is the problem. It is an unusual concern for a nation historically concerned with the emigration of its young and more talented (Akenson 1993). It is projected that there will be 200,000 new job openings over the next five years (Nyhan 2000). This is just not the issue. From a handful in the early years of the 1990s, the emigration of asylum-seekers and those wanting work, many from Eastern Europe and Africa, had reached an average of 1,000 per month by the turn of the century. Most of the newcomers are unskilled, poorly educated and speak little to no English. The government's policy has been to distribute them to towns and villages around Ireland (on the contention that Dublin can hold no more) and to subsidise their housing (in designated buildings) and their food. At the same time, the newly arrived immigrants are prohibited from working for up to 18 months while their applications are processed.

The policy has not been well received. The locals resent the influx of foreigners into areas that have little to offer them and the public subsidies made available to newcomers. The latter in turn feel uncomfortable in their new surroundings and frustrated by the prohibitions against their working. It is a curious position and, reasonable to say, an uncomfortable one for all concerned. No acceptable solution appears imminent.

Ireland also has begun to experience the social ills that accompany prosperity, from suburban sprawl, pollution and choked roads to, among other things, the increases in crime and drugs that the country has witnessed in recent years. The country's social tolerance and good will may be tarnished by the increasing differences in wealth and economic opportunities experienced by some and not others and by the influx of newcomers strange to a people long associated with the continued emigration of their own.

A fundamental transformation is underway, one that affects all aspects of the society including its relations with Europe and the rest of the world. Much of what is occurring is beneficial; yet at the same time fissures have begun to appear that may test the cohesiveness of the nation's social fabric.

Introducing the chapters

Within broad parameters, the chapters that follow develop themes and issues related to the points raised and their ramifications. An introduction to the chapters and the basic approaches taken in the presentations follows.

In *Chapter 2*, 'Irish foreign policy', Ben Tonra addresses the 'cosmopolitanism' of Irish society, its secularisation and Europeanisation and how these have contributed to a redefinition of Ireland's international perspective, one directly associated with the transformation taking place in Irish identity. The focus is on foreign policy and the structures important in decision-making processes. The canvas includes government bureaux, NGOs (non-government organisations), the major political parties and the role of a more informed public in all of this. The challenge may rest in further democratising the process while operating within the constraints of a European community.

In *Chapter 3*, 'The Irish economy in international perspective', John Bradley argues that small countries need to design their economies to take advantage of international currents. He questions whether, given Ireland's comparatively poor performance up to the 1980s, the spectacular economic growth since then has simply been a product of playing 'catch-up'. In developing his points, Bradley makes reference to other economies, including the approaches taken by the Asian Tigers and the reason for the differing levels of success. Ireland has emphasised inward investment. Bradley compares the nations in terms of their economic context, centrality/peripherality and other geographical characteristics, and internal issues of governance as they impact economic policy. He also reviews the earlier and more recent periods of Ireland's economic performance in relation to such issues as receptivity to the global economy, improvements of physical infrastructure and human capital, the role of the state and the climate for industrial cooperation.

In *Chapter 4*, 'Ireland – a multicultural economy', John Fitz Gerald traces Ireland's economic development from the days of Sinn Féin ('Ourselves Alone') up to the contemporary period's open economy and international marketplace. Distinguishing features of the Irish experience are the efforts put into attracting foreign multinationals, successful to the point where one-half of the industrial output and one-half of those engaged in industry work for foreign firms (with about 50 per cent of these being American). In addition, the changing emigration flows have helped fuel the economic expansion. Fitz Gerald draws attention to the still largely nascent but certainly productive rise of the Irish multinationals. Ireland has in fact fostered a 'multinational' economy, but one also that has contributed to the indigenous development of domestic international corporations, a process that will be of increasing importance.

In *Chapter 5*, 'Ireland and the European Union', Brigid Laffan reviews the rise of Ireland from a 'peripheral' in the European scheme of things to its present position in the EU. Today the EU is seen as 'an integral part of our future', in the words of Taoiseach Bertie Ahearn. Surveys indicate that the Irish people agree. Laffan examines the extent to which EU membership has promoted national goals through, for example, financial transfers and the degree to which regional associations may place a strain on national priorities (such as in the relation to security and military issues). Ireland's modernisation and prosperity are changing its relationship with the EU and raise concerns of consequence to both Ireland and other smaller nations relevant to the future direction of EU policy.

In *Chapter 6*, 'Irish–American relations', Richard Finnegan sheds light on the once distant but presently close official relationship between Ireland and America. Finnegan discusses early ambiguity over recognising the newly independent state and later the pressure placed by the United States on Ireland to drop its neutrality and enter World War II on the side of the Allies. Most of the attention is given to the period since 1968, when relations have been close, culminating in the Clinton Administration's instrumental role in achieving the Good Friday Agreement in Northern Ireland, bringing the warring parties to the negotiating table. These developments are particularly riveting and constitute one of the most impressive and successful examples of a cooperative international approach (Ireland, the US and Great Britain). While the future remains uncertain, the outline for a peaceful resolution of the Northern Ireland problem may be in place. Meanwhile, the association between Ireland, and the US is stronger and warmer than it has ever been.

In *Chapter 7*, 'The Northern Ireland conflict and the impact of globalisation', Joseph Ruane and Jennifer Todd approach the situation in the North from a different perspective. They argue that the effects of globalisation differ in relation to how it interacts with a country's social structures and cultural mores. For Northern Ireland, the impact of globalisation is contradictory. On the one hand, it facilitates negotiations by eroding the underlying causes of conflict and older patterns of interactions while providing a broader stage, the EU being an example, for Ireland and Northern Ireland to pursue their goals. Yet the international flow of ideas and resources can serve to both recast the struggles and prolong them. The dynamics of the global community and those that have contributed to the Good Friday Peace Agreement could also challenge the peace process by fostering a new and uncertain political environment.

In *Chapter 8*, 'Northern Ireland and the international system', Adrian Guelke addresses the impact on the parties and the peace process in Northern Ireland of evolving conceptions of the state and individual rights related to the advent of globalisation. The argument is qualified in relating it to Northern Ireland, but Guelke draws a distinction between colonial conceptions of self-determination and the sovereignty of the state, both related to territorial interpretations of states with fixed boundaries. Globalisation has eroded traditional beliefs about state sovereignty and rearranged the political landscape and international norms have influenced developments in Northern Ireland. Similarly, minority rights have become more firmly protected through international convention.

In *Chapter 9*, 'Ireland and the international security environment: changing police and military roles', Eunan O'Halpin analyses the changing role of Ireland's military obligations, security needs, international policing and contributions to international peace. The changes have been necessitated by the country's emergence as an outward-looking partner in regional and super-regional military and economic organisations and alliances. The internationalisation of Irish society is as evident in the approach to foreign affairs as it is in any other aspect of Irish life. The distinction is that for Ireland this is primarily a new and uncharted area. O'Halpin traces the emergence of Ireland in this context, some of the successes enjoyed and problems encountered. He concludes that Ireland's interaction with other nations in these areas has increased significantly leading to the beginning of a redefinition of the country's historic commitment to neutrality and a reorientation of its military and defence outlook in order to better integrate its mission and level of preparedness with regional and global forces promoting interdependence.

In *Chapter 10*, 'Ireland and human rights', Eilis Ward assesses human rights issues in Ireland, in terms of both the substantive policy positions taken and the efficacy of the mechanisms and organisations used to implement them. Ireland's experiences in the colonial and post-colonial periods contributed to a concern with human rights on an international level and the adoption of strong policy positions in its foreign relations. Ireland's assumption of the presidency of the EU in the mid-1990s and its efforts through this position to focus attention on the situation in East Timor is an example of the concerns expressed.

Ward argues that NGOs have pressed the state on these issues and that Ireland, while small in size relative to most other countries, might be more active internationally in promoting the protection of human rights.

In *Chapter 11*, 'The political economy of growth', Niamh Hardiman argues that capitalist countries are marked by significant variations in their institutional structures in responding to the forces associated with the globalisation of economies. Wage levels, industrial organisation, tax and welfare programmes, and approaches to international trade and reactions to market forces can take a variety of forms. The argument has also been made that political choice and control over economic matters has been threatened by the new world order. While it is true that the evolution of the EU has lessened national diversity, the adoption of a one-form-fits-all neo-liberal model is not a predetermined outcome.

Hardiman looks at the economy of growth in Ireland and the institutional arrangements that support it and draws attention to a 'concentrative' model of policy-making that in contrast to other European nations has led to wage modernisation and the continuation of social welfare programmes. She ends with a discussion of the likelihood of the continuation of such policies in a globalised marketplace and analyses both the strength and fragility of Ireland's 'consensual' model of economic development.

In *Chapter 12*, 'Ireland on the world stage: conclusions and challenges', David E. Schmitt concludes the volume by reviewing and integrating the themes developed in the earlier chapters into a statement of Ireland's place in the world today – its web of economic relationships, its foreign policy priorities, its approach to foreign aid and the changes to cultural identity and the problems being encountered. Schmitt traces the reciprocal nature of a changing international order and the conscious (as well as the unintended) consequences of government policy. The emphasis is on adaption and change. The manner in which cultural and identity issues have transformed the nature of Ireland's elites, government and society is explored and the Irish experience is placed in comparative perspective. The chapter ends with a discussion of Ireland's international impact, its achievements and the challenges it faces in the future.

References

The Agreement: Agreement Reached in Multi-Party Negotiations (1998), mimeo 10 April.

Akenson, Donald Harman (1993) *The Irish Diaspora: A Primer* (Toronto: P.D. Meaney Company).

Anderson, James and James Goodman (1995) 'Euro-regionalism: national conflict and development', in Peter Shirlow (ed.), *Development Ireland: Contemporary Issues* (London: Pluto Press).

Berger, P. (1973) *The Social Reality of Religion* (Harmondsworth: Penguin).

Breen, Richard and Christopher T. Whelan (1996) *Social Mobility and Social Class in Ireland* (Dublin: Gill and Macmillan).

Breen, Richard, Damian F. Hannan, David B. Rottman and Christopher T. Whelan (1990) *Understanding Contemporary Ireland: State, Class and Development in the Republic of Ireland* (Dublin: Gill and Macmillan).

Brown, Terence (1985) *Ireland: A Social and Cultural History 1922–1985* (London: Fontana Press/HarperCollins).

Burke, Andrew E. (ed.) (1995) *Enterprise and the Irish Economy* (Dublin: Oak Tree Press).

Coakley, John (1993) 'Society and political culture', in John Coakley and Michael Gallagher (eds), *Politics in the Republic of Ireland*, 2nd edn (Dublin: Folens/PSAI Press).

Corish, M. (1996) 'Aspects of the secularisation of Irish society', in Eoin G. Cassidy (ed.) *Faith and Culture in the Irish Context* (Dublin: Veritas).

Cox, Michael (1998) 'Northern Ireland: the war that came in from the cold', *Irish Studies in International Affairs*, vol. 9 (Dublin: Royal Irish Academy).

Crotty, William (1998) 'Democratization and political development in Ireland', in William Crotty and David E. Schmitt (eds), *Ireland and the Politics of Change* (London: Longman).

Crotty, William (2000) 'Ireland: economics and the reinventing of a nation', Symposium on the changing state in Ireland and Northern Ireland: perspectives on the transitions underway, *Policy Studies Journal*, vol. 28, no. 4, pp. 779–814.

Crotty, William and David E. Schmitt (eds) (1998) *Ireland and the Politics of Change* (London: Longman).

Curtin, Chris, Trutz Haase and Hilary Tovey (eds) (1996) *Poverty in Rural Ireland: A Political Economy Perspective* (Dublin: Oak Tree Press).

D'Arcy, Michael and Tim Dickson (eds) (1995) *Border Crossings: Developing Ireland's Island Economy* (Dublin: Gill and Macmillan).

Dempsey, George T. (1998) 'Myth-making and missing the point: largely Irish perceptions of American foreign policy', *Irish Studies in International Affairs*, vol. 9 (Dublin: Royal Irish Academy).

Dooge, James and Ruth Barrington (eds) (1999), *A Vital National Interest: Ireland in Europe 1973–1998* (Ireland: Institute of Public Administration).

Drudy, Sheelaugh and Kathleen Lynch (1993) *Schools and Society in Ireland* (Dublin: Gill and Macmillan).

Dwyer, T. Ryle (1988) *Strained Relations: Ireland at Peace and the United States of America at War 1941–1945* (Dublin: Gill and Macmillan).

Fahey, Tony (1994) 'Catholicism and industrial society in Ireland', in J.H. Goldthorpe and C.T. Whelan (eds), *The Development of Industrial Society in Ireland* (Oxford: Oxford University Press).

Fahey, Tony (1998) 'Progress or decline?: demographic change in political context', in William Crotty and David E. Schmitt (eds), *Ireland and the Politics of Change* (London: Longman).

Fahey, Tony and John Fitz Gerald (1997) *Welfare Implications of Demographic Trends* (Dublin: Oak Tree Press).

Fanning, Ronann (1998) 'Small states, large neighbors: Ireland and the United Kingdom', *Irish Studies in International Affairs*, vol. 9 (Dublin: Royal Irish Academy).

Fisk, Robert (1985) *In Time of War: Ireland, Ulster, and the Price of Neutrality, 1939–1945* (Philadelphia: University of Philadelphia Press).

Fitz Gerald, Garrett (1998) 'The origins, development, and present status of Irish "Neutrality"', *Irish Studies in International Affairs*, vol. 9 (Dublin: Royal Irish Academy).

Galligan, Yvonne (1993) 'Women in Irish Politics', in John Coakley and Michael Gallagher (eds), *Politics in the Republic of Ireland*, 2nd edn (Dublin: Folens/PSAI Press).

Galligan, Yvonne (1998a) 'The changing role of women', in William Crotty and David E. Schmitt (eds), *Ireland and the Politics of Change* (London: Longman).

Galligan, Yvonne (1998b) *Women and Contemporary Politics in Ireland: From the Margins to the Mainstream* (London: Cosswell).

Garvin, Tom (1981) *The Evolution of Nationalist Politics* (Dublin: Gill and Macmillan).

Garvin, Tom (1996) *1922: The Birth of Irish Democracy* (Dublin: Gill and Macmillan).

Gillespie, Paul (ed.) (1996) *Britain's European Question: The Issues for Ireland* (Dublin: Institute of European Affairs).

Girvin, Brian (1997) 'Political culture, political independence and economic success in Ireland', *Irish Political Studies*, 12, pp. 48–77.

Goldthorpe, J.H. and C.T. Whelan (eds) (1994) *The Development of Industrial Society in Ireland* (Oxford: Oxford University Press).

Guelke, Adrian (1998) 'Northern Ireland: international and North/South issues', in William Crotty and David E. Schmitt (eds), *Ireland and the Politics of Change* (London: Longman).

Guiomard, Cathol (1995) *The Irish Disease and How To Cure It: Common-Sense Economics for a Competitive World* (Dublin: Oak Tree Press).

Hardiman, Niamh (1994) 'The state and economic interests: Ireland in comparative perspective', in J.H. Goldthorpe and C.T. Whelan (eds), *The Development of Industrial Society in Ireland* (Oxford: Oxford University Press).

Hardiman, Niamh (1998) 'Inequality and the Representation of Interests', in William Crotty and David E. Schmitt (eds), *Ireland and the Politics of Change* (London: Longman).

Hardiman, Niamh (2000) 'Taxing the poor: the politics of income taxation in Ireland', Symposium on the changing state in Ireland and Northern Ireland: perspectives on the transitions underway, *Policy Studies Journal*, vol. 28, no. 4, pp. 815–842.

Hardiman, Niamh and Christopher T. Whelan (1998) 'Changing values', in William Crotty and David E. Schmitt (eds), *Ireland and the Politics of Change* (London: Longman).

Hartley, Steven (1987) *The Irish Question as a Problem in British Foreign Policy, 1914–1918* (New York: St. Martin's Press).

Haughton, Jonathan (1998) 'The dynamics of economic change', in William Crotty and David E. Schmitt (eds), *Ireland and the Politics of Change* (London: Longman).
Hoge, Warren (2000) 'Money, jobs, big cars: how's an Irishman to cope?', *New York Times*, 17 July, p. A3.
Hornsby-Smith, Michael P. (1994) 'Social and religious transformation in Ireland: a case of secularisation?', in J.H. Goldthorpe and C.T. Whelan (eds), *The Development of Industrial Society in Ireland* (Oxford: Oxford University Press).
Hornsby-Smith, Michael P. and Christopher T. Whelan (1994) 'Religious and moral values', in Christopher T. Whelan (ed.), *Values and Social Change* (Dublin: Gill and Macmillan).
Inglis, Tom (1987) *Moral Monopoly: The Catholic Church in Modern Irish Society* (Dublin: Gill and Macmillan).
Inglis, Tom (1998) *The Moral Majority: The Rise and Fall of the Catholic Church in Modern Ireland* (Dublin: University College Dublin Press).
Jacobsen, John Kurt (1994) *Chasing Progress in the Irish Republic* (Cambridge: Cambridge University Press).
Kearney, Richard (1997) *Postnationalist Ireland: Politics, Culture, Philosophy* (London: Routledge).
Keatinge, Patrick (1973) *The Formulation of Irish Foreign Policy* (Dublin: Institute of Public Administration).
Keatinge, Patrick (1996) *European Security: Ireland's Choices* (Dublin: Institute for Foreign Affairs).
Keatinge, Patrick (1998) 'Ireland and European security: continuity and change', *Irish Studies in International Affairs*, vol. 9 (Dublin: Royal Irish Academy).
Kennedy, Kiernan A., Thomas Giblin and Dierdre McHugh (1994) *The Economic Development of Ireland in the Twentieth Century* (London: Routledge).
Kennedy, Liam (1996) *Colonialism, Religion and Nationalism in Ireland* (Belfast: Institute of Irish Studies, The University of Belfast).
Keogh, Dermot (1988) *Ireland and Europe: 1919–1948* (Dublin: Gill and Macmillan).
Laffan, Brigid (1997) 'Constitutional change in the European Union: the small state/large state issue', *Irish Studies in International Affairs*, vol. 8 (Dublin: Royal Irish Academy).
Laffan, Brigid and Rory O'Donnell (1998) 'Ireland and the growth of international governance', in William Crotty and David E. Schmitt (eds), *Ireland and the Politics of Change* (London: Longman).
Lane, Jan-Erik, David McKay and Kenneth Newton (1997) *Political Data Handbook*, 2nd edn (Oxford: Oxford University Press).
Lee, Joseph (1995) *Ireland 1912–1985: Politics and Society* (Cambridge: Cambridge University Press).
MacGréil, M. (1991) *Religious Practice and Attitudes in Ireland* (Maynooth: Survey and Research Units, Department of Social Studies, St Patrick's College).
McCarter, Willie (1997) 'Irish businesses and America', in Pat McArt, Colm McKenna and Donal Cambell (eds), *Irish Almanac and Yearbook of Facts: 1998* (County Donegal: Speenoge).
McSweeney, Bill (1998) 'Identity, interest, and the Good Friday agreement', *Irish Studies in International Affairs*, vol. 9 (Dublin: Royal Irish Academy).
Mitchell, George J. (1999a) *Making Peace* (New York: Alfred A. Knopf).
Mitchell, George J. (1999b) 'Peace and reconciliation in Northern Ireland', *Boston Sunday Globe*, 19 December, p. C7.
Munck, Ronnie (1993) *The Irish Economy: Results and Prospects* (London: Pluto Press).
Murphy, Gary (1997) 'Government interest groups and the Irish move to Europe, 1957–1963', *Irish Studies in International Affairs*, vol. 8 (Dublin: Royal Irish Academy).
Nolan, Brian and Tim Callan (eds) (1994) *Poverty and Policy in Ireland* (Dublin: Gill and Macmillan).

Nyhan, David (2000) 'The spoils of Irish prosperity reach many a hand', *Boston Sunday Globe*, 29 May, p. E4.
Ó Gráda, Cormac (1995) *Ireland: A New Economic History 1780–1939* (Oxford: Oxford University Press).
Ó Gráda, Cormac (1997) *A Rocky Road: The Irish Economy Since the 1920s* (Manchester: Manchester University Press).
O'Hagan, J.W. (ed.) (1995) *The Economy of Ireland* (Dublin: Gill and Macmillan).
O'Neill, Helen (1998) 'Ireland's foreign aid in 1997', *Irish Studies in International Affairs*, vol. 9 (Dublin: Royal Irish Academy).
O'Neill, Helen (1999) 'Ireland's foreign aid in 1998', *Irish Studies in International Affairs*, vol. 10 (Dublin: Royal Irish Academy).
OECD (Organization for Economic Cooperation and Development) (1997) *The World in 2000: Towards a New Global Age* (Paris: OECD).
OECD (Organization for Economic Cooperation and Development) (1998a) *Economic Development* (Paris: OECD).
OECD (Organization for Economic Cooperation and Development) (1998b) *Main Economic Indicators* (Paris: OECD).
OECD (Organization for Economic Cooperation and Development) (1998c) *OECD Economic Outlook* (Paris: OECD).
Rapaport, Richard (1999) 'When Irish IT [International Technology] is smiling', *Forbes ASAP*, 31 May, pp. 114ff.
Rees, Nicholas (1998) 'Ireland's foreign relations in 1997', *Irish Studies in International Affairs*, vol. 9 (Dublin: Royal Irish Academy).
Rees, Nicholas (1999) 'Ireland's foreign relations in 1998', *Irish Studies in International Affairs*, vol. 10 (Dublin: Royal Irish Academy).
Ruane, Joseph and Jennifer Todd (1996) *The Dynamics of Conflict in Northern Ireland: Power, Conflict, and Emancipation* (Cambridge: Cambridge University Press).
Ruane, Joseph and Jennifer Todd (1998) 'Peace processes and communalism in Northern Ireland', in William Crotty and David E. Schmitt (eds), *Ireland and the Politics of Change* (London: Longman).
Schmitt, David E. (2000) 'Internationalization and patterns of political change in Ireland', Symposium on the changing state in Ireland and Northern Ireland: perspectives on the transitions underway, *Policy Studies Journal*, vol. 28, no. 4, pp. 784–98.
Shirlow, Peter (ed.) (1995) *Development Ireland: Contemporary Issues* (London: Pluto Press).
Sloan, Geoffrey (1997a) 'Geopolitics and British strategic policy in Ireland: issues and interests', *Irish Studies in International Affairs*, vol. 8 (Dublin: Royal Irish Academy).
Sloan, Geoffrey (1997b) *The Geopolitics of Anglo-Irish Relations in the Twentieth Century* (London: Macmillan).
Sommers, Frans (1995) *European Community Economics: A Comparative Study*, 2nd edn (London: Longman).
Sweeney, Paul (1998) *The Celtic Tiger: Ireland's Economic Miracle Explained* (Dublin: Oak Tree Press).
Tansey, Paul (1998) *Ireland At Work: Economic Growth and the Labour Market, 1987–1997* (Dublin: Oak Tree Press).
Tonra, Ben (1999) *The Europeanization of Irish Foreign Affairs*, vol. 10 (Dublin: Royal Irish Academy), pp. 149–68.
Townshead, Charles (ed.) (1988) *Consensus in Ireland: Approaches and Recessions* (Oxford: Clarendon Press).
United Nations, Economic Commission for Europe (1998a) *Economic Survey of Europe: 1998, No. 1* (New York: United Nations).
United Nations, Economic Commission for Europe (1998b) *Economic Survey of Europe: 1998, No. 2* (New York: United Nations).

United Nations, Economic Commission for Europe (1998c) *World Economic and Social Survey 1998: Trends and Policies in the World Economy* (New York: United Nations).
Walsh, James (1995) 'EC structural funds and economic development in the republic of Ireland', in Peter Shirlow (ed.), *Development Ireland: Contemporary Issues* (London: Pluto Press).
Westarp, Karl-Heinz and Michael Boss (1998) *Ireland: Towards New Identities?* (Oxford: Alden Press).
Whelan, Christopher T. (ed.) (1994) *Values and Social Change in Ireland* (Dublin: Gill and Macmillan).
Whelan, Christopher T. and T. Fahey (1994) 'Marriage and the family', in C.T. Whelan (ed.), *Values and Social Change in Ireland* (Dublin: Gill and Macmillan).
Whelan, Christopher T., Richard Breen and Brendan J. Whelan (1994) 'Industrialization, class formation and social mobility in Ireland', in J.H. Goldthorpe and C.T. Whelan (eds), *The Development of Industrial Society in Ireland* (Oxford: Oxford University Press).
Whyte, J. (1980) *Church and State in Modern Ireland, 1923–1979*, 2nd edn (Dublin: Gill and Macmillan).
World Bank (1997) *World Development Report 1997: The State in a Changing World* (New York: Oxford University Press).
World Bank (2000a) *2000: Little Data Book* (Washington DC: World Bank).
World Bank (2000b) *2000: World Bank Atlas* (Washington DC: World Bank).
World Bank (2000c) *2000: World Development Indicators* (Washington DC: World Bank).

Chapter 2

Irish foreign policy

Ben Tonra

Introduction – small state in a big world

After decades of disillusionment, the people and government of the Republic of Ireland (hereafter, 'Ireland') have begun to reassess their role and identity in the international system. The Irish state is no longer exclusively defined through its position (mental and geographic) as an 'island behind an island'. While a shared and complex history may always make relationships with Ireland's nearest neighbour problematic, the pursuit of, or flight from, British norms is a decreasing feature of debates in public policy. In its stead is a greater self-confidence, an attempt to reach out to other European and small state models and a general ambition to orient the state and its society outwards towards all azimuths rather than eastwards.

All of this has a bearing on how the Irish see themselves in the wider world. On the one hand this has been welcomed as an overdue normalisation of Irish society. The increasing 'cosmopolitanism' and internationalisation of Irish culture, secularisation of its society and the 'Europeanisation' of Irish public policy-making are three of the most widely (and often positively) cited features of this development. At the same time, however, notes of caution have also been sounded. Rapid economic growth and a cultural predisposition towards holding authority in contempt has, it is argued, made Irish society more selfish, less open and less sensitive to the plight of those marginalised at home and abroad.

In foreign policy terms this has been translated as marking the start of a 'Europeanised' phase in Irish foreign policy. Irish policy-makers – whether ministers or newly minted civil servants – are swiftly incorporated into a dense, highly structured and intensive foreign policy-making framework of consultation, coordination and joint action. This does not assume that a 'national' foreign policy is being lost or that policy-makers have abrogated their duty to defend the national interest. Instead, it argues that the definition and pursuit of national interest is now managed through a European context that has implications for the content and conduct of Irish foreign policy.

Those who study and write on Irish foreign policy appear to be divided. Some argue that Ireland's changing place in the world has been a function of individual choices. Thus, they map Ireland's course through the choppy seas of international politics by reference to the personalities and preferences of its political leaders and senior officials. These detailed, narrative stories centre, for example, around the efforts of W.T. Cosgrave to redefine the British Empire (Harkness 1969; Mansergh 1969), Eamon de Valera's determination to rewrite the 1921 Anglo-Irish Treaty and to sustain Irish neutrality (Bowman 1982; McMahon 1984; Keogh 1990), Sean MacBride's fusion of partition with neutrality (McCabe 1991), Frank Aiken's stewardship of the golden age of Irish diplomacy at the UN (MacQueen 1983; Skelly 1997) and Ireland's introduction to the global economy by Sean Lemass.

Other writers look for their explanations in Ireland's geo-strategic position. Here the predominant issue is Ireland's relationship with the United Kingdom. It is argued that the roots of Irish foreign policy are to be found in the necessary fixation of Irish foreign policy-makers with their closest neighbour. This fixation is not one of choice but one of political geography (Sloan 1997) and it thereby determines the range of available foreign policy choices. Irish policy, for example, has been analysed as being an attempt to fabricate independence from meaningless UN votes and vacuous political declarations (Sharp 1990). Similarly, the most striking feature of Irish foreign and security policy – its neutrality – has been dismissed as being devoid of real substance and an almost adolescent effort to distinguish the state from its ancient enemy (Salmon 1989).

Finally, some writers see domestic factors as illuminating the course of Irish foreign policy. In these analyses, foreign policy is a function of competing domestic claims that are adjudicated through government. Such writers focus upon the manipulation of foreign policy issues for party political gain (Keatinge 1984), the role of interest groups in defining the policy agenda (Hederman 1983) and the capacity of bureaucratic and political elites to rethink Irish economic and political interests (Maher 1986).

What all of these approaches lack, however, is an interest in linking changes in the Irish state's international role with a transformation of its identity. If such a linkage were to be made then the story of Irish foreign policy would not simply be based upon an historical excavation of individual, strategic or domestic interests but would be rooted in a changing sense of self and an evolving set of collective beliefs. This is also a point evident to policy-makers. In 1996 the then Foreign Minister, introducing the first comprehensive White Paper on Irish Foreign Policy, argued that it 'is about much more than self-interest. The elaboration of our foreign policy is also a matter of self-definition – simply put, it is for many of us a statement of the kind of people that we are' (Dáil Debates, 463: 1273).

If the 'Irish' define themselves differently at the start of this century than they did at the beginning of the last, then surely this has had consequences for the way in which that people, through their state, relates to the rest of the world? Moreover, what is the impact of these changing international relationships (and perceptions thereof) upon collective understandings of what it is to be Irish? Simply by making this linkage we open up new questions in the study of Irish foreign policy and present a new framework from which Irish foreign policy can be analysed.

Structures – an overburdened system

The central constitutional place of the Government in the conduct of the state's external relations makes the cabinet an obvious starting point in any analysis of the structures behind the Irish foreign policy process. In constitutional terms, the cabinet is collectively responsible for all government policy while individual ministers are responsible before the Dáil for all decisions and actions of their departments. Within the cabinet a number of departments and ministers are involved in the broad sweep of Irish foreign policy formulation. While specific foreign policy proposals are brought for approval to the cabinet table by the Minister for Foreign Affairs, these may require extensive consultation and subsequent negotiation with other departments responsible for some aspect of that proposal's implementation. Crucially, while policy may be initially defined collectively around the cabinet table, it is more often than not executed through the collective policy-making structures of the EU.

Within the cabinet itself there are no permanent, dedicated structures for foreign policy-making. The only exception here are various cabinet subcommittees which have been responsible either for EU policy coordination on specific issues (such as the 1992 EU Single Market Plan, the 1996 and 2000 Intergovernmental Conferences on EU treaty reform or the Agenda 2000 negotiations on EU budgetary and policy reform) or administrative issues such as preparation for an Irish Presidency of the EU Council of Ministers. The membership of these committees has varied from government to government, and they have had no permanent status or any independent secretariat.

Turning to individual government departments with specific duties related to the conduct of foreign policy, the Department of Finance is a significant actor at both the European and national levels. In its European context it has responsibilities through the Economics and Finance Ministers' Council (ECOFIN) for setting and agreeing the parameters of the EU budget. In foreign policy terms this impinges upon EU spending on development cooperation, emergency relief operations, technical aid and assistance programmes and the funding of certain types of actions under the Common Foreign and Security Policy of the Union. The Department also has specific responsibilities for the operation of structural and cohesion funds in Ireland and works through ECOFIN and its subcommittees in support of the monetary and fiscal policies underpinning the euro as Europe's single currency.

At national level the Department has the central role in setting government spending plans and overseeing individual departmental budgets and personnel policies. This gives the Department a direct input to foreign policy. It is centrally involved in decisions on issues such as the opening and closure of overseas missions, the size of the bilateral Overseas Development Aid budget, the scope and extent of training offered to members of the Diplomatic Service and the shape of promotional structures within the Department. In sum, any foreign policy proposal that involves a charge upon public funds must be approved by the Department of Finance and, if not, by the cabinet as a whole.

The Department of Enterprise, Trade and Employment also has an input to Irish foreign policy at both European and national levels. Within the Union, the Department has, alongside its EU partners, key policy-making functions in respect of bilateral trade agreements, multilateral trade negotiations and regulation of the single market. At the national level the Department chairs meetings of the Foreign Earnings Committee (FEC). It is the FEC that seeks to coordinate the activities of Irish trade and investment promotion agencies overseas. The FEC also has a crucial role to play in advising on the establishment of Irish diplomatic missions overseas. Here the Department's contribution is based upon its judgement of the economic potential that any new mission might be able to offer. This, in turn, is based upon the views of the executive agencies involved in trade and investment promotion. The Department also has an important national role in licensing the export of goods that have dual (military/civilian) use to third countries.

The Department of Agriculture and Food's contribution to foreign policy-making is centred upon its European involvement. Here, the Department is involved in decision-making that has the effect of setting product prices in major sectors of the European agricultural market. It also contributes significantly to collective Union policy-making in bilateral and multilateral trade and agricultural assistance programmes to third countries. The Department is also active at the national level of policy-making through its direct involvement with the multilateral agencies of the United Nations such as the Food and Agriculture Organisation. Many of the executive agencies for which the Department is responsible are also actively engaged in trade promotion overseas.

The Department of Justice, Equality and Law Reform is another with foreign policy responsibilities rooted in its European activities. With the 1993 establishment of the 'Third Pillar' of EU policy responsibility in the area of Justice and Home Affairs, the Department formally participates in European-level policy-making in areas related to migration, refugees, asylum, cross-border police cooperation and cooperation between criminal law agencies (Barrett 1996; Regan 2000). At the national level the Department takes lead responsibility for handling requests for asylum status and dealing with refugees. It is also deeply involved in security issues related to the peace process in Northern Ireland and here its work is directly and closely coordinated with the Departments of Foreign Affairs and that of the Taoiseach.

The role of the Department of Defence in foreign policy-making is rooted primarily in the national level but it also has an emerging European focus. EU defence ministers first met collectively in 1998. Within the institutional frameworks established under the 2000 Nice Treaty, they meet more regularly alongside their counterparts in national foreign ministries to establish and develop the 60,000-strong European Rapid Reaction Force. Contributing to the political and operational direction of that force, senior military staffs now also participate in a range of new institutional structures based in Brussels. At national level the Department has a key function in supporting Irish participation in various international peacekeeping missions and maintaining security along the land border. Traditionally, peacekeeping missions were restricted under Irish law to duties of a police character. However, the 1993 Defence Act dropped this restriction to facilitate an Irish contribution to the UN Operation in Somalia (UNOSOM). It also made possible participation in UN-mandated but NATO-led operations in Bosnia and Kosovo and other multilateral operations such as that in East Timor. The budget of the Permanent Defence Forces (PDF) is also administered and managed through the Department.

For its part, the Department of the Taoiseach is in somewhat of a unique position. As 'first among equals' within the cabinet, it is the Taoiseach who chairs the weekly cabinet meetings and who is ultimately responsible for setting the overall political agenda of the Government. In a European context, the Department contributes to Irish foreign policy-making through the European Council and its six-monthly summit meetings. Among many other functions, the European Council is responsible for setting the strategic parameters of the Union's own Common Foreign and Security Policy and its emerging Common European Security and Defence Policy. At a national foreign policy level, the Department takes the lead in all negotiations on Northern Ireland and associated constitutional issues. Officials within this department work closely with colleagues in the Department of Foreign Affairs to coordinate negotiating positions through the Anglo-Irish Conference/British–Irish Council, bilaterally with the British Government and with other parties in Northern Ireland.

The striking feature of cabinet and departmental involvement in the foreign policy process is its fragmented nature. There is no equivalent of a National Security Council or any sustained, co-ordinated approach to foreign policy formulation. The only substantial cabinet-level foreign policy structures relate to the EU and even here the approach is largely an *ad hoc* one. Senior policy-makers argue that this lack of cabinet and interdepartmental structures reflects the small size of the Irish administration, the high degree of personal familiarity at senior levels within that administration and an underlying political hostility towards hierarchies and 'heavy bureaucracies'.

Minister for Foreign Affairs and Ministers of State

In common with all other government ministers, the Minister for Foreign Affairs is formally appointed by the President, on the nomination of the Taoiseach. From 1921 to 2000 just 20 men have held this post and in that 79-year period ministers from just one party, Fianna Fáil, have held office for a total of about 50 years.

The Minister for Foreign Affairs may be said traditionally to have had four key roles. The first is a managerial one in which the Minister directs, and is held accountable to the Dáil for, the actions of the Department and of the officials within that Department. The second role is that of policy-maker. The Minister's responsibility here is to offer direction to the state's external relations and to work with cabinet colleagues in pursuit of agreed foreign policy objectives. The third role is that of spokesperson. Here the Minister represents the interests of the Department and its staff around the cabinet table, in negotiation with other ministers, in the Oireachtas and to the broader public. Finally, the Minister's role is that of a representative of the state. The Minister's function in this instance is to negotiate with the representatives of other governments both bilaterally and through multilateral forums in pursuit of policy objectives.

These roles have changed over time and become increasingly complex as the Department has grown both politically and physically. As Minister for External Affairs in the late 1950s and throughout the 1960s, for example, it was unremarkable for Frank Aiken to spend upwards of six to eight weeks in New York attending the General Assembly of the United Nations. At that time the Minister's policy responsibilities were quite narrow, were seen to be distant from day-to-day political priorities at home and were seen largely within the context of just one major international organisation. At the start of the 21st century, by contrast, the Minister for Foreign Affairs' policy responsibilities are broad and deep, impact directly and often immediately upon domestic political interests and are conducted within a much denser institutional framework centred upon membership of the EU.

The managerial role has perhaps been the subject of the least substantive change. The Minister continues to direct the actions of officials within the Department of Foreign Affairs and continues to be held accountable for those actions before the Dáil. However, participation in the EU's policy-making machinery has contributed to pressure for departmental reform such as additional training demands from staff and to some increases in resources. Second, although the direct accountability of the Minister to the Dáil is formally unchanged, it has been argued that foreign policy formulation at EU level has made it more difficult to hold ministers to account (Tonra 1996).

It is in the Minister's role as policy-maker that perhaps the greatest evolution has occurred. While the Minister continues to work with cabinet colleagues in offering direction to Ireland's external relations and the pursuit of agreed national policy objectives, the Minister pursues many of these within a European context. The Minister is responsible for working with the Taoiseach at the level of the European Council to offer a political direction to the Union as a whole that fits in with Ireland's own strategic interests. He also acts as a policy advocate within the General Affairs Council when it discusses issues under the Union's Common Foreign and Security Policy.

In the role of spokesperson, the Minister's duties have also expanded in a European context. The Minister for Foreign Affairs is now an advocate of the Union in Ireland and of Ireland in the Union. The former function is especially important in the context of successive referenda to ratify Irish accession to amending EU treaties. The Minister for Foreign Affairs, alongside the Taoiseach, has traditionally taken a leading political role in referenda campaigns to support ratification of the various European treaties.

The Minister's representative role has been partially redefined by virtue of EU membership. In the first instance, the successful conduct of EU Council Presidencies has been a top priority of Irish governments since accession to the European Communities in 1973. A key ministerial function of such presidencies is the representation of the Union internationally. This representative function is a highly prized aspect of EU membership since it is one that offers a level of international profile to the Minister, the Department, the government and the state that would otherwise be unobtainable. Senior officials argue that this has the effect of increasing the political weight of Irish foreign policy-makers in third countries.

With such an expansion and change in the role of Ministers it is hardly surprising that a major challenge is their capacity physically to fulfil all of these roles as well as those deriving from an exclusively Irish context – and in particular the pursuit of peace in Northern Ireland. To date, however, the only structural assistance provided has been the appointment of one or more junior ministers (Ministers of State) assigned either exclusively or partly to the Department of Foreign Affairs.

Since the early 1980s junior ministers at the Department of Foreign Affairs have tended to cover one of two functional areas of responsibility, either development aid or European affairs. In neither area have such junior ministers succeeded in achieving for themselves a significant political profile although the European affairs portfolio – which has been either jointly or exclusively assigned to the Department of the Taoiseach – has been perceived as a platform for later ministerial preferment. To date, no junior minister responsible for development aid has made it to the cabinet table.

Department of Foreign Affairs

The Department of External Affairs was established by legislation in 1923. By 1934 there were just 15 officials accommodated in a hallway of the Department of Agriculture building while the Department's budget amounted to just 0.34 per cent of government expenditure (Keogh 1982). Sixty-six years later the full complement of officials in the Department amounted to just under 1,000 persons divided almost equally between headquarters staff based at Iveagh House and those posted to overseas missions. Expenditure on the Department and its activities in 1999 amounted to just under 0.5 per cent of total government spending while the Department oversaw diplomatic relations with a total of 107 countries through a network of 53 overseas resident missions.

The Department's early political profile was initially built around its pursuit of what might be called constitutional diplomacy. Until the state was declared to be a Republic in 1948, the Department and its officials played a comparatively significant role in establishing the legal and political status of the state within the League of Nations, the British Empire and later the British Commonwealth (McMahon 1984; Kennedy 1996). At the end of the 1939–45 war the Department was essentially re-tooled as a public relations agent whose aim was to direct international attention to the inequities of the partition of the island of Ireland and to support the Irish Government's position on the re-unification of the 'national territory' (Cruise-O'Brien 1969). With UN membership in 1956 the Department's horizons were broadened and it played a key role in developing Ireland's international profile on issues such as disarmament, support for UN peacekeeping missions and decolonisation (MacQueen 1983; Holmes *et al.* 1992).

It was membership of the European Communities, however, that brought the Department into the mainstream of Irish government. The newly titled Department of Foreign Affairs led the accession negotiations for EC entry in 1970–72 and was given the central coordinating role for policy towards the EC by taking over the chair of the Cabinet's European Community Committee. This had the effect of putting the Department at the heart of domestic socioeconomic policy-making (Sharp 1990: 111). At the same time the gradual development of foreign policy cooperation among the EC member states provided an additional rationale for an expansion in the diplomatic infrastructure of the Department and increased staffing levels within the Political Division.

The small size of the diplomatic corps (less than 300 individuals), the limited number of overseas postings (53 resident missions), and the linkage of specific postings to specific grades poses major staffing difficulties for Departmental managers. In the first instance, recruitment to the Department has occurred in episodic waves. This has given rise to demographic bulges within certain grades. As a result, the scope for highly competent and otherwise ambitious officials to be 'stranded' at mid-level grades is considerable.

Another problematic issue for departmental managers is gender. Until 1972 all women were required by law to resign from the civil service upon marriage. This policy had the obvious effect of eliminating most women from senior grades in both the general service and the diplomatic corps. The end of the marriage 'bar', however, did not result in equality within the Department. A review of data for headquarters staff in 1998 reveals that, on average, men occupied 75 per cent of all diplomatic grade posts. The situation was even worse overseas. At the Assistant Secretary (Ambassador) grade 90 per cent of overseas posts were held by men compared to 70 per cent at the same grade among headquarters staff.

The eight Divisions in the Department reflect its functional duties. The Administration and Consular Division is responsible for the consular needs of Irish citizens overseas and for the management of the Department's own resources, both human and material. The Anglo-Irish Division is primarily occupied with the conduct of policy towards Northern Ireland and, as a consequence, bilateral relations with the United Kingdom. The Development Cooperation Division manages and evaluates all official aid and assistance programmes to the developing world. The Economic Division directs policy on external economic relations and also takes lead responsibility for coordinating the Irish position on EU domestic policy issues, including treaty and institutional reform. The Inspectorate Division was set up in 1992 and is tasked with the performance evaluation of departmental units and the conduct of a rolling 4-year programme of on-the-spot audits of all overseas missions. The responsibility of the Legal Division is to provide advice on matters of international law and treaty obligations. The Political Division is responsible for the conduct of bilateral and multilateral diplomacy in areas such as security and disarmament policy and human rights. It is also tasked with leading the Irish contribution to the EU's Common Foreign and Security Policy. Finally, the Protocol and Cultural Division manages all state and official visits, advises on protocol issues and is responsible for bilateral cultural relations.

The focus of Irish foreign policy is directed towards Anglo-Irish relations and general political issues – including the United Nations and the EU's Common Foreign and Security Policy. Approximately one half of all headquarters' diplomatic staff are assigned almost equally between the Anglo-Irish and Political Divisions. The

Economic Division and the Development Cooperation Division with 18 and 13 diplomatic grade staff respectively are the other substantial units within the Department. Others, such as Administration, may have more staff, but these are overwhelmingly drawn from the general service rather than diplomatic grades.

A dedicated Human Rights Unit, which was established in 1997 within the Department's Political Division, is significant for what it illustrates about the growing links between the Department and the NGO community. Through the 17, member Joint Department of Foreign Affairs/NGO Standing Committee on Human Rights the Unit has established a vigorous bilateral dialogue with the NGO community. Since 1998 the unit also sponsors an annual NGO Forum on Human Rights which brings together NGO activists as well as academics, politicians and Department officials to discuss human rights issues and to nominate two NGO representatives onto the Standing Committee (the other 15 members being nominated by the Department). The Unit's significance rests particularly upon its positive and direct engagement with the NGO community. As the Minister of State, Liz O'Donnell argued at the 1998 conference 'modern governments can only be enhanced by strong links and regular dialogue with the NGO community' (Dáil Debates, 489: 812).

Throughout the 1990s there were debates on structural reform in the Department. One of the most significant of these is related to its functional sub-division. The primary distinction is that between the 'political' and 'economic' divisions. The perceived utility of such a division is related to a traditional diplomatic distinction between foreign policy and foreign economic policy. The question that arises is whether or not a geographic 'desk' system might be more logical where regional or country 'desks' bring together diplomats responsible for both economic and political relations.

In the EU, so long as a clear distinction was maintained between the Common Foreign and Security Policy of the Union and the conduct of its external economic relations, the rationale for maintaining a functional differentiation within the Department was a strong one. However, following the Maastricht, Amsterdam and Nice treaties, these two policy realms are increasingly being brought together. For example, diplomats from Iveagh House are now participating in a single set of Brussels-based foreign policy working groups constructed from two previously parallel systems. In addition, the General Affairs Council now deals with a single agenda drawn up by the Committee of Member States' Permanent Representatives in Brussels (COREPER) instead of facing two – one dealing with EC international trade matters and a second on CFSP. The logic of such a development would suggest that the Department will have to consider its own structural change so as to engage effectively with those in Brussels. The Danish foreign ministry, for example, was reorganised along this principle in 1991 and, according to the Department's Permanent Secretary, Henrik Wohlk, this was in direct response to the evolution in EU foreign policy structures (Jørgensen 1997).

Another major structural issue is the position of the Development Cooperation Division. That Division manages a spending programme three times the size of the Department's own budget. Despite the sometimes specialised nature of activity in this Division, officials working there are rotated with the same regularity and with the same determination to avoid excessive 'specialisation' as those elsewhere in the Department. Some senior officials and many spokespersons for major development NGOs see a logic in spinning that Division off from the Department and establishing it as a stand-alone executive agency. Such an agency would have its own management structure, hire its own professional staff and be held accountable to the Dáil on the same basis as other executive agencies. One central counter-argument raised by senior departmental officials is the impact of such a move on the promotional prospects of diplomats. The loss of diplomatic posts from that Division and its associated overseas assignments would seriously exacerbate existing staff difficulties.

Policy process – a modest democratisation in view

The starting point for any analysis of democratic control of the foreign policy process is parliament. Despite constitutional claims to the contrary, the Oireachtas (parliament) is a servant of the executive rather than its master (Gallagher 1996: 126). Weak committees, powerful party whips and an electoral system that is seen to reward local constituency work over national legislative activism all serve to undermine the capacity of the Oireachtas to hold the executive to account. Thus, traditional analyses of Irish foreign policy have tended to downplay both the role and the significance of the Oireachtas in the conduct of foreign policy (Keatinge 1973).

In 1990 one former Minister for Foreign Affairs described the Oireachtas as being 'the least developed legislature in the European Community' and noted that it was unique in Europe in having no parliamentary committee to consider foreign affairs (Dáil Debates, 396: 1638). The 1974 establishment of the Joint Oireachtas Committee on Secondary Legislation of the European Communities had been the first parliamentary foray into what might be described as foreign policy and this was only the second Joint Oireachtas Committee ever to be established. That committee did not, however, succeed in developing a strong political profile for itself.

Not until 1993 was a Joint Committee on Foreign Affairs (FAC) finally established. It was constructed from the creation of two parliamentary select committees – one each from the Dáil and the Seanad and provision was also made for Irish members of the European Parliament and the Parliamentary Assembly of the Council of Europe to attend but not vote in meetings.

Meeting very often weekly during the parliamentary term, the new committee quickly established its own precedents and working methods. Initially, its work included that previously conducted by the Joint Oireachtas Committee on the Secondary Legislation of the European Communities and a subcommittee was established for that purpose. By 1995, however, it was judged that this division of labour was unsatisfactory and a separate Joint Committee on European Affairs (EAC) was established. The remit of the latter was also extended beyond European legislative scrutiny to include any matter arising from Irish membership of the Union. In addition, this committee was given the mandate to represent the Oireachtas in meetings and activities of the inter-parliamentary Conference of European Affairs Committees (COSAC) within the EU.

According to its members, the Foreign Affairs Committee can be characterised as being only a partially successful experiment in parliamentary supervision. The committee's strengths flow from its ability to set its own agenda, to review policy in greater detail than is possible within either the Dáil or the Seanad and the committee's generally non-partisan approach. At the same time, the committee's weaknesses are seen to be rooted in its limited resources, its consequent dependence upon the executive, the broad and shallow nature of its agenda and its failure to engage successfully with the public through the media.

Many of the central weaknesses identified by members are a function of the committee's structure. In 1999 it was composed of 20 Oireachtas members (14 from the Dáil and 6 from the Seanad). Despite its size, the committee has no substantial secretariat, no independent research staff and, until the appointment in 2000 of a parliamentary law officer, it had to rely upon the Government's own Attorney General for any legal advice. The senior staff that work with the committee are often seconded from the Department of Foreign Affairs. The committee itself can offer no long-term job security or career advancement to its staff since its life span is limited to the 5-year maximum constitutional life of the Dáil itself.

This paucity of back-up support means that the agenda of the committee tends to be broad but shallow. Unlike most other committees, it does not have a ready-made agenda flowing from the passage of legislation and members, therefore, rarely have the chance to involve themselves in the nitty-gritty of legislative amendment and formulation. In reaction to this limitation and its lack of resources, the committee has come to rely upon the contribution of consultant experts commissioned to write draft reports on issues of interest. These reports are debated within the committee and may or may not be linked to public hearings. They are then published as formal reports of the committee.

Apart from any direction provided by the Chairperson, the committee's focus is in large part driven by the organisations that contact it according to several members. TDs and Senators receiving communications from NGOs tend to pass these on to the committee as specific agenda items that then may form the basis of a hearing or even a series of hearings. The witnesses or experts brought before such hearings are themselves often identified or even provided by the NGOs that made the initial contact. This creates what was described by one member as a 'somewhat incestuous circle' of policy insiders and was a process that, according to another member, was a boon to 'professional sore-heads'.

The breadth of the committee's agenda is illustrated well in its 1998 work programme, characterised by one member as looking more like a 'wish list rather than a programme'. It covered 28 separate topics divided among five categories of issues (both thematic and geographic). The size of the committee's agenda meant that there wasn't, according to another member, 'a hope in hell of getting through it and little point even if we did'. This latter point underscores serious dissatisfaction, often expressed as a sort of weary resignation, that the work of the committee, while worthy, has little or no substantive policy impact or public profile.

Many members feel that the work of the committee is rarely if ever a factor in policy formulation. The general view appears to be that at best the committee is treated 'with respect and politeness'. For some, the fault is seen to rest at least in part with the committee itself. One member argues that the committee's tendency to flit from one issue to the next with no concrete follow-up and little original research leaves very little for the media to get their teeth into. Most members, however, feel that the media, both print and broadcast, give the Oireachtas as a whole very little attention and parliamentary committees even less so.

More traditional mechanisms of parliamentary oversight reflect many of the same weaknesses evident in the work of the committees. The use of Parliamentary Questions in the Dáil, for example, highlights the fact that members' interests tend to be driven by media and NGO interest. What is especially striking in the pattern of Parliamentary Questions addressed to the Minister for Foreign Affairs is that the contemporary focus of Irish parliamentary interest in foreign policy is to be found in the Asia Pacific region. Of approximately 551 individual Parliamentary Questions (written and oral) submitted to the Minister for Foreign Affairs in 1998 just under 20 per cent focused on this single region and especially East Timor and Indonesia, Tibet and China and Burma–Myanmar.

Questions related to Northern Ireland accounted for 14 per cent of the total with those directed towards Anglo-Irish relations making up an additional 11 per cent. The majority of questions in these two categories were concerned with ongoing peace negotiations and the position of the Irish Government on many of the matters associated with them. A significant minority, however, were preoccupied with what might be categorised as 'sovereignty' issues: alleged border incursions by Northern Ireland and British security forces, delays in re-opening border roads, general complaints against the security forces and specific queries about the status of Irish prisoners in UK jails. The balance of questions concerned political issues in other parts of the world: the Middle East and Africa 12 per cent, Western Europe (including Turkey) 10 per cent, Central and Eastern Europe and Latin America both 8 per cent.

When questions are categorised on the basis of functional (rather than geographic) interest it is evident that political issues predominate overwhelmingly. More than 22 per cent of questions in 1998 asked the Minister for his political assessment of events in areas of tension or conflict. Many if not most of these questions appear to have been driven by media reports. The second major category of questions, 17 per cent of the total, related specifically to human rights issues. Security and disarmament were the focus of 14 per cent of questions with a substantial proportion here related to Irish neutrality and perceived threats thereto.

At the interface between parliament and executive it is also interesting to note that while Ministers for Foreign Affairs (in the period 1993–99) have devoted between 20 and 30 per cent of their annual estimates' speech to issues related to EU membership, less than 8 per cent of parliamentarians' contributions have touched upon this set of issues. For them, the areas of greatest interest were related to security and defence (26 per cent), Northern Ireland (23 per cent), departmental structures and administration (23 per cent), human rights (11 per cent) and the United Nations (9 per cent).

In sum, while the scope for parliamentary scrutiny over foreign policy has expanded considerably, the depth of its penetration into the policy process is as yet marginal. The potential of the parliamentary committees has not been fully exploited. They are seen by their members and by officials and ministers as being peripheral to the policy process and, as a consequence, they have not achieved the kind of political profile that is seen to accrue to similar committees in other parliaments. While access and relevance to the policy process are crucial, the committees' limited profile is also seen to be a function of its lack of resources and the limited dedication of members.

Many parliamentarians take an active part in raising foreign policy issues through Parliamentary Questions. However, it is evident from the content of these interventions that members' interests are quite narrow, are poorly focused and are more often than not the product of either a recent news report or effective NGO lobbying. Only in rare instances can they be seen to be part of an ongoing policy commitment and when they are such members may often be seen – quoting one long-serving parliamentarian – as 'cranks and bores' by their colleagues. At the same time, the pattern of parliamentary intervention does indicate certain lines of predominant interest – in human rights, in the developing countries of Asia, Latin America and Africa and in disarmament issues.

An informed public

Political parties lie at the intersection of policy formulation and democratic consent. Whatever their flaws as mechanisms for aggregating interest, representing public opinion, mobilising public participation and offering leadership, Irish political parties are key to an understanding of the public policy process. The analysis here seeks to identify the significance of foreign policy issues for all of the major parties represented in the Oireachtas by looking at their policy documents, press releases and the profile they give to their international linkages with trans-national party organisations. In looking at this documentation, attention will then focus upon the pre-eminent foreign policy narratives that may be seen to emerge.

The largest party in the state, Fianna Fáil, would appear to direct comparatively little attention to foreign policy matters. In its electronic archive of party statements and press releases for the first six months of 1999 just two out of 54 such documents (4 per cent) were primarily concerned with such issues (Fianna Fáil 1999). However, this limited activity was largely a consequence of its position as the leading party within the Government with the result that most of its press efforts were directed through official rather than party channels. In reviewing archived party policy documents a greater level of interest does indeed emerge. In the nine policy chapters of its 1999 European Parliament election manifesto, for example, three were directly related to foreign policy issues: reform of the EU, the peace process in Northern Ireland and European security. In 1995 the party also published a comprehensive policy statement on foreign policy (Fianna Fáil 1995). This document, which was issued while the party was in opposition, was published in advance of the Government's own White Paper on the subject (Government of Ireland 1997). On the party's web site, however, no specific linkage or mention was made in 1999 to or of the party's links in the European Parliament with the Gaullist-led Union for Europe group.

The party's policy documents do not reveal any clearly dominant foreign policy narrative. The 1999 EP election manifesto, for example, identifies the central purpose of Fianna Fáil's approach as being the pursuit of Irish national interests at both European and international levels through an 'enlightened foreign policy' (Fianna Fáil 1999). That document also goes to some lengths to assert the party's commitment to neutrality and to demote foreign policy cooperation at EU level to those occasions 'that may require decisions with the other like-minded countries in the EU, including the neutrals' (Fianna Fáil 1999). Alongside this very sovereignty-conscious and independent approach, the moral and ethical dimension of foreign policy is also highlighted. In its earlier policy document, Ireland's 'particular affinity' with the developing world is asserted and the ambition that Ireland might be 'a voice for the Third World in the chambers and corridors of power' is also expressed (Fianna Fáil 1995).

For the second largest party, Fine Gael, foreign policy appears to be an area of some considerable interest. Just under 20 per cent of its 141 electronically archived press releases and statements issued in the first six months of 1999 related to foreign policy issues. The focus of these was Northern Ireland (40 per cent), security and defence (30 per cent) and the EU (15 per cent). Of its 29 archived policy documents and 'consultation' papers, five were foreign policy related. These dealt with the Amsterdam Treaty, Irish membership of the Partnership for Peace, development cooperation, the European Parliament elections and the proposal of a Transatlantic Institute to be established in Ireland to analyse EU–US relations. Furthermore, within its European Parliament manifesto the party devotes 13 chapter headings from a total of 27 directly to foreign policy issues. On its web site the party vigorously promotes its linkage to the European People's Party within the European Parliament but makes no mention of its participation in the Christian Democrat International (CDI) of which it is also a member.

The dominance of a European narrative in the party's documentation emerges very strongly indeed. Its commitment to Irish membership of the EU goes beyond the fulfilment of specified national interests (although these are frequently invoked). It also includes the pursuit of collective European interests, summarised as 'the cause of a peaceful, prosperous and stable Europe' and invokes the increased political and institutional capacity of the 'Union' as a necessary condition to that end (Fine Gael 1999). Membership of the EU is presented as requiring a fundamental rethink of 'how we can participate more effectively in the evolving post-Cold War European security architecture' (Fine Gael 1996: 8). Finally, the values underpinning Irish foreign policy are frequently presented as being rooted in collective European principles rather than being something that is uniquely or exclusively Irish.

The Labour Party too devotes considerable attention to foreign policy. Of the 241 press statements and news releases archived by that party in the first six months of 1999 more than 25 per cent were devoted to foreign policy issues. The European Union was the preoccupation of nearly 40 per cent of statements, with Northern Ireland (20 per cent), security and defence (20 per cent) and human rights and asylum issues (8 per cent each) being the other central issues. With only three policy documents electronically archived it was difficult to assess the extent of the party's ongoing research into foreign policy issues. Only one of these documents directly related to foreign policy and that was its European Parliament election manifesto. However, in a statement of the party's general priorities and principles, more than 35 per cent of the text was devoted to foreign policy issues, primarily Northern Ireland, human rights, international economic justice, European security, international environmental cooperation and EU development. On its web site, the party also highlights both its European and international party linkages through the Party of European Socialists and the Socialist International respectively.

Two narratives emerge strongly from the Labour Party's published documentation and statements. First, the party clearly has a strong self-image as being dedicated to international justice, development and peace. Direct linkage is made between social and economic development at home and that same development overseas. The 'moral obligation' of work against global poverty is also invoked but, interestingly, this is immediately placed within a European context where 'the European Union should take the leading role'. Ireland should then 'play its part in this development' (Labour 1999a). The Union is thus presented here and elsewhere as the means through which Irish foreign objectives are to be pursued since 'action taken in conjunction with our European neighbours is far more effective than any action we might take on our own' (Labour 1999b). Ireland's distinctive contribution to global development is then later defined as its contribution to UN reform, diplomatic support for international debt relief and a greater allocation to the Irish bilateral Official Development Assistance (ODA) programme. By contrast, sovereignty issues are not highly valued. In Northern Ireland the party looks forward to the removal of nationalist and sovereignty issues from the political agenda.

The fourth largest party in the state – based upon its parliamentary representation in the period 1997–2000 – is the Progressive Democrats (PD) who show comparatively little interest in foreign policy issues. Of 76 statements issued to the press and electronically archived by that party in the first six months of 1999, just 10 per cent related to foreign policy issues. Of these, half were concerned with developments in Northern Ireland while the remainder related to EU issues and security and defence. Of 13 archived policy papers just one dealt with foreign policy and this too was devoted to Northern Ireland. Finally, there was no acknowledgement of the party's linkage with the Liberal group in the European Parliament nor with the Liberal International.

There is no decisive indication of dominant narratives emerging from this limited pool of source documents. PD party statements on Northern Ireland speak in generally vague terms about the need for consensus, mutual respect and accommodation and an equivalence of rights. They decisively reject the language of sovereignty, nationalism and independence. At the same time, however, the party does extensively employ the language of national interests towards developments within the EU.

Of the remaining parties represented in the Dáil in 1999 – the Green Party, Sinn Féin and the Socialist Party – all devote some attention to foreign policy issues and all are anxious to highlight their linkages with parties and political groups internationally. They also share, to a very large extent, the same dominant foreign policy narrative. All three focus upon what they see as the threats posed to an independent and sovereign foreign policy by cooperation at EU level which has already turned Ireland into 'a puppet of the main western powers' (Green Party 1999a). All three maintain that consecutive governments have engaged in a long-term strategic effort to undermine Irish neutrality in the interests of a 'European military superstate' (Sinn Féin 1999), the imperialist ambitions of several of the larger EU member states (Socialist Party 1999) and the United States and/or major arms manufacturers (Green Party 1999b). The EU itself is seen to be fundamentally undemocratic or at least critically deficient in terms of democratic accountability and all three parties opposed ratification of both the Maastricht and Amsterdam treaties. They see the roots of a progressive, positive and engaged Irish foreign policy to be found in its neutrality and the conduct of a sovereign and independent foreign policy. Finally, all three highlight Ireland's experience of colonialism as giving the Irish state and people a unique capacity to speak and act alongside countries in the developing world.

While political parties are an important part of the framework in the policy process another is that provided by NGOs. There is no agreed definition of NGOs and the label has been acknowledged by several analysts to be imprecise and unsatisfactory (Sheriff 1996: 33). In an Irish context the term has been used to include everything from a four-person, all-volunteer single-issue solidarity campaign group to a professionally staffed development agency with an annual budget running into the tens of million of pounds annually.

The first and largest 'cluster' of NGO activity (at least in terms of budgets and professional staff) is perhaps that of NGO development organisations. These might be said to be involved, either directly or indirectly, in the pursuit of development issues either at home (in terms of development education) and/or overseas (the provision of long- or short-term aid). In the Irish context, NGOs such as Concern, Trocaire, Christian Aid, Gorta, the Irish Red Cross, ActionAid Ireland and World Vision Ireland might be included here.

A second cluster is centred upon single-country solidarity campaigns and single-issue interest groups. Such groups, often small, poorly resourced and reliant upon volunteer staff or government-sponsored social employment schemes, campaign to raise public consciousness towards oppression or perceived injustice in specific parts of the world such as East Timor, Nicaragua, Tibet, Mozambique, Nigeria, Peru, Cuba, Burma, El Salvador, Liberia–Sierra Leone, Brazil or Bosnia. Alternatively, they might be very specifically related to a single, often development-related, issue. Organisations in the latter category might be said to include Baby Milk Action, the Debt and Development Coalition, Fair Trade, Tools for Solidarity, etc.

A third cluster of NGOs might be identified that focus upon broader issues of peace, welfare and human rights. Their campaigns may focus on particular trouble spots, campaigns or individual issues but, in the main, they try and keep an eye on what might be perceived to be the wider and inter-related issues of global politics and/or development. They may also come from a particular philosophical or religious perspective and seek to bring this perspective to bear upon contemporary global issues. Organisations in this category might include Pax Christi, Irish CND, Amnesty International, Action from Ireland (Afri) and the Irish Commission for Justice and Peace.

A fourth cluster of NGOs might be said to focus very closely upon either informing or moving major and specific public policy debates. Organisations such as the Institute for European Affairs, the National Platform, the European Movement, the Peace and Neutrality Alliance or umbrella associations such as Dochas would see their roles perhaps as one of education, information and/or mobilisation on a particular public policy issue. Such organisations may present themselves as either grassroots membership/campaigning organisations or as forums for education/research.

A fifth and final cluster could be seen as providing more of a social or even professional service to its members. While many solidarity campaigns and support groups provide an important social link for expatriate members, other organisations are perhaps more tightly focused upon this service-related goal. Examples of such NGOs include Comlámh, Irish–Argentine Society, Irish–Finnish Society, Islamic Relief Agency and the Overseas Institute.

There has been some spectacular growth in the NGO community over the last number of years. By its very nature the NGO community is difficult to keep track of. As noted above, while there are large, professional and well-funded NGOs these are a minority of the population. The majority have less than 100 members, rely heavily upon cooperative and volunteer structures and frequently operate within larger supportive 'umbrella' associations. However, using an annual register of social, political and other organisations it is possible to sketch a rough map of the growth of Irish foreign policy NGOs from the mid-1960s (IPA 1999).

In 1999 it was possible to identify more than 80 organisations that were dedicated to participating in, to influencing or to challenging the foreign policy-making process in Ireland. In 1966 there were four such organisations that might be seen as directing their attention beyond Irish borders. Looking at the subsequent annual data it is possible to identify several 'waves' of NGO development. In the period 1970–80, for example, a three-fold increase in the number of foreign policy NGOs was largely a result of the proliferation of overseas development aid agencies sparked by the 1974 inauguration of an Irish bilateral aid programme. From 1980 to 1985 a doubling in the number of foreign policy NGOs resulted from the growth of Latin American solidarity groups and the anti-nuclear/peace movement. This was associated with heightened East–West tensions from 1979–80, the resulting proliferation of 'proxy' Cold War conflicts in Latin America and the politicisation of debates surrounding Irish neutrality in the early 1980s. The third identifiable wave is to be found in the period from 1995 with the establishment of refugee and asylum support organisations and various solidarity campaigns associated with other specific areas of conflict.

The role of NGOs is substantially greater at the start of the 21st century than it was in the early 1970s when it was argued that outside the arena of Anglo-Irish relations there was no discernible public constituency of interest in foreign policy (Keatinge 1973: 293). NGOs are actively engaged across a range of issues and campaign both publicly and privately to shift the course of Irish policy-makers. While the content of such efforts is unremarkable – personal lobbying, letter writing, advertising, charity collections, petitions, demonstrations and direct action such as boycotts – the access of some groups to the policy process is quite remarkable.

Despite the best efforts of parliamentarians, parties and partisan interest groups, however, the level of direct public interest in foreign policy issues in Ireland is limited and narrow. For one long-time development aid campaigner this leads to frustration when she views the '. . . absence of public debate on foreign policy matters during [the] recent election campaign' (Mary van Lieshout, *Irish Times*, 14 June 1997). Even when, as in the case of EU treaty reform, the implications for citizens are direct and meaningful it can be difficult to generate any serious public attention. Within six weeks of the 1998 referendum on the Amsterdam Treaty less than half of the electorate had decided to vote either 'yes' or 'no' with 36 per cent still in the 'don't know' category and only 38 per cent of the entire electorate 'genuinely interested' in the issues involved (*Sunday Independent*/IMS, 5 April 1998). Even in that foreign policy sector where popular support is highest – development cooperation – public opinion is ambiguous. While, according to a poll conducted by the Advisory Council on Development Co-operation, there is broad and enthusiastic support for development aid, understanding of the core issues associated with it is lacking (Holmes *et al.* 1993: 58). For one commentator, the explanation for all of this lies close to home: 'Northern Ireland and, by extension, Anglo-Irish relations absorbs much of such limited public attention as is directed beyond our boundaries' (Ronan Fanning, *Sunday Independent*, 2 April 1995).

When fingers are then pointed, in search of an explanation for a perceived public apathy, the media is usually to be found at the sharp end of the digit. Several arguments are to be found floating in this intellectual ether. The first is that the media has been captured by minority interests, that it reflects a radicalised and unrepresentative sample of opinion and that through either laziness or complicity it allows the agenda to be driven by small unrepresentative NGOs. One reflection of this, it is argued, is to be found in issues related to neutrality and defence where one commentator asks the rhetorical question 'can any reader remember even one article arguing that there are sound moral political and economic reasons why we should support NATO . . .'. His answer is that '. . . to argue any of that is totally taboo in Irish journalism' (Eoghan Harris, *Sunday Times*, 14 April 1996). Another, more establishment voice, echoes some of these concerns when – in relation to the same issues – he identifies a 'visceral anti-Americanism' in much of what passes for analysis of major international events (Garret FitzGerald, cited in Kirby 1992: 163–4).

From the other side of the political trenches similar brickbats are lobbed in the direction of Irish print and broadcast journalism. The corporate and/or state control of all the mass media outlets, the penetration of US and UK information providers in the Irish media market and the scale of market share captured by UK broadcast and print journalism have all conspired to create an establishment-backed consensus on major foreign policy issues. For Patricia McKenna MEP – a visceral critic of the EU – this has meant that the Irish media has 'sold out' to pro-EU arguments and refuses to publish sceptical views on EU-related issues (*Irish Times*, 20 October 1997).

There is certainly no doubt that the media has a crucial role to play in generating public debate around foreign policy issues. Certainly the Government recognised this when, ten days in advance of the formal publication of its 1996 White Paper on foreign policy, it sent draft copies to the media and provided briefings to select journalists four days prior to its launch and distribution to parliamentarians (*Irish Times*, 28 March 1996). According to a study by John Horgan (1987) the media is indeed the first source of public information followed by Church and formal political debates. The Irish media is also credited by that report as being considered fair and even-handed by its audience.

In meeting the challenge of public disinterest, Irish governments have begun to claim that public engagement in the policy process is a necessary part of a healthy and effective foreign policy. Through the construction of the 1996 White Paper, Irish policy-makers tried directly to engage the general public and foreign policy activists in a broader dialogue on the nature and direction of Irish foreign policy (Government of Ireland 1996). Explicitly intended to vest the 'ownership' of Irish foreign policy in the hands of the people, the drafting process was based upon a series of seven open public meetings in 1994 and 1995. On average, these brought together more than 200 government ministers, politicians, officials from the Department of Foreign Affairs, foreign policy activists and members of the public to debate the principles and purpose of Irish foreign policy in a number of specific issue areas. In addition, public written submissions were invited through press advertisements and more than 60 individuals and organisations sent in their views.

For the Tánaiste and Minister for Foreign Affairs, Dick Spring TD, the effort was central to engaging public involvement and was a response to popular demand. He insisted that 'a revolution is taking place in Ireland . . . slowly but with growing resolution the people are seizing power . . . through demands for greater accountability from their elected representatives, more openness in government and wider access to information' (Spring, *Irish Times*, 16 January 1995). In the case of the White Paper he argued that '*Above all I want the white paper to contribute to a real sense of ownership of policy*. Secondly I want the white paper to demonstrate that our foreign policy is about defending our *interests* but *also* is capable of reflecting *values* that are deep-seated in Ireland and the Irish people' [emphasis in original] (Spring, *Irish Times*, 26 March 1996). Whether that clarion call to democratisation has yet taken root – or indeed is allowed to – has yet to be determined.

Conclusion: the Europeanisation of Irish foreign policy

Just after Ireland joined the European Communities in 1973 a new Minister for Foreign Affairs convened the first ever conference of all of Ireland's Heads of Mission from its embassies worldwide. Part of its purpose was to study the implications of this new European context for the conduct and principles of Irish foreign policy. Nearly 25 years later another Minister for Foreign Affairs reflected upon that impact by noting that membership of the EU '. . . has become the biggest single factor in our international relations and is crucial to our economic development . . . [it] also enhances our ability to exert an influence on the wider international stage' (Government of Ireland 1997: 3).

Membership of the EU has undoubtedly expanded the horizons of Irish diplomats. Their involvement in global issues today is both substantively wider and deeper than at any time in the history of Irish diplomacy. Through EU foreign policy working groups and the CFSP Secretariat, through presidency activities, through the Political Committee, Political and Security Committee, the Military Committee, the Military Staff Committee, COREPER and in support of the General Affairs Council, Irish diplomats and military personnel now engage with their European colleagues across the entire range of global issues.

The socialisation of Irish diplomats into a European diplomatic regime is also evident. This is most obvious at the level of Political Director and European Correspondent, but also at official level through the many EU foreign policy working groups. The commitment to something like a 'European foreign policy' is identifiable. While some officials will speak in terms of the Union as being an amplifier for 'national' policy, others – especially younger diplomats – tend to speak more in terms of the credibility and efficacy of the collective European policy where that would have greater impact in reflecting Irish foreign policy 'values' and 'concerns'.

This internalisation of norms can sometimes be made explicit. Department officials, for example, have said that there is a '. . . habit of thinking in terms of [an EU] consensus'. Another notes that '. . . where there is ever any new foreign policy initiative in the making, the first reflex is European. The question is now "what will our European partners say – what is the opinion in Europe"'. Some even more senior officials insist that it is this EU context that gives meaning, substance and significance to Irish foreign policy.

The structural changes wrought in the Department of Foreign Affairs as a result of EU membership have been noted above. Both the Presidency of the Council of Ministers and the responsibilities associated with EPC were initially linked with more than doubling the number of Irish overseas missions (from 20 in 1970 to 51 in 1998) as well as organisational adaptation within the Department. The impact on individual embassies has also been significant – and has been paralleled by a reassessment of the role of Irish embassies. As the White Paper on Irish foreign policy puts it: 'Embassies now have an important additional function in influencing the relationship between their host country and the European Union; ensuring that the host country's policies towards the European Union are as favourable as possible to Irish interests and that the (host) country is familiar with and responsive to Irish policies across the whole spectrum of activities covered by the European Union.'

In this respect, scope is left open for some level of cooperation with EU partners and institutions. On a value-for-money basis, flexibility and innovation are invoked as a basis for the possible co-location of Irish missions with those of EU partners. According to the White Paper this is an option which '. . . will be fully explored' in further consideration of diplomatic expansion. There has also been discussion of the possibility of co-location with European Commission delegations overseas where Ireland is without direct diplomatic representation.

The key outstanding question for Irish policy-makers is the extent to which they can reconcile their ambition for greater democratic input to the policy process with the reality of an emerging European identity to foreign policy. While in principle there is no necessary inverse correlation between democratisation and Europeanisation, it is certainly true to say that Europeanisation – with its spatial and psychological distance from the 'national' political arena – will increase the challenge of democratisation. Some smaller European states, such as Denmark, have made explicit efforts to square that political circle by investing significant policy responsibilities in their national parliament. It remains to be seen what strategy, if any, will be adopted by their Irish colleagues.

References

Barrett, G. (1996) *Justice Co-operation in the European Union*, IEA Studies in European Union (Dublin: Institute of European Affairs).

Bowman, J. (1982) *De Valera and the Ulster Question 1917–1973* (Oxford: Oxford University Press).

Cruise-O'Brien, C.C. (1969) 'Ireland in international affairs', in Owen Dudley Edwards (ed.), *Conor Cruise O'Brien Introduces Ireland* (New York: Andre Deutsch).

Fianna Fáil (1995) *Policy Statement on Irish Foreign Policy* (Dublin: Fianna Fáil).

Fianna Fáil (1999) http://www.fiannafail.ie/whatsnew/index.html

Fine Gael (1996) *Beyond Neutrality: Ireland's Role in European Defence and Security* (Dublin: Fine Gael), http://www.finegael.ie/main.htm

Fine Gael (1999) http://www.finegael.ie/main.htm

Gallagher, M. (1996) 'Parliament', in John Coakley and Michael Gallagher (eds), *Politics in the Republic of Ireland* (Dublin: PSAI Press).

Government of Ireland (1996) *Challenges and Opportunities Abroad: White Paper on Foreign Policy* (Dublin: Department of Foreign Affairs).

Government of Ireland (1997) http://www.irlgov.ie/iveagh/default.htm

Green Party (1999a) http://www.imsgrp.com/greenparty/neutral.htm

Green Party (1999b) http://www.imsgrp.com/greenparty/a-treaty.htm

Harkness, D.W. (1969) *The Restless Dominion: The Irish Free State and the British Commonwealth of Nations, 1921–31* (London: Macmillan).

Hederman, O'Brien, M. (1983) *The Road to Europe: Irish attitudes 1948–61* (Dublin: Institute for Public Administration).

Holmes, M., Rees, N. and Whelan, B. (1992) 'Increased Horizons, Increased Constraints: Dilemmas of a Small State Within EPC', paper prepared for inaugural Pan-European Conference in International Studies, Heidelberg, 16–20 September.

Holmes, M., Rees, N. and Whelan, B. (1993) *The Poor Relation: Irish Foreign Policy and the Third World* (Dublin: Trócaire/Gill and Macmillan).

Horgan, J. (1987) 'Explaining the media', in *Trócaire Development Review* (Dublin: Trócaire).

IPA (1999) *Administration Yearbook and Diary 2000* (Dublin: Institute for Public Administration).

Jørgensen, K.E. (1997) 'Denmark', in Brian Hocking and David Spence (eds), *EU Member State Foreign Ministries*, vol. 1 (Brussels: Directorate General 1A).

Keatinge, P. (1973) *The Formulation of Irish Foreign Policy* (Dublin: Institute of Public Administration).
Keatinge, P. (1984) 'The Europeanisation of Irish foreign policy', in P.J. Drudy and Dermot McAleese (eds) *Ireland and the European Community: Irish Studies 3* (Cambridge: Cambridge University Press).
Kennedy, M. (1996) *Ireland and the League of Nations, 1916–1946* (Dublin: Irish Academic Press).
Keogh, D. (1982) 'Ireland: the Department of Foreign Affairs', in Zara Steiner (ed.), *Times Survey of Foreign Ministries of the World* (Times Books).
Keogh, D. (1990) *Ireland and Europe: 1919–1989* (Dublin: Hibernian University Press).
Kirby, P. (1992) *Ireland and Latin America: links and lessons* (Dublin: Trócaire and Gill and MacMillan).
Labour (1999a) http://www.labour.ie/policy/demprog.tmpl
Labour (1999b) http://www.labour.ie/policy/amster.tmpl
MacQueen, N. (1983) 'Ireland's entry to the United Nations 1946–1955', in Tom Gallagher and James O'Connell (eds), *Contemporary Irish Studies* (Manchester: Manchester University Press).
Maher, D.H. (1986) *The Tortuous Path: The Course of Ireland's Entry to the EEC, 1948–1973* (Dublin: Institute of Public Administration).
Mair, P. (1995) *Representative Government in Modern Europe* with Michael Gallagher and Michael Laver (New York, London: McGraw-Hill).
Mansergh, N. (1969) 'Irish foreign policy 1945–1951', in Kevin B. Nowlan and Desmond T. Williams (eds), *Ireland in the War Years and After* (Dublin: Gill and Macmillan).
McCabe, Ian (1991) *A Diplomatic History of Ireland 1948–1949: The Republic, the Commonwealth and NATO* (Dublin: Irish Academic Press).
McMahon, D. (1984) *Republicans and Imperialists: Anglo Irish Relations in the 1930s* (New Haven, CT: Yale University Press).
Regan, E. (2000) *The New Third Pillar: Cooperation against Crime in the European Union* (Institute for European Affairs).
Salmon, T.C. (1989) *Unneutral Ireland: An Ambivalent and Unique Security Policy* (Oxford: Clarendon Press).
Sharp, P. (1990) *Irish Foreign Policy and the European Community: A Study of the Impact of Interdependence on the Foreign Policy of a Small State* (Aldershot: Dartmouth).
Sheriff, A.P. (1996) 'Non Governmental Organisations and Irish Politics', in *Irish Political Studies*, vol. 11 (Dublin: PSAI Press).
Sinn Féin (1999) http://www.sinnfein.ie/
Skelly, J.M. (1997) *Irish Diplomacy at the United Nations 1945–1965: National Interests and the International Order* (Dublin: Irish Academic Press).
Sloan, G.R. (1997) *The Geopolitics of Anglo-Irish Relations* (London: Leicester University Press).
Socialist Party (1999) http://www.dojo.ie/socialist/home.html
Sunday Independent
The Irish Times
The Sunday Times
Tonra, B. (1996) 'Ireland: the internal dissenter', in Stelios Stavridis and Christopher Hill (eds), *The Domestic Sources of Foreign Policy: A Study of the West European Reactions to the Falklands Conflict* (Oxford: Berg).

Chapter 3

The Irish economy in international perspective

John Bradley

Introduction

In a remarkable comment on the state of the Irish economy today, Intel president Craig Barrett recently reflected on why his firm had come to Ireland. Speaking to Thomas Friedman, author of *The Lexus and the Olive Tree* (1999), Barrett said:

> We are there because Ireland is very pro-business, they have a very strong educational infrastructure, it is incredibly easy to move things in and out of the country, and it is incredibly easy to work with the government. I would invest in Ireland before Germany or France. (Friedman 1999: 188)

It was not always like this. Any Irish person born in the immediate aftermath of World War II has seen their country undergo an extraordinary transformation. Once upon a time Ireland was an inward-looking, inefficient, economic basket case, haemorrhaging their population through emigration. Today, it attracts the admiration of the nations and businesses of the developed and developing world. How did this come about, when as recently as 1988 *The Economist* magazine portrayed Ireland as a beggar nation seeking alms?

Today Ireland enjoys the many economic advantages that come with membership of the EU. Among the chief of these is that Irish policy-makers – in both the public and private sectors – are able to plan in a more stable environment, with the cooperation as well as with the active financial support of other member states, mediated through the European Commission. However, in today's increasingly internationalised economy, policy-making autonomy has been progressively ceded by small states to supranational organisations. The policy-making autonomy of any small country wishing to be part of this international economy is now heavily circumscribed and recognising this fact, and exploiting the consequences, is a wise exercise of national sovereignty. Since Ireland belongs to the euro zone, monetary policy, as well as the responsibilities for defending the euro against speculative attack, are decided in Frankfurt by the European Central Bank. The task in Ireland is to embrace with enthusiasm whatever the outcome happens to be, and the outcome so far has been remarkably favourable.

Against this background I examine the Irish economy in an historical and international perspective. In doing so, there is a temptation to focus exclusively on the past decade of rapid growth and convergence and to attribute most of this improvement to EU Structural Funds. This, indeed, is an interesting story that has attracted considerable international attention. However, in this chapter I wish to place the recent Irish experience in a wider context by comparisons that range across space, across time and across ideas. For example, the United Kingdom provided the encompassing economic context for Ireland until almost two decades after the end of World War II. Political independence (achieved in 1922) had only a modest impact on Irish economic development and the then Irish Free State (to become the Republic of Ireland in 1949) continued to function as a regional economy of the British Isles.

During the decade and a half after Ireland joined the then EEC in 1973, the small developed core European states became obvious touchstones of comparison, at a time when attempts were being made to diversify the economy away from excessive reliance on the United Kingdom towards wider European norms and standards. Later, the so-called cohesion states (Greece, Ireland, Portugal and Spain) became standards of comparison during the 1980s and the 1990s, a period when substantial development aid was forthcoming to these countries from the EU under the enlarged Structural Fund programmes. Today Ireland has many (but not all) of the characteristics of a modern developed economy and its recent performance has itself become the object of international interest by less developed countries. For example, the Irish developmental model is closely studied by the newly liberalised states of Central and Eastern Europe as they make their transition from Communist autarky and central planning to full integration into an enlarged EU.

The historical economic perspective

The 1960s represented a watershed in economic terms in Ireland. Policy actions taken from the late 1950s and early 1960s onwards launched the economy on a development path that differed radically from that pursued before and after independence. The core policy dilemma was not about whether the Irish economy should be open to trade and factor flows with the wider world economy, since Ireland already had a relatively open economy when compared to the other small European states in the late 1950s (Table 3.1). Rather, the issue was the nature of this involvement and whether there was to be a break with the heavy dependence on the UK market as the destination for exports of a very restricted variety of mainly agricultural products.

We touch on only three key factors that served to condition economic performance prior to 1960. The first concerns demographics, emigration and the openness of the Irish labour market. The second concerns economic geography and the emergence of a North–South divide in the economy, with the industrialising North achieving a much higher degree of prosperity than the mainly agricultural South. The third concerns the manner in which the economy of the island of Ireland, and later the separate economy of the Irish Free State, came to be almost totally dominated

Table 3.1 Small EU economies: measures of openness in 1960 (1999)

Country	Exports of goods and services (% of GDP)	Imports of goods and services (% of GDP)
Luxembourg	85.6 (93.6)	72.4 (80.8)
The Netherlands	45.7 (56.6)	44.2 (49.8)
Belgium	39.0 (73.8)	39.2 (69.1)
Denmark	32.7 (34.6)	34.5 (31.8)
Ireland	*30.4 (85.8)*	*35.5 (66.1)*
Austria	23.7 (46.2)	24.4 (45.8)
Sweden	22.7 (46.0)	23.3 (40.1)
Finland	22.5 (41.1)	23.2 (32.2)
Portugal	16.0 (33.2)	21.3 (40.3)
Greece	7.1 (16.0)	14.2 (23.3)

Source: Commission of the European Communities (1998) *European Economy*, no. 66, statistical appendix (Brussels).

by trade and other policy links with Britain, the difficulty in breaking free from this embrace, and the consequences of the British link for Irish policy-making.

Demographics, emigration and decline

Two unique features of Irish demographics stand out clearly. First, of the 10 European comparison countries used by Lars Mjøset in his seminal National Economic and Social Council (NESC) report (Mjøset 1992), Ireland was unique in that it experienced a major decline in population between 1840 and 1960. Secondly, if a comparison is made with the only three other European nations that displayed significant migration behaviour sometime during the period 1851–1960 (namely, Denmark, Norway and Sweden), only for a short period towards the end of the 19th century did emigration rates (i.e. emigration per thousand of the population) come anywhere near the persistently high Irish rates. The tradition of migration continued into more recent decades (Figure 3.1), and Ireland now has the most open labour market in the EU. Today, migration is net inwards, and this has served to reduce pressure on wages in a fast-growing economy.

Historically, emigration was both a cause and an effect of slow growth originating from other wider failures in the economy. Causes and effects become circular, and the real challenge is to include emigration in a broader study of the Irish pattern of development. Mjøset introduces the notion of a *vicious circle* linking two key Irish characteristics: population decline via emigration and a weak national system of innovation (Mjøset 1992: 50–67). He suggests that in Ireland these two mechanisms reinforced each other negatively through the social structure: the pastoral bias of agrarian modernisation, paternalistic family structures, sluggish growth of the home market, and a further marginalisation through weak industrialisation. In a range of other small European states, *virtuous circles* tended to operate and

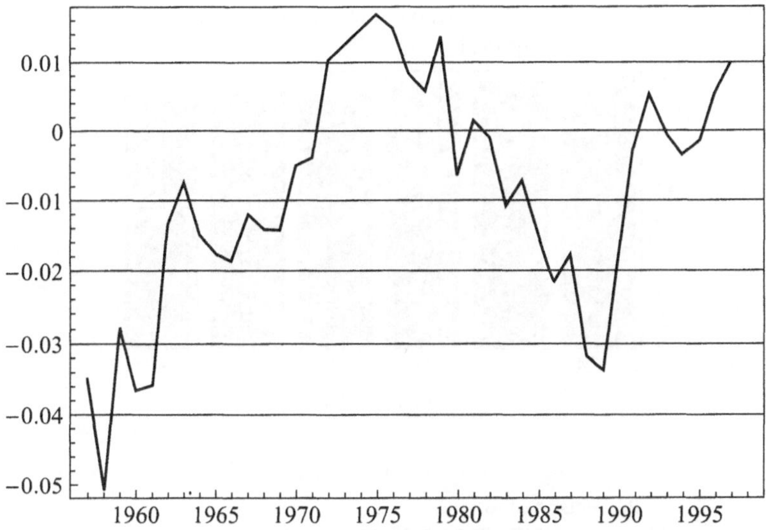

Figure 3.1 Recent migration in Ireland (expressed as fraction of total labour force)
Note: Negative sign indicates net outward flow.

promote development. Many of the elements in the weak national system of innovation arise in the context of the economic geography of 19th- and early 20th-century Ireland.

Economic geography and the island's North–South divide

A striking feature of economic growth is that it often occurs unpredictably and in forms that are highly concentrated spatially. The reasons behind the tendency towards concentration have been traditionally associated with the presence of increasing returns to scale and agglomeration economies that come from the more intense economic interactions that are encouraged by close proximity. Hence, it was not entirely surprising that when the Industrial Revolution came to Ireland in the latter half of the 19th century, it developed in a geographically concentrated form (Ó Gráda 1994).

However, Ireland's industrialisation did not emulate Britain's more generalised economic and technological leap forward. Rather, it came to involve a few specific sectors (brewing, linen, shipbuilding) and selected locations (mainly Dublin and Belfast), and bypassed much of the rest of the island. The spatial theory of economic growth provides suggestive insights into the process whereby Belfast developed rapidly as the only region in Ireland that fully participated in the latter phases of the Industrial Revolution (Krugman 1995; Ó Gráda 1994). In fact, the greater Belfast region took on all the attributes of an 'industrial district', a geographically defined productive system characterised by a large number of firms that were involved, at various stages and in various inter-related ways, in the production of relatively

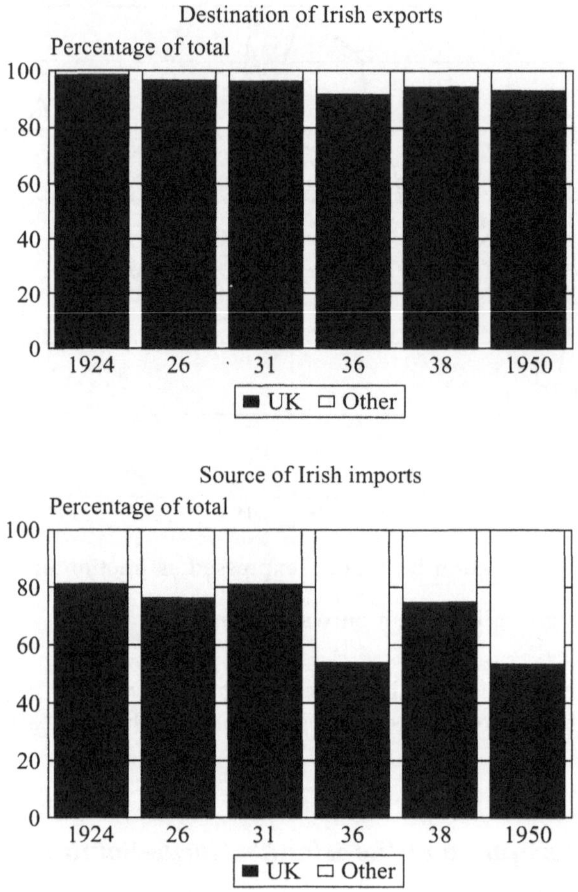

Figure 3.2 Southern trade shares with Britain and the North

homogeneous products. More generally, the north-east region eclipsed the rest of the island and established a clear edge in terms of industrial dynamism and economic strength.

Relations with the rest of the world

The political incorporation of Ireland into the United Kingdom in 1801 eventually generated forces that led to comprehensive economic and trade integration as well. The full extent of this integration after more than one hundred years of Union is illustrated in Figure 3.2, which illustrates the UK–Irish trade position from just after partition to the year 1950. The proportion of Southern exports going to the UK showed a very small reduction from 98.6 per cent in 1924 to 92.7 per cent by 1950.

The failure of Ireland to diversify its economy away from an almost total dependence on the UK had serious consequences for its economic performance when compared to a range of other small European countries and has been the subject of research and comment.[1] The reluctance of the new Irish public administration to deviate too much from British policy norms has been well documented (Fanning 1978). The nature of the difficulties faced by Irish policy-makers in attempting to break free from the economic embrace of the UK was a reflection of the wider behaviour of trade within the EU over the past 30–40 years. Thomsen and Woolcock (1993) point out that the exports from individual countries to the rest of Europe are still highly concentrated in only a few markets. Export market proximity is a key factor, but market size, distance, common borders and similar languages strongly influence intra-industry trade and the pattern of overall trade in Europe.

Wijkman (1990) has extended the analysis of geographical factors by looking at what he calls 'webs of dependency'. He suggests that there are three sub-regional trade blocs in Europe. The first is the *North* periphery, consisting of the UK, Ireland and Scandinavia. The second is the *South* periphery, comprising the Iberian peninsula, Greece and Turkey. The remaining countries are clustered around Germany and called *Core Europe*. Comparing the trade pattern of 1958 with that in 1987, Wijkman found that in many cases these clusters have become more, rather than less, clearly defined as a result of greater EU integration. However, Ireland's relationship with Britain, which had been among the very strongest webs of dependency prior to 1960, weakened considerably thereafter for very specific reasons.

It was hardly surprising that Ireland and Britain formed a particularly strong web of dependency, continuing from independence well into the 1960s. While policies and policy-makers in Ireland may have been less assertive and innovative than might have been desired, in the absence of a competitive and export-oriented industrial sector there is probably very little that could have been achieved to accelerate an earlier economic decoupling from the UK. The consequences followed inexorably. In the words of Mjøset:

> Ireland became a free rider on Britain's decline, while Austria and Switzerland were free riders on Germany's economic miracle. (Mjøset 1992: 9)

The strong web of dependency between Ireland and the UK only began to weaken after the shift to foreign direct investment (FDI) and export-led growth that followed the various Programmes for Economic Expansion in the late 1950s and during the 1960s. Figure 3.3 shows the behaviour of the shares of Irish exports going to the UK, and Irish imports originating in the UK, for the period 1960–95, after which shares tended to stabilise. The forces that brought about this changed pattern of behaviour – mainly export-oriented FDI – are examined in the next section.

Internationalisation and foreign direct investment

The early Industrial Revolutions of the 18th and late 19th centuries bypassed most of the island of Ireland, with the exception of the Belfast region of what is now

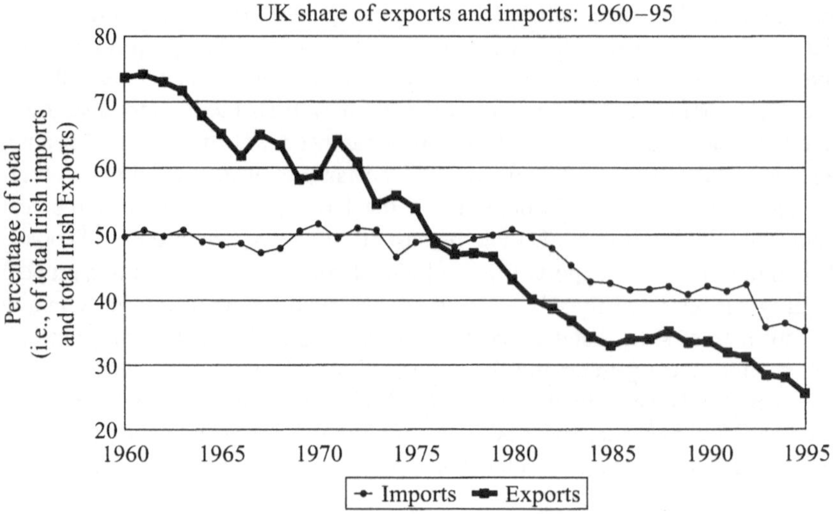

Figure 3.3 Southern trade with the UK: export and import shares, 1960–95

Northern Ireland. Our modern economic age only dawned in the late 1950s. The successes and challenges that we face today are an extraordinary reversal of the failures and problems faced by policy-makers at that time. In the words of Dr Ken Whitaker, the senior civil servant in the Irish Department of Finance, writing in the late 1950s, we had 'plumbed the depths of hopelessness'. Today, we bask in success.

The 1960s represented a watershed for the Irish economy. Policy changes made from the late 1950s and early 1960s onwards launched the economy on a development path that differed radically from that pursued before and after independence. The central policy dilemma was not whether the Irish economy should be open to trade and investment flows with the wider world economy, since – as we showed in Table 3.1 – Ireland already had a relatively open economy when compared to the other small European countries in the late 1950s. Rather, the issue was the nature of this involvement and whether there was to be a break with an almost total dependence on the British market as the destination for exports of a very restricted variety of mainly agricultural products.

The failure of the policy of industrialisation behind protective tariff barriers that was pursued from 1930 to 1960, became apparent during the economic crises of the 1950s (Kennedy *et al.* 1988; O'Malley 1989). A case can be made that union within the United Kingdom – at a time when Britain was the dominant world economic superpower – had been economically beneficial to Ireland during most of the 19th century, except for the period of the Great Famine of 1847–49 and its immediate aftermath (Ó Gráda 1994). But the problems that beset the much weakened UK economy in the straitened circumstances that followed World War II, the birth of the European community with the signing of the Treaty of Rome in 1956,

Table 3.2 GDP per head of population: (PPS), EU15 = 100

Country	1960	1973	1986	1999
Belgium	98.6	104.5	104.2	112.5
Germany	122.1	114.5	116.8	109.1
France	105.3	110.5	109.8	103.7
Italy	87.3	94.0	102.5	101.2
Luxembourg	168.7	153.1	138.8	165.9
The Netherlands	112.1	107.1	102.2	105.3
Denmark (73)	119.9	114.4	117.9	114.6
Ireland (73)	*60.8*	*58.9*	*63.7*	*111.0*
United Kingdom (73)	123.9	104.4	101.9	98.4
Greece (82)	*42.5*	*62.4*	*61.4*	*68.7*
Portugal (86)	*43.2*	*61.1*	*54.0*	*74.1*
Spain (86)	*56.9*	*74.8*	*69.7*	*80.2*
Austria (95)	94.8	98.5	105.4	110.9
Finland (95)	87.8	94.3	100.6	101.8
Sweden (95)	122.7	115.0	112.5	96.5

Source: Commission of the European Communities (1998) *European Economy*, no. 66, pp. 80–1, statistical appendix (Brussels).

as well as the fact that the United States was the new hegemonic economic power, were factors to which Irish strategic policy formulation was not indifferent.

To measure the extent to which Ireland lagged behind the other small European states in the late 1950s is a difficult task, since comparisons based on the simple conversion of domestic prices to a common currency are beset by problems. However, from the year 1960 we have standardised data that makes this comparison in terms of purchasing power parity (Table 3.2). Ignoring the special case of Luxembourg, the original six member states of the then EEC formed a relatively homogeneous group, with Germany leading (at 122 relative to the average of 100) and Italy lagging (at 87). In the case of Italy, the low average concealed the fact that the Northern sub-regions were well above the European average, while the Southern (or *Mezzogiorno*) sub-region was well below. The other nine future members of what is now the EU consisted at that time of five wealthy countries (Denmark, Austria, Finland, Sweden and the UK, ranging from a high of 124 (UK) to a low of 88 (Finland)) and four much poorer countries (Greece, Spain, Ireland and Portugal, ranging from a high of 57 (Spain) to a low of 43 (Greece)).

At the time of the first enlargement in 1973, the Danish and Irish GDP per head figures had changed very little relative to the EU average, but the UK had declined in relative terms to about the EU average. Since Ireland was a heavily agricultural country even as late as 1973, debate on the wisdom of its entry into the then EEC focused attention on the likely benefits from higher prices of agricultural produce under the Common Agricultural Policy (CAP) rather than on regional policy. In the early years of its membership, the main benefits to Ireland came from the CAP in terms of greatly increased transfers under the price guarantee section (McAleese 1975).

An aspect of modern Irish economic development that has attracted considerable attention internationally is the dynamic role played by FDI. Ireland is a case study of the effects on a small developing host economy of export-oriented FDI and this phenomenon has been the subject of much detailed research (O'Malley 1989; Barry *et al.* 1999). The economy emerged in the late 1950s from a heavily protectionist regime and the switch to openness was more dramatic than in the other European states and was implemented in terms of a vigorous industrial incentive package consisting of a very low corporate tax regime and generous capital and training grants. After a slow start in the 1960s, the foreign sector grew very rapidly during the 1980s and now accounts for about one half of Irish manufacturing employment and over two-thirds of gross manufacturing output (Barry and Bradley 1997). Directly as well as indirectly, FDI has affected every corner of the Irish economy.

FDI inflows into Ireland did not go primarily into the more traditional sectors in which the economy had a comparative advantage (e.g. food processing, clothing, footwear) mainly because many indigenous manufacturing sectors are largely non-tradeable (i.e. directed mainly at serving the small local market), and the substantial high technology FDI inflows that came to Ireland turned out not to depend on local comparative advantage. Although the outward orientation occurred at a time when the concept of growth poles was universally popular as a spur to development (Buchanan and partners 1968), the normal processes of clustering and regional concentration in Ireland were impeded both by the branch-plant nature of the investment and by a public policy that encouraged geographical dispersal almost certainly at some expense to strict economic efficiency criteria. However, after more than three decades of exposure to FDI, Ireland eventually succeeded in attracting sufficient firms in the computer, instrument engineering, pharmaceutical and chemical sectors to merit a description of sectoral 'agglomerations' or 'clusters'.

The long overdue switch to an outward orientation from the 1960s was an enlightened response to changes in the world economy. The engine of subsequent Irish growth was the manufacturing sector, and the engine of the manufacturing sector was the foreign-owned multinational subsector. Experience led to a better understanding of the role of small regions and small states in the increasingly integrated international economy, where:

> In Adam Smith's day, economic activity took place on a landscape largely defined – and circumscribed – by the political borders of nation states: Ireland with its wool, Portugal with its wines. Now, by contrast, economic activity is what defines the landscape on which all other institutions, including political institutions, must operate. (Ohmae 1995: 129)

On the global economic map, the lines that now mattered were rapidly becoming those defining 'natural economic zones', where the defining issue is that each such zone possesses, in one or other combination, the key ingredients for successful participation in the international economy. Thus, the rise of the EEC, the development of the Pacific Rim and the progressive liberalisation of world trade under successive General Agreement on Tariffs and Trade (GATT) rounds, presented both opportunities and threats to Ireland. But the eventual dominance of the Irish manufacturing sector by foreign multinationals was unexpected and quite unique by OECD experience. With falling transportation and telecommunication costs, national economies were destined to become increasingly interdependent, and in the words of President Clinton's former Labour Secretary, Robert Reich:

> the real economic challenge . . . [of a country or region] . . . is to increase the potential value of what its citizens can add to the global economy, by enhancing their skills and capacities and by improving their means of linking those skills and capacities to the world market. (Reich 1993: 8)

Perhaps the most striking consequence of foreign investment inflows was that it hastened the de-coupling of the Irish economy from its almost total dependence on the United Kingdom. Ireland's development dilemma had always been that it could either stick closely to UK economic policy and institutional norms and be constrained by the erratic UK growth performance, with little prospect of rapid convergence to a higher standard of living. The alternative was to implement an economically beneficial and politically acceptable degree of local policy innovation that offered hope of a faster rate of growth than its dominant trading partner. The Irish economic policy-making environment during this period can be characterised as having shifted from one appropriate to a dependent state on the periphery of Europe to that of a region more fully integrated into an encompassing European economy. FDI renovated and boosted Irish productive capacity. The Single Market provided the primary source of demand. All that remained was for a big push on improvement in physical infrastructure, education and training, and this arrived in the form of a dramatic innovation in regional policy at the EU level.

Facilitating Irish convergence: EU regional policy

In his 1975 paper examining the evidence for and against Ireland's membership of the EEC, McAleese concluded that:

> At this stage, more than ever before, attention will have to focus on regional policy. Ireland, as one of the least developed regions of the Community, has a particular active interest in the evolution of such a policy. . . . Paradoxically, therefore, the strongest long-run economic argument in favour of Ireland's joining the Community is based on a policy which does not yet exist. (McAleese 1975)

The importance and emphasis given to regional policy within the EU has greatly increased since the late 1980s, a time when major policy reforms and extensions were introduced in the lead-up to the implementation of the Single Market (SEM) and Economic and Monetary Union (EMU). After the turbulence of the 1970s and the 1980s, economic analysts tended to be more preoccupied with stabilisation (very much a national issue) rather than with growth (which usually has a regional dimension). It was not until the latter part of the 1980s, when inflation and unemployment disequilibria were brought more under control (nominal convergence), that a range of longer-term issues (such as real convergence and regional policy) moved towards the top of the EU agenda.

The rise of EU regional policy

Three major driving forces of EU regional policy set the scene for public policy-making in the lagging regional states of the EU.

1. The progressive *enlargement* of the EU from its foundation in 1956 – when there had been a degree of homogeneity at the national level – brought about an ever-increasing degree of socio-economic heterogeneity with the entry of Ireland, Greece, Portugal and Spain, the imminent entry of some low-income states from Central Europe, as well as a growing desire to address regional disparities within nation states as well as between states.
2. In addition to the simple aspect of enlargement, the *internal and external socio-economic challenges* faced by the member states and regions became more complex and forced EU policy-makers to address the task of preparing weaker states and regions to handle such initiatives as the SEM, EMU and more recently the need to prepare for the transition of economies of Central and Eastern Europe to EU membership.
3. While nation states have always operated internal regional policies of various types, what is different about EU regional policy is that significant *financial resources* were made available by the wealthier member states to fund regional policy initiatives in a limited number of the poorer member states. The available EU budget was initially dominated by the need to support the CAP, but there were major expansions in resources to fund the reformed Community Support Frameworks of 1989–93, 1994–99 and 2000–06.

If the original customs union of the Treaty of Rome had never deepened – in the sense of moving towards greater economic and monetary integration – the simple process of enlargement in itself would have required greater attention to be given to regional policy (see Table 3.2 above). After the entry of Ireland in 1973, the next two enlargements (Greece in 1982; Portugal and Spain in 1986) faced the EU with the danger of developing a two-tier community. In 1986, a very pronounced gap existed between four states (Greece, Ireland, Portugal and Spain) and the other eight. At that time, and using the measure of GDP per head, Spain was the wealthiest in relative terms (at 70) and Portugal lagged most (at 54). Ireland (at 64) and Greece (at 61) lay between these extremes.

If living standards are more accurately measured by private consumption per capita, as shown in Table 3.3, relative living standards are found to have improved only modestly in all four peripheral member states between 1973 and 1991. Ireland, on this measure, lay much closer to the lower levels of Portugal and Greece than to the relatively high level of Spain. With respect to unemployment rates, only in the

Table 3.3 Economic indicators in the periphery

	Greece	Ireland	Portugal	Spain	EU15
Unemployment rate – Eurostat definition (%)					
1960	6.1	5.8	1.7	2.4	2.3
1973	2.0	6.2	2.6	2.6	2.6
1991	8.6	15.6	5.7	22.8	10.7
1999	9.1	7.4	5.1	17.2	10.2
Private consumption/capita (PPS)					
1960	57	77	46	64	100
1973	70	65	62	81	100
1991	72	72	66	80	100
1999	78	83	74	79	100

Source: Commission of the European Communities (1998) *European Economy*, no. 66, statistical appendix (Brussels).

1990s did the Irish rate start to fall and converge towards the lower rates in Greece and Portugal, leaving Spain as the high unemployment outlier. The early convergence experience is therefore a little ambiguous.

Internal and external challenges and EU regional policy

It is well known that economic disparities tend to increase during recessions and to lessen when growth is high and pervasive. The economies of the EU were hit by two major world recessions in the aftermath of the oil price crises of 1973 and 1979. Not only did national growth rates decline and diverge, but the fortunes of regions of nation states also diverged. Thus, some of the UK regions (including Northern Ireland, Scotland and Wales) suffered badly relative to the more prosperous southern regions as traditional manufacturing declined precipitously. Although there was some response to the greater challenges faced by the EU, and regional policy was reformed and extended in various modest ways, the major reforms and extensions of EU regional policy were initiated only in the context of planning for the development of the Single Market that took place during the years 1985–88.

Progressive trade liberalisation within Europe was always likely to entail substantial industrial disruption in the periphery, either defined as the member states on the western and southern edge of the EU or as those sub-regions of member states that were located far from the centres of population and economic activity. Adjustment problems were therefore likely to be greater in the periphery.

A massive shake-out of jobs in Irish and Spanish 'traditional' industry occurred as trade liberalisation progressed during the 1980s, even before the formal initiation of the Single Market. The low productivity sectors in Greece and Portugal also faced increasingly intense pressures. One of the potential difficulties faced by peripheral economies like Ireland in adjusting to EU membership was the possibility that as trade barriers fell, industries that had a high share of the plants that exhibit increasing returns to scale (i.e. plants where productivity increases with size) would be attracted away from the periphery towards the densely populated core markets. This process led to the decline of many traditional Irish indigenous industries. However, the influx of multinational companies more than offset this decline. Foreign firms locating in Ireland have tended to be in sectors where there are increasing returns to scale (IRS) at the industry level (computer equipment, pharmaceuticals, instrument engineering) but constant returns (CRS) at the plant level, so the share of Irish employment in IRS sectors has increased substantially.

The reform of EU regional aid programmes into the so-called *Community Support Framework* (CSF) in the late 1980s presented EU as well as national policymakers and analysts in countries like Ireland with major challenges. The political rationale behind the CSF came from the fear that not all EU member states were likely to benefit equally from the SEM, whose purpose was to dismantle all remaining non-tariff barriers within the Union. In particular, the less advanced economies of the southern and western periphery (mainly Greece, Portugal, Spain and Ireland) were felt to be particularly vulnerable unless they received development aid (Cecchini 1988).

What was special about the reformed regional policies was their goals, i.e. to design and implement policies with the explicit aim of transforming the underlying structure of the beneficiary economies in order to prepare them for exposure to the competitive forces about to be unleashed by the SEM. Thus, CSF policies moved far beyond a conventional demand-side stabilisation role, being directed at the promotion of structural change, faster long-term growth, and real convergence through mainly supply-side processes.

Was Ireland a case study of successful EU regional policy?

By the time Ireland and Greece joined the EU – in 1973 in the case of Ireland, and in 1982 in the case of Greece – the programme that led to the completion of the SEM had not yet begun. The then European Economic Community was effectively a customs union. It was evolving slowly, but it remained more or less a customs union. Portugal and Spain joined in 1986, just when serious consideration was being given to deepening the level of economic integration by means of the SEM initiative, i.e. removing all the non-tariff barriers to trade (such as border controls, nation-specific product standards, etc.). The larger, wealthier countries feared that the four poorest member states in the EEC at that time – Greece, Ireland, Portugal, Spain – where development lagged behind the average, might be vulnerable to the introduction of the SEM. In effect, they feared that the industrial and service sectors of the poorer member states would not be able to withstand the competitive forces that would come from the larger, richer core member states.

To help these poorer so-called 'cohesion' countries, very generous development aid was made available, targeted at facilitating their participation in the SEM, as well as accelerating their convergence towards EU average income per head. We have seen that in 1986, just before the Structural Funds were expanded, if you set an index of the European average GDP per capita at 100, Greece was at 61; Ireland was at 64; Portugal was at 54 and Spain was higher, at 70. These four countries had many other common characteristics in 1986. They had high actual and hidden unemployment and large agricultural sectors (in the case of Ireland, about 18 per cent of the labour force and in the case of Greece and Portugal, much higher). They had underdeveloped physical infrastructure (in 1986 there were no motorways in Ireland). The unfavourable structure of their manufacturing sectors left them with a preponderance of traditional products (such as food processing, clothing, textiles), and a lack of modern sectors (such as electronics, pharmaceuticals, etc.). They also had a greatly underdeveloped market service sector, in particular producer services (i.e. services to industry, rather than consumer services). From her entry into the EU in 1973 until the year 1988, Ireland remained at 60 per cent of the EU average GDP per head. The Irish level of income per head was about the same as Greece, a bit higher than Portugal, but somewhat lower than Spain.

With the advent of the SEM, the EU deepened in many different ways. For example, intra-EU trade grew and trade in intermediate goods (i.e. sales to firms by other firms) grew particularly quickly. In the late 1980s, Spain and Ireland had intermediate levels of this type of intra-industry or firm-to-firm trade. Portugal and Greece had very low levels. However, this type of trade is a measure of the differing degree of the integration of these countries into the EU and wider global economy. It is a much better measure than simple trade data.

A gradual restructuring of European industry took place, with the evolution of strategic alliances in manufacturing and services between countries. From being a customs union, Europe evolved towards being a SEM. A big shake-out of traditional industry had already taken place in Ireland and Spain prior to the advent of the Structural Funds in 1989. This shake-out is still underway in Portugal and Greece. In the case of Ireland it had catastrophic economic effects. The Irish unemployment rate rose to 20 per cent in the mid-1980s. The debt-to-GDP ratio rose to 130 per cent. Ireland at that time was in serious economic and social difficulties.

It was in this context that the reorganisation and massive increase in the EU Structural Funds took place. The process started for the five years from 1989 to 1993 (in what was called the Delors I package, after Jacques Delors, then President of the Commission). The next round of Structural Funds (called Delors II) ran from 1994 to 1999. Each of the four main 'cohesion' countries who were the recipients of most of the aid have had 10 years of sustained high development aid from the EU. In the case of Ireland, under the Delors I package this ran at some 3 to 4 per cent per annum of Irish GDP. In the second period the aid fell slightly as a share of GDP to some 2 to 3 per cent. By any standards, this was generous aid. Taken together with the domestic co-financing element, it allowed major investment schemes to go ahead.

The purpose of the Structural Funds was to generate permanent improvements in economic competitiveness and performance, rather than just impart a transitory stimulation that would vanish after the aid was cut off. There were three main channels through which the supply-side effects of the Structural Fund aid operated.

The first channel is to improve the physical infrastructure such as roads, rail, ports, telecoms. A country cannot communicate with the global economy unless these channels operate efficiently and effectively. The second channel is to improve the level of education and training, and to enhance the skills of the labour force. You cannot produce world-class goods unless your labour force is well educated and trained. The third channel is to directly assist private sector firms by subsidising investment, improving marketing and design skills, research and development (R&D), etc. A fourth channel (intra-national regional aid) did not apply to Ireland under Delors I and II since we were such a small and relatively homogeneous country. Portugal, Spain and Greece have poor regions that suffer relative to others, as does Southern Italy (the Mezzogiorno) and the former East Germany.

The goal of the Structural Funds was to transform the underlying structure of the beneficiary economies and to prepare them to face the competitive forces that were about to be unleashed by the SEM. The details and modalities of the implementation have been described elsewhere (Bradley *et al.* 1995), and the outcome was very interesting. Remember that in 1986, just before the Structural Funds were reformed and expanded, Greece was at 61 relative to a European average of 100. By 1999 it was at 69. There had been a modest, but quite significant, increase in living standards. Portugal started at 54 in 1986 and is now at 74. Spain started at 70 and is now at 80. But Ireland started at 64 and is now at 111. Those figures flatter the Irish performance to some extent, but it represented a massive improvement. We summarise briefly a logical sequence of interconnected effects that brought about that impressive Irish result.

First, the Irish economy in the late 1970s and for the first half of the 1980s was seriously and massively destabilised – high unemployment, relatively high inflation and the public finances almost out of control.

Secondly, there were the effects of the Structural Funds. These had demand and supply effects. As you actually build a road, it injects income and expenditure into your economy. But the long-lasting benefits of building a road come when it is available to connect your cities and to transport goods more efficiently into and out of your economy.

The third event was the beneficial effect of Ireland joining the European Monetary System (EMS). This was the exchange rate mechanism that was instituted in 1979 and served as a precursor of EMU. But the credibility benefits of Ireland's membership of the EMS were delayed by about a decade. To put it quite bluntly, the world's financial markets did not believe that the Irish economy could be stabilised successfully and could perform within the constraints of the EMS. So, the lower Deutsche Mark interest rates did not become available to the Irish economy until the late 1980s when eventually credibility was established.

The fourth event was the massive inflow of mainly US FDI, most of it in high technology areas. This was in part a spin-off benefit of the Structural Funds, making use of the improved infrastructure and human capital. It was also due in part to Ireland's access to EU markets for exports produced by multinational companies

Table 3.4 Relative GDP per capita in purchasing power parity terms (EU15 = 100)

	1991	1992	1993	1994	1995	1996	1997	1998	1999
Ireland	75.7	79.0	82.2	88.5	93.8	94.5	100.7	107.1	111.0
Spain	79.8	77.8	78.4	76.4	76.9	77.6	78.3	79.2	80.2
Greece	61.2	62.5	64.4	65.2	66.3	67.6	68.3	68.1	68.7
Portugal	64.7	65.4	68.3	70.0	70.7	70.3	71.3	72.7	74.1

Source: Commission of the European Communities (1998) *European Economy*, no. 66, statistical appendix (Brussels).

located and producing in Ireland. Additionally, of course, one of the long-term elements of Irish policy was a low rate of corporate taxation, designed to attract inward investment.

The fifth event, producing a reinforcement of the fiscal stabilisation benefits, came as a result of the Irish government strongly signalling its firm intention to join the EMU from the start-up in January 1999, even in the absence of our largest trading partner, the United Kingdom, from EMU membership.

Finally, in Ireland there was an evolving social partnership (involving employers' organisations, trade unions and government) that eased the distribution conflicts and disputes that come with recovery and rapid growth.

After a full decade of Structural Funds and the SEM, how have the cohesion countries performed? In Table 3.4 we show the convergence experience of these four countries, where it is seen that some quite rapid convergence has taken place in recent years. Adaptation to the competitive rigours of the SEM and efficient use of Structural Funds underpin the dramatic convergence of Ireland that coincided with the implementation of the new EU regional policies. One is tempted to suggest that the combination of openness and the use of Structural Funds was the primary force driving Irish convergence, but of course the full picture is more complex. Nevertheless, it is the policy of openness and the use of Structural Funds that served to distinguish Ireland from, say, Greece, which had a similar development distance to travel but which has only recently set its wider policy framework in the context of embracing internationalisation. Portugal, on the other hand, is in the process of repeating Irish success. It remains to be seen if these countries can sustain their convergent behaviour in times of recession as well as in times of growth.

Conclusions

The opening of the economy and the removal of tariff barriers were necessary policy changes if we were to be kick-started from stagnation. Free trade with the UK – our dominant trading partner until the late 1960s – gave us our first opportunity of 'testing the water' of outward orientation. Free trade with Europe came later when we joined the then EEC in 1973. The strategic orientation of Irish economic policy-making over the past three decades has emphasised the need to face the consequences of the extreme openness of the economy, to encourage export orientation towards fast growing markets and products, and to align the economy with European initiatives. We joined the EMS in 1979, breaking a long link with sterling and escaping from economic and psychological dependency on the United Kingdom. We embraced the SEM of 1992 and, most recently, EMU from January 1999. Perhaps this is the main legacy bequeathed to us by the prescient policy-makers of the time of Taoiseach (Prime Minister) Seán Lemass. The enthusiastic embrace of openness provides the strong and enduring strategic backbone of our economic planning.

But Ireland was not a very attractive investment location in the early 1960s. It was remote, unknown, had little by way of natural resources, and had no industrial heritage. To offset these handicaps, the main inducement provided to inward investors was initially a zero rate of corporation tax on exports of manufactured goods. Under pressure from the EU, this was later replaced by a low 10 per cent tax rate on all manufacturing profits. This tax policy, combined with aggressive and sophisticated marketing initiatives designed by the Industrial Development Authority (IDA) to attract and aid inward investors, provided the main driving force for the modernisation of the economy through export-led growth.

However, the attractive tax rate and the absence of tariffs were only a start, and would not in themselves have made Ireland a major destination of high-quality FDI. Other factors came together to reinforce Ireland's success and interacted to create a virtuous circle of superior performance that replaced the previous vicious circle of decades of under-performance. Educational standards in the Irish workforce had lagged behind the world. Policies were urgently needed to bring about a steady build-up of the quality, quantity and relevance of education and training, and this had been initiated by far-seeing educational reforms starting in the 1960s. These reforms were extended by the emphasis given to scientific and technical skills through the use of generous EU Structural Funds from the late 1980s. Although issues of social inequality are still of concern, the general level of educational attainment in Ireland rivals that of other wealthier European countries.

Low taxes and bright people combined with an inefficient road network and an unreliable telephone system result in an incomplete and unsatisfactory recipe for success. Here, Ireland was remarkably lucky because it was granted so-called Objective 1 status for EU regional policy aid. As a result of a generally low standard of living in the late 1980s (less than two-thirds of the EU average), as well as a peripheral location far away from the rich European markets, generous aid was made available to improve infrastructure, train young people and stimulate the business sector. Few would claim that everything is perfect today, and, indeed, growth itself has brought congestion in its wake. But dramatic improvements have taken place in the quality of roads, airports and telecommunications. A recent American consultancy report included Ireland among the highly desirable 'broadband four' (USA, Canada, UK and Ireland), these being countries best prepared by infrastructure and deregulation to meet the challenges of the new age of e-commerce (Legg Mason Precursor Group 2000).

These were the building blocks of the new Irish economy, and they brought success through their interaction and combination. The far-sighted targeting by the Irish Industrial Development Agency of inward investment in clusters of industries in computer equipment, software and pharmaceuticals was pursued with a degree of diligence and professionalism that became the envy of all aspirant developing countries. Such firms needed highly skilled workers, and these were available in ever-increasing numbers from the universities as well as from the assertive and bustling Regional Technical Colleges. Business and knowledge spillovers from the initial clusters encouraged further growth in the high technology areas, and provided the basis for additional benefits, often in the older, more traditional areas (such as food processing and clothing) that needed injections of new strategies and technologies.[2] The eponymous *The Economist*, which had painted so damning a portrait of the Irish economy as recently as 1988, now – a mere nine years later – told a very different story (*The Economist* 1997).

However, there are risks associated with the development path chosen by Ireland. First, the dynamic foreign manufacturing base is concentrated on a narrow range of technologies that can quickly move through maturity and into decline. Secondly, the policy initiatives that ensured that Ireland enjoyed an advantageous 'first mover' status in the early 1960s are unlikely to benefit other smaller economies to the same extent.

Using a business (as distinct from an economic) research perspective, Michael Porter in his most recent work has returned to the sources of national and regional competitive advantage and places greater stress on the role of government policy than in his earlier work (Porter 1990, 1998). Porter examined national competitiveness analysis from a systematic integration of previous disaggregated analysis at the level of the individual firm and sector. In future national and regional planning, policy-makers are going to have to think increasingly in this way rather than in aggregate macroeconomic terms. For example, cluster development in the Irish case was seeded and reinforced by foreign direct investment, mainly by an industrial policy that distorted competition in our favour. However, future clustering will need to focus on removing constraints to productivity growth in a far wider range of indigenous industries; dramatic economic changes always have serious social consequences. Young people, with their superior education, are easily absorbed by burgeoning high technology sunrise sectors and the spin-off professional and other services. Older people, however, are locked into traditional skills in sunset industries, and tend to lose out. During the 1980s the Irish unemployment rate soared to 20 per cent, threatening to tear apart the social fabric of the nation. Prompted by the terrible recession of the 1980s, employers, trade unions and government came together in the mid-1980s to design a consensual process of social partnership. They understood the urgent need to ensure that there would be as few losers as possible in the economic dislocation that accompanied modernisation. Unlike the United Kingdom – which had been wracked by violent class conflict during the

1980s – in Ireland the social democratic institutions of Sweden, Germany and the Netherlands were emulated and adapted to local conditions. In this way, Ireland became a remarkable and slightly exotic blend of American business efficiency and European social equity.

The path chosen by Ireland for its economic development is not without risks. The most dynamic part of our manufacturing is almost completely foreign owned and is concentrated in a narrow range of technologies that are fast moving towards maturity. For example, Ireland excels in making personal computers, but who knows what new devices will be used to surf the Internet five years from now? Will they be made in Ireland? The policy initiatives that ensured Ireland had an advantageous head start in the early 1960s may not be sufficient to facilitate the inevitable switches to newer technologies since other countries have been learning by watching Ireland doing! Until recently, we could rely on an abundant supply of highly trained Irish workers. But birth rates fell dramatically in the 1980s, and if economic growth is to continue, we may have to rely on inward migration to supply the labour. We have long had a manufacturing sector dominated by multinational firms. But how easily and gracefully will we make the transformation to a multinational society?

Meanwhile, Irish businesses compete in a global economy and only the most innovative and efficient will survive and prosper. Global competition is organised today mainly by multinational firms and not by governments. Production tends to be modularised, with individual modules spread across the globe so as to exploit the comparative advantages of different regions. Hence, individual small countries like Ireland (as well as small regions like Northern Ireland, Scotland and Wales) have less power to influence their destinies than in earlier eras. Today, they must focus their economic policies on location factors, especially those which are relatively immobile between countries: skills, infrastructure, the efficient functioning of labour markets and superior economic and social governance.

In stark contrast to my time as an undergraduate in the 1960s, college students today no longer aspire to pensionable jobs in the public sector, but are more likely to be planning business ventures and dreaming of how stock market flotations will make their fortune. This is the very best time to be Irish, when our rapid economic progress has catapulted us from the role of poor laggard to successful Tiger. Our society is at once traditional and modern, and the tension between these forces serves to animate our thought and artistic expression. The Irish economy may be very small in size, but its policy experiences during the 20th century provide a rich source of information and guidance for other small countries that seek to develop and prosper.

Endnotes

1. Mjøset (1992) is a study of Irish economic under-performance that draws carefully from a wide European literature on social and economic development.
2. For example, a recent television programme on the Irish fashion industry showed computer-controlled knitting machines being used by native Irish speakers on Inishman to produce high-quality, high value-added customised Aran sweaters for export to fashion-conscious customers in the USA and Japan!

References

Barry, F. and Bradley, J. (1997) 'FDI and trade: the Irish host-country experience', *Economic Journal*, 107 (445), pp. 1798–1811.

Barry, F., Bradley, J. and O'Malley, E. (1999) 'Indigenous and foreign industry: characteristics and performance', in F. Barry (ed.), *Understanding Ireland's Economic Growth* (London: Macmillan).

Bradley, J., O'Donnell, N., Sheridan, N. and Whelan, K. (1995) *Regional Aid and Convergence: Evaluating the impact of the Structural Funds on the European Periphery* (Aldershot: Avebury).

Buchanan, C. and partners (1968) *Regional Studies in Ireland*, Report Commissioned by the United Nations on behalf of the Irish Government, Dublin: An Foras Forbatha.

Cecchini, P. (1988) *The European Challenge 1992: The Benefits of a Single Market* (London: Wildwood House).

Commission of the European Communities (1998) *European Economy*, no. 66, statistical appendix (Brussels).

Fanning, R. (1978) *The Irish Department of Finance 1922–58* (Dublin: Institute of Public Administration).

Friedman, T. (1999) *The Lexus and the Olive Tree* (New York: Farrar Straus Giroux).

Kennedy, K., Giblin, T. and McHugh, D. (1988) *The Economic Development of Ireland in the Twentieth Century* (London: Routledge).

Krugman, P. (1995) *Development, Geography, and Economic Theory* (Cambridge: Massachusetts: The MIT Press).

Legg Mason Precursor Group (2000) *The Building Blocks of Growth in the 'New Economy'*, Spring, Philadelphia.

McAleese, D. (1975) 'Ireland in the enlarged EEC: economic consequences and prospects', in John Vaizey (ed.), *Economic Sovereignty and Regional Policy* (Dublin: Gill and Macmillan).

Mjøset, Lars (1992) *The Irish Economy in a Comparative Institutional Perspective*, Report No. 93 (Dublin: National Economic and Social Council).

Ó Gráda, C. (1994) *Ireland: A New Economic History 1780–1939* (Oxford: Clarendon Press).

Ohmae, Kenichi (1995) 'Putting global logic first', in K. Ohmae (ed.), *The Evolving Global Economy* (Harvard: Harvard Business Review Books).

O'Malley, E. (1989) *Industry and Economic Development: The Challenge for the Latecomer* (Dublin: Gill and Macmillan).

Porter, M. (1990) *The Competitive Advantage of Nations* (London: Macmillan Press).

Porter, M. (1998) *On Competition* (Mass.: HBR Press).

Reich, Robert (1993) *The Work of Nations: A Blueprint for the Future* (London: Simon and Schuster).

Rodrik, D. (1999) *The New Global Economy and Developing Countries: Making Openness Work* (Washington, DC: Overseas Development Council).

The Economist (1997) 'Europe's shining light', 17 May 1997.

Thomsen, S. and Woolcock, S. (1993) *Direct Investment and European Integration* (London: Pinter).

Wijkman, P. (1990) 'Patterns of production and trade', in W. Wallace (ed.), *The Dynamics of European Integration* (London: Pinter).

Chapter 4

Ireland – a multicultural economy

John Fitz Gerald

Introduction

To many outsiders today looking at the Irish economy the question on their lips is how can it be such a success? However, probably a much more interesting question is why did it stop being a failure? When looked at in the context of its 80 years of independent existence the success is clearly very recent. Even in the early 1990s, official reports were still being published considering the source of the country's weak economic performance (Mjøset 1993). Since that date a large literature has grown up about the success.

With the benefit of hindsight, it is clear that Ireland made many mistakes in the period up to 1960. However, since then three important strategic policies have been pursued with consistency by all governments:

- The opening up of the economy and society to the outside world.
- Promotion of foreign direct investment into Ireland.
- Investment in education.

These policies have contributed in a major way to the success that is seen today. Their importance was disguised by some self-inflicted wounds in the 1980s, which delayed their fruition to the 1990s. The recovery that was already under way in 1989 was halted in late 1990 by the wider economic effects on the EU of German unification. It is only since 1994 that the full benefits can be seen from these policies.

This chapter focuses on the process of 'opening up' the economy and society, one aspect of which has been the role of FDI. The effect of this policy has been to transform a very insular and rather claustrophobic economy into the multicultural economy that it is today. The chapter first considers the change that has occurred from Ireland being an economic failure to becoming an economic success. It then discusses the process of 'opening up' and the key role that this has played. One key aspect of this change has been the reversal of the traditional pattern of emigration. The phenomenon of the 'homing pigeons' (returning emigrants), and the even more recent rapid growth in immigration by people who are not Irish citizens, has played a very important role in bringing about change.

From economic failure to success

While people today talk of the Irish economic success it is probably better understood as a story of belated success after prolonged failure from the time of independence in 1922. That failure was sustained in the face of the post-war European recovery and, while economic growth began again in the post-1960 era, it was not until the 1990s that the economy made up much of the lost ground of the previous 70 years of independence. Writing in 1989, in a very influential work on Irish history, Lee strove to explain Ireland's economic failure. He was slightly unfortunate to publish just when the economy was on the threshold of success, but he was right to focus on the poor performance of independent Ireland. However, he also failed to see some of the seeds of success that were already apparent in the late 1980s (Bradley *et al.* 1987).

Lee's explanations for the economic failure placed considerable emphasis on institutional factors. This chapter focuses instead on two aspects of economic policy that were important to the failure and subsequent success of the economy – investment in education (human capital) and the positive industrial policy related to the process of EU integration. The failure to follow the rest of Western Europe in beginning the process of freeing trade in the 1950s was a serious lost opportunity. Also the Irish state, unlike governments in the rest of Europe, failed to invest in education from 1950 onwards. In both cases Ireland was 10 or 20 years behind the rest of Europe in realising its mistakes. As a result, while the post-war boom in Europe peaked in the 1960s and 1970s, in Ireland it reached its zenith in the 1990s, 10 to 20 years after its neighbours. Inappropriate policy helped postpone the convergence in living standards to the EU average until the end of the 20th century. Better-informed policy could have seen an earlier realisation of this dream.

As shown in Figure 4.1, average earnings in manufacturing, which had risen substantially relative to Britain in the late 19th century (O'Rourke and Williamson 1995), fell soon after independence, as protection was introduced. In spite of the

Figure 4.1 Relative wage rates in manufacturing

opportunities for emigration (and free movement of capital to and from the UK), wage rates remained around 50 per cent of UK levels up to 1960. It was only with the freeing of trade and the opening up of the economy that wage rates began to gradually converge on UK rates, approaching 90 per cent of those levels by the end of the 1970s. While exchange rate fluctuations have muddied the waters since 1980, it seems apparent that, on average, wage rates in Ireland have followed trends in the UK since then.

The process of EU integration was not an easy one for the traditional manufacturing sector in Ireland (including clothing, textiles, furniture, motor vehicle assembly, etc.). Many of the firms that were in business in the 1960s failed to make the transition to the free trade environment. While EU membership occurred in 1973, the full impact of market liberalisation was not felt until the 1980s when the prolonged recession aggravated the problems faced by the sector. Figure 4.2 shows employment in the more traditional sectors of manufacturing. It peaked in 1970 and it reached a trough in the early 1990s, with employment at under half of the 1970 level. This meant that the process of EU integration, while essential for future prosperity, was far from painless.

The collapse of old firms, and old ways of doing business, was painful for the owners of those firms, but more particularly for the large number of unskilled workers who lost their jobs along the way. In firms in traditional sectors, like clothing and textiles, the bulk of employees had very limited skills and, when the jobs disappeared in the 1980s, the demand for unskilled labour generally in the economy was falling. This contributed to a high level of unemployment.

In the non-tradable sector, such as financial and business services, business had more time to adjust. Competition had already been creeping in in the 1960s and the transition to a more open environment was more gradual. In many cases the existing businesses had time to make the transition and to survive in the new more competitive environment. Today many sectors, that in the past were not subject to competition through trade or new entry, now find themselves facing a new more

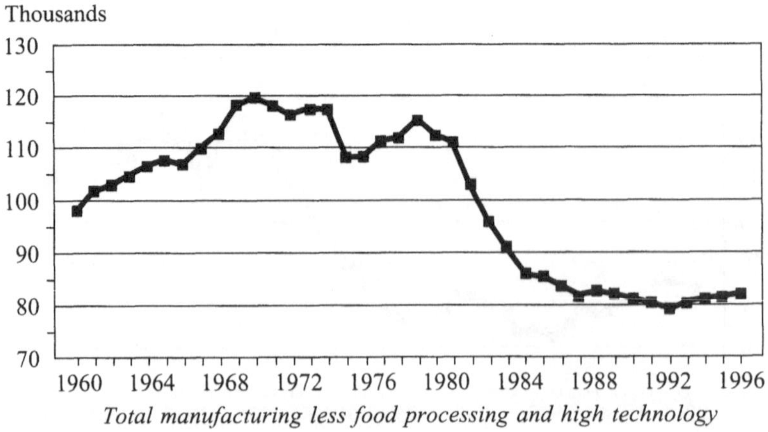

Figure 4.2 Employment in traditional manufacturing

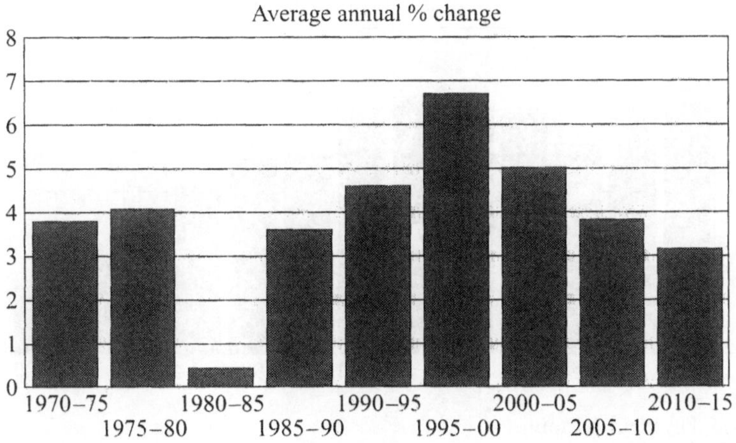

Figure 4.3 Growth in GNP

bracing environment. However, because they had time to prepare, they are coping successfully with the new situation.

Figure 4.3 shows the growth rate for GNP for each of the five-year periods from 1970 to 1990. With the exception of the first half of the 1980s, when the delayed effects of market liberalisation hit the economy at the time of a necessary fiscal retrenchment, there was relatively little deviation from an apparent trend growth of 4 per cent a year. For the more recent period, 1990–95, the growth rate picks up to 5 per cent and the economy is currently growing at a rate well above its past trend. It looks as if the average growth rate over the five years 1995–00 will be around 7 per cent a year.

The 1990s have seen an exceptionally rapid growth in the numbers employed at an average of over 3.5 per cent a year (see Figure 4.4). In the second half of the decade the rate of increase has risen to 5.2 per cent a year. What makes this all the

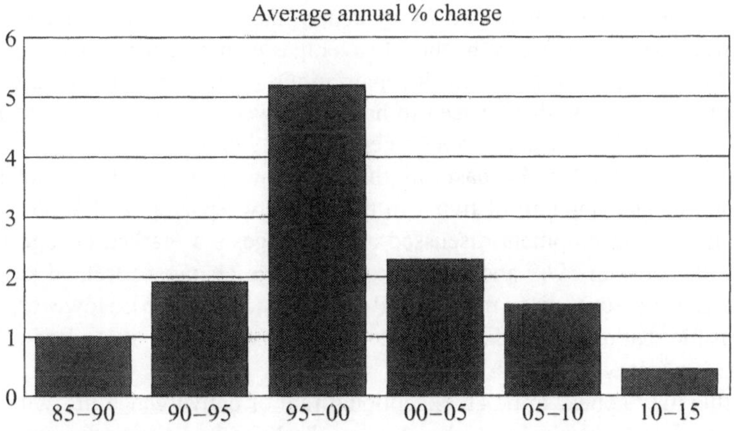

Figure 4.4 Employment growth

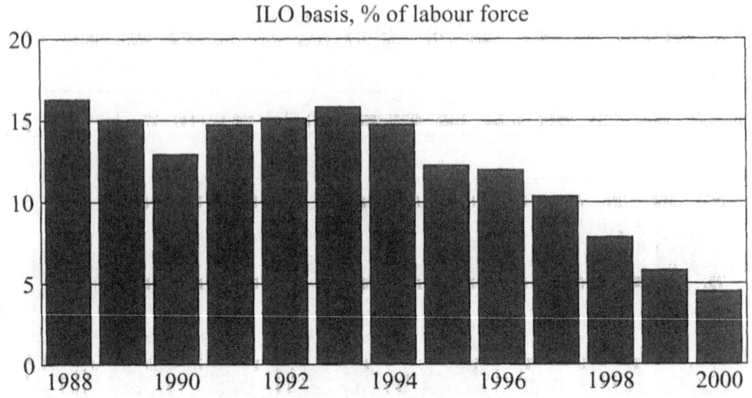

Figure 4.5 Unemployment
Source: CSO Labour Force Survey.

more remarkable is that the vast bulk of the new jobs being created are for skilled people. In the most recent years, at the height of the boom, there has been some increase in demand for unskilled labour. But throughout much of the decade the numbers of unskilled in employment continued to fall.

As shown in Figure 4.5, the unemployment rate, which had been high for over a decade, has fallen dramatically over the last four years. The fall in the unemployment rate began after the rapid rise in employment had already commenced. The reason for the delay was the very high rate of growth in the labour force, due to the large number of young people entering the labour market, the rapid rise in female labour force participation and skilled immigration. However, in the last two years the slow growth, rather than decline, in the demand for unskilled labour, at a time when supply of unskilled labour is falling due to the investment in education, has meant that the unemployment rate has finally fallen rapidly.

The result of this relatively rapid period of growth will be that Ireland, which in 1990 had a GDP per head of around 74 per cent of the EU average, will, by the year 2000, be well over 100 per cent of the EU average. A more appropriate measure is GNP per head (which excludes profit repatriations by foreign multinationals); on this measure Ireland can also be seen to have narrowed the gap in living standards compared to the EU as a whole from 67 per cent in 1990 to an expected 95 per cent in 2000 (Figure 4.6). On the basis of this forecast, using GNP, Ireland should achieve the average standard of living in the EU between 2000 and 2005.

The pattern of development discussed above suggests a marked change in gear around 1990; between 1960 and 1990 there was little change in Ireland's position within the EU measured in terms of GNP per head (Figure 4.6). However, it now seems possible that over the next 15 years Ireland may achieve a standard of living among the highest within the EU.

While this may appear to be an exceptional rate of convergence in living standards measured as GNP per head, the situation looks rather different when considered in terms of output per person employed – national productivity, broadly defined.

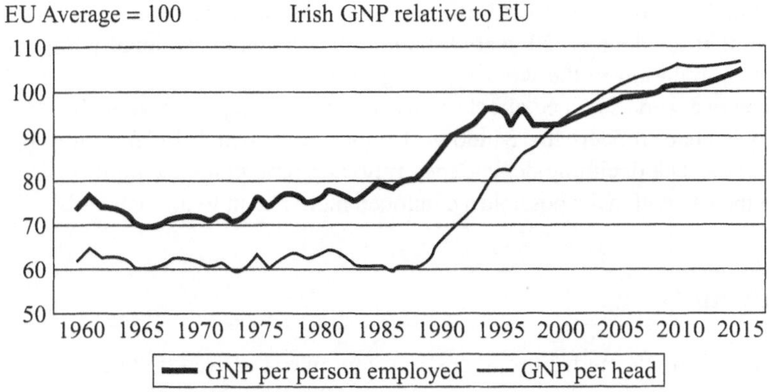

Figure 4.6 Relative living standard

On this measure the Irish economy has been converging towards EU standards of productivity fairly steadily since the 1970s. While we are presently seeing some acceleration in the rate of convergence, this is not out of character with the past 30 years. The explanation for the contrast between the two measures, GNP per head and GNP per person employed, lies in the movement in the economic dependency ratio – the ratio of the population not in paid employment to those who are at work.

As shown in Figure 4.7, while Ireland had an economic dependency ratio that was exceptionally high relative to the EU level in the 1980s, it has now fallen to the EU level, and will fall below it in the near future. The reason for this 'demographic windfall' is the combined effect of high emigration in the 1950s, which left the working-age population depleted for the following 30 years, and a high birth rate

Figure 4.7 Economic dependency ratio

up to 1980. The rapid fall in the birth rate after 1980 and the reversal of emigration will mean that for the next 20 years Ireland will have an exceptionally high proportion of its population in the working age groups.

This contrast, and its related effects on living standards represented by the movement in GNP per head, reflects the window of opportunity which Ireland faces over the next 20 years. The declining dependency ratio at a time when the ratio is rising elsewhere in the EU will make possible a continued rapid rise in living standards in Ireland.

Opening up

While the rest of Western Europe entered into an era of free trade and developing economic cooperation in the years immediately after World War II, Ireland slumbered on, maintaining prohibitive barriers to trade with its neighbours until the 1960s. Though capital did flow freely between Ireland and the UK, and there was also free movement of labour, the outmoded 'ourselves alone' (Sinn Féin) economic policy of the 1920s and 1930s still held sway.

The continuation of this isolationist economic policy followed on the neutral stance adopted by Ireland throughout World War II. Whatever the merits or demerits of the policy of neutrality, it contributed to a situation where Ireland was left behind politically by developments in the immediate aftermath of the war. While the 1950s saw the formation of the EEC consisting of Benelux, France, Germany and Italy, Ireland was not involved. Of course Ireland did not have the burden of physical reconstruction after the war, but the political isolation tended to reinforce the self-imposed economic isolation.

This economic isolation was reflected in the literature of the time and many Irish authors chose emigration rather than continuing to live at home. The anger and bewilderment of some of the emigrants are also reflected in the literature of the time, for example in the works of Brendan Behan and Edna O'Brien. Whereas in earlier generations emigration was accepted as the natural course for many young people, in a post-war Europe that was thriving it was increasingly seen as a symptom of failure by the Irish state.

The 1950s in Ireland were a period of slow growth and continuing very high levels of emigration, as much of the younger generation sought a better future outside the country. It took some time for the political system to recognise that the contrasting fortunes between Ireland and all of the rest of north-western Europe were not preordained. The economic and social stagnation forced new thinking, so that from the end of the 1950s onwards a new outward-looking economic policy was gradually adopted.

The first manifestation of a change in strategy came in 1957 with the abolition of corporation tax on profits made from exporting goods. This initiative was combined with a positive policy of trying to attract foreign firms to set up in Ireland. However, it was only from 1960 onwards, with the gradual abolition of the exceptionally high tariff barriers (and corresponding changes by partner countries), that the scope for supplying a wider market from Ireland increased. It was access to this wider market that was important to new foreign firms looking to Ireland as a potential European base. The logical conclusion of this policy occurred in 1973 when Ireland joined the EEC, now the EU, guaranteeing equal access to the large European market for all foreign (and Irish) firms operating in Ireland.

Membership of the EU represented a tremendous cultural change in its widest sense. For example, for most civil servants in the previous 50 years the economic relations with the outside world meant a trip to London to find out how they did things there. From 1 January 1973 all the files dealing with bilateral relations with London were sent to the basement and never again opened. Instead, many young civil servants found themselves at meetings in Brussels with equal rights and status to their opposite numbers, generally much older, from all over the rest of the EU. It is not surprising, therefore, that for the administration EU membership represented the culmination of Ireland's journey to independence.

This process was mirrored throughout Irish society. For the social partners, the trade unions and the employers, they suddenly found themselves playing in a major league. While initially it may have been intimidating, it rapidly opened their eyes to the diversity of European experience. While some of the leading trade unions were still branches of British trade unions, the trade union movement as a whole developed new ways of progressing their objectives over the course of the 1980s. This process of learning from the wider European culture of industrial relations and policy-making bore fruit in the 'partnership process', launched in 1987. Following on many years of economic adversity and industrial conflict, the social partners recognised that a more European model, whereby all sides agreed a common way forward for the economy, could benefit all parties. This partnership process helped underpin the stirring economic recovery of the late 1980s.

The inflow of foreign direct investment into Ireland that the economic policy of openness has produced has grown over the years. Ruane and Görg (1997) highlight the consistency with which this policy of attracting FDI was pursued. All governments over the last 40 years have pursued the same policy and the commitments on the rate of corporation tax payable many years ahead have been honoured by successive governments. This has helped create an environment where foreign investors feel welcome, and it reduces the level of uncertainty that is inherent in all foreign investment decisions.

The high proportion of FDI in the Irish manufacturing sector and its export-oriented development makes the Irish economy quite unique among the EU peripheral members. At this stage foreign-owned firms account for over half of all output in manufacturing and almost half of all employment (Barry *et al.* 1999). Foreign-owned manufacturing firms export almost 90 per cent of their output whereas Irish-owned manufacturing firms export around 36 per cent of output. Thus the influx of foreign-owned firms over four decades has played a vital role in opening up the economy directly.

By 1997 a quarter of all those employed in manufacturing were employed in US-owned firms and another quarter were employed in other foreign firms.[1] This has contributed to a situation where foreign-owned firms are treated equally and are clearly made welcome. While in many other countries there is some ambivalence

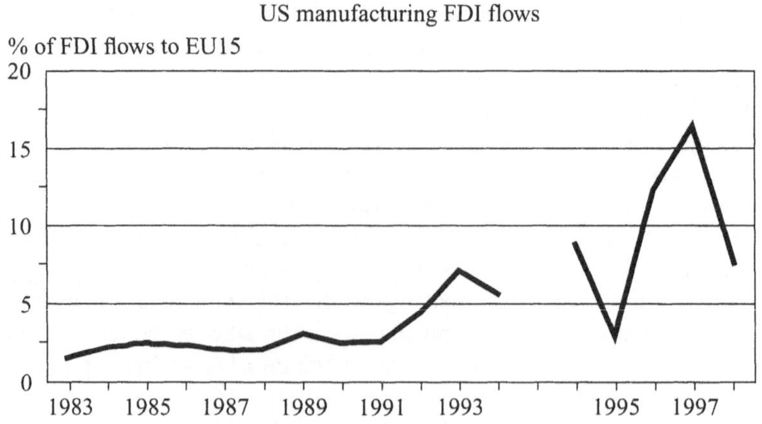

Figure 4.8 Foreign direct investment in Ireland

about the presence of foreign multinationals operating locally, in Ireland this has not been an issue in recent decades. This acceptance, and even welcoming of the global nature of the economy has, in turn, helped increase Ireland's attractiveness as a destination for further foreign investment.

In terms of nationality of origin of the foreign firms, the US is clearly dominant. This means that for a European economy, the Irish economy is unusually exposed to the US economic cycle. Thirty years ago UK firms played a much bigger role in the economy but, over time, they have not expanded, and many have even contracted, while the new investment has tended to come from the US and from the rest of the EU. To date the presence of Japanese and other Asian-based multinationals is quite low in the Irish economy.

The 1990s have seen a further rise in Ireland's success in attracting investment by foreign firms. Figure 4.8 shows how Ireland's share of US FDI in the EU has grown in the 1990s. While in the 1980s Ireland was already attracting more than its share of this investment, the 1990s saw the long-term policy achieve major success.

There have been significant benefits arising from the large inflows of FDI into the Irish manufacturing sector since accession to the EU. First, it has helped develop a high-growth, export-oriented sector and has led to a shift towards more high-skilled production. Secondly, it has reduced dependence on the UK as the main market for Irish exports. Thirdly, Ireland has become a major conduit of US technological innovation into Europe, especially in the 1990s. Fourthly, the policy of concentration on a small group of sectors has meant that Ireland has now become a major location for specific industries – information technology and pharmaceuticals. This leads to spill-over effects into the domestic economy, both in terms of received expertise and technological know-how, and via direct linkages with the domestic economy and the local labour market.

In the 1950s management and ownership of the very limited scale of domestic industry was dominated by a very small number of families (Kelleher 1987). Traditionally businesses were handed on from father to son (not daughters) and there was limited scope for professional management. Industry aimed to supply a heavily protected domestic market and future profitability depended more on success in lobbying for high tariff barriers than on any underlying business acumen.

Left to its own devices such a small-scale business sector, where management achieved their position through birth rather than ability, had little chance of succeeding in the much more sophisticated developing global market of the post-war world. Instead of continuing to protect this position, public policy aimed to attract foreign firms, not just to bring new capital, but probably more importantly to introduce new technologies and management skills to the Irish economy.

The new foreign firms setting up in Ireland in the 1960s and the 1970s brought with them foreign management and foreign business expertise, as well as the technical know-how and access to markets that their individual businesses specialised in. They naturally recruited young Irish staff to work with the senior management. In the course of time these younger staff tended to move on within the multinational organisation, moving to postings outside of Ireland. The willingness of young Irish people to move abroad meant that they were reasonably successful within their chosen enterprise. Over time many of them moved jobs but all of the time they developed their expertise.

As discussed later, a new pattern of migration developed over the last 40 years where, just as in the past, young Irish people moved abroad in search of a higher standard of living, but as they grew older they tended to return. The availability of a pool of skilled Irish managers working throughout the world has been tapped over the last 20 years by many new firms coming to Ireland. As a result, in contrast with the 1960s and the 1970s, many of the top management of the foreign multinationals operating in Ireland today are Irish. The combination of familiarity with the local culture and a wide experience of business practice abroad has made them an important asset, and even an ally, in attracting new business to the country.

In the early 1980s it had been hoped that a concentration on attracting foreign firms in the computer and pharmaceutical sectors would see the development of a 'silicon valley' type effect. However, this did not really happen in the way that was intended. While the volume of foreign investment reached critical mass in the late 1980s and has been extremely successful, there was little spin-off in terms of new Irish start-ups. However, where there has been a notable growth in new Irish business has been in the computer software industry. This was very small in the late 1980s but now up to one per cent of the labour force work in the business, over half of them in Irish-owned firms (O'Gorman *et al.* 1997).

A final phenomenon, which has evoked little domestic comment, is the rise of the Irish multinational. While small by world standards, the growth of these firms is nonetheless important for the future of the Irish economy in a global market. It is reducing the exposure of Irish firms to shocks to the Irish economy and it is widening the range of Irish economic interests. For example, today three of the top 200 multinationals in Poland are Irish owned.

The process of attrition in the traditional manufacturing sector has, in a sense, seen the survival of the fittest. For example, in the food-processing sector, where the industrial structure had been dominated by farmer-owned cooperatives since independence, the 1980s saw major changes. Most of the main players transformed themselves into public companies. Whereas in the past the owners – the farmers – wanted the highest possible price for their inputs into the industry, squeezing profitability, the new shareholders wanted to see the firms themselves prosper and expand. This change in governance has seen a transformation in the sector.

As a result of this process of change in the manufacturing sector, a substantial number of firms have emerged that are significant players in their sectors at a European, or even a world level. However, the growth of such firms is not confined to food-processing. Other more traditional industrial sectors, such as cement production, and the financial sector have also seen the growth of firms operating on a wider canvas than that of the Irish economy. In the past the inflow of capital and management expertise was seen as a one-way process, from abroad into Ireland; it is now a two-way process with Irish firms investing in subsidiaries elsewhere in the EU, in the US, and increasingly in the economies in transition in Central Europe.

This process is likely to make the economy more resilient in the face of shocks to the domestic economy. The more diversified regionally are the companies' interests, the less vulnerable they will be to a purely Irish recession in the future.

The growth of the Irish multinational is also continuing the process of globalising Irish management. Now Irish staff of Irish firms are gaining experience of new markets and new business challenges in the same way that they benefited in the past from working for foreign multinationals.

The homing pigeons

An unusual feature of the Irish experience has been the mobility of the population. Whereas in most of the rest of the EU the bulk of the indigenous population do not tend to migrate across national boundaries, in Ireland there is a tradition of migration stretching back to the 18th century. The diaspora of the last 150 years is common knowledge but the radical change in this phenomenon in recent times is less well known. Whereas up to the 1950s those who went never came back, since the 1960s we have seen the development of a 'homing pigeon' phenomenon. Today, while a large number of young Irish people still leave the country each year when they graduate, the bulk of them return in their late 20s or early 30s, bringing with them new skills and a new way of doing business. Developments in modern technology are strengthening the ties between emigrants and their home through increasing their ability to maintain daily contact with domestic cultural and social developments – the era of the 'email emigrant' who reads the *Irish Times*[2] daily and listens to the radio news headlines from RTE has arrived.

Ireland has traditionally been a very homogeneous society with the bulk of the population having the same blood group[3] – O, the same ethnic background, practising the same religion. Until the 1970s Irish people left and never came back and very few foreigners came to Ireland. This made for a rather claustrophobic society with

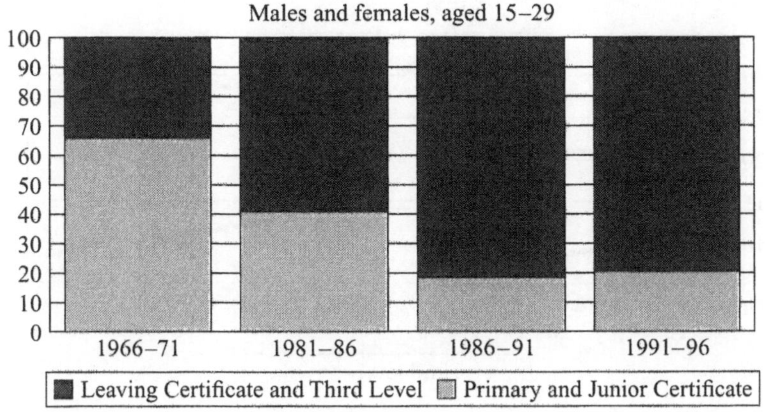

Figure 4.9 Educational attainment of emigrants

very limited cultural diversity. This claustrophobia was reflected in the choice by many Irish writers of a life outside Ireland in Britain, France or elsewhere in Europe.

From 1960 onwards, with the bulk of the population having access to British television, the modern media played an important role in increasing knowledge and understanding of the rapid changes elsewhere in Europe. However, possibly more important than the media in changing the economic culture of the country has been the direct experience by a substantial proportion of the population of life elsewhere. In the most restricted sense, for the bulk of the population, tourism has provided an initial experience of foreign cultures.

Traditionally those who emigrated were relatively unskilled and they sought to improve their standard of living by moving to the United Kingdom or the United States. This remained the position until the 1970s. As shown in Figure 4.9, in the late 1960s over two-thirds of those emigrating had not completed high school.[4] However, this began to change by the end of the 1970s and by the late 1980s 80 per cent of emigrants had at least completed high school. From a situation where emigrants traditionally tended to be among the less skilled in Irish society the situation was transformed to one where they were among the most skilled.

This change in the pattern of emigration in the 1980s raised considerable concerns about a 'brain drain'. There were fears that the state, having invested considerable resources in educating the emigrants, was then losing the benefits of this investment as their skills were harnessed by the wider EU or US economies.

However, the reality has turned out to be rather different. While in the past the 'American wake'[5] was an important feature of the Irish culture, it has ceased to be the case today as the majority of emigrants are 'homing pigeons' – they will eventually return. The phenomenon of returning emigrants only really began in the 1970s. In the years up to World War II many emigrants, especially those going to the US, expected never to see Ireland again. However, with the fall in the cost of transport and the shift in destination for most emigrants to the UK, those leaving in the post-war years expected to return to Ireland at some stage on holidays.

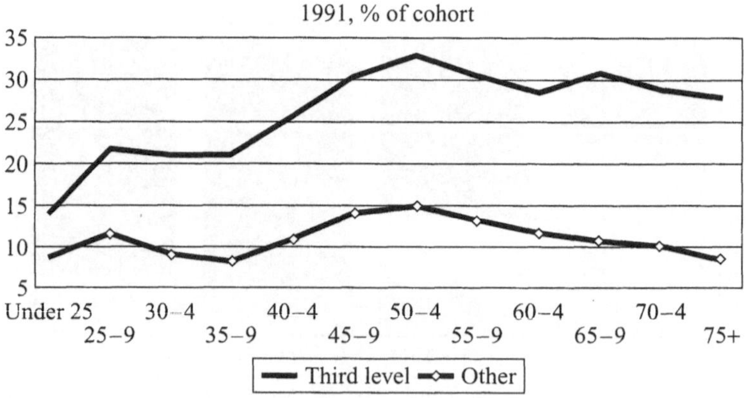

Figure 4.10 Males who have resided abroad, 1991

In a more lasting way, the fact that such a high proportion of the population are returned emigrants has helped transform the economy and society generally. This has contributed to a wide range of changes – from a change in eating habits, forms of entertainment and cultural interests to an increase in the productivity of the workforce. Barrett and O'Connell (2000) show that for males who emigrate and return, controlling for education and other characteristics, they earn around 10 per cent more in Ireland as a result of their experience abroad. This provides a striking quantification of the benefits to Ireland of labour mobility and it is an important confirmation of the role that migration has played in opening up the economy.

While those with a good education are now more likely to emigrate than those with only a primary education, they are also more likely to come back. As shown in Figure 4.10, in 1991 over a quarter of all males in the country (the figures are similar for females) with a third-level education had lived abroad for at least a year. For all other educational categories the proportion was 10 or 15 per cent. It means that even in the face of continuing substantial gross outflows, the fact that individuals return with additional experience from working abroad may actually enhance the return from education.

In addition to the returning emigrants there is now a very substantial inflow of non-Irish workers. Over the last five years they have accounted for just under half of all the gross immigration into the country. Barrett and Trace (1998) have shown that an even higher share of the inflow of persons not born in Ireland have a third-level education than returning Irish emigrants. Thus immigration, whether or not those involved are returning emigrants, has been a very important source of skilled labour in the 1990s and it has played a significant role in helping the economy to grow at such a rapid pace. The high level of education of immigrants contrasts with the experience of other EU countries.

From an economic point of view, this high degree of mobility, especially for skilled labour, greatly increases the elasticity of labour supply. This has tended to keep Irish skilled labour costs from rising too rapidly. It makes the Irish labour

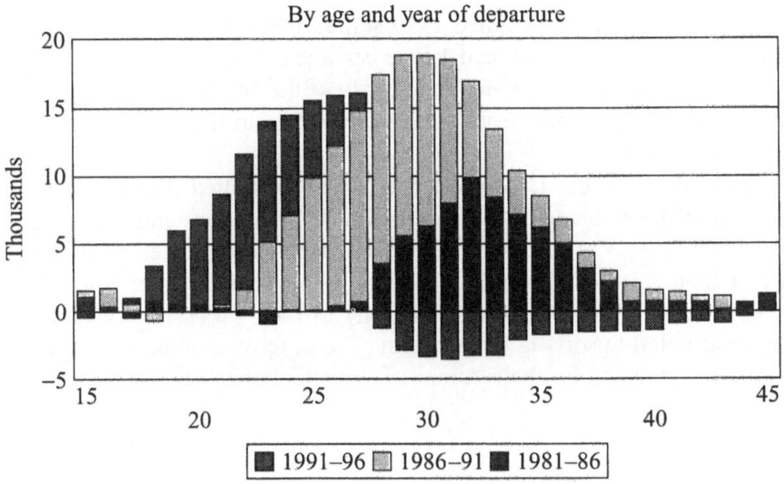

Figure 4.11 Stock of emigrants abroad
Source: Census of Ireland.

market closer to that of the US than that of other EU national labour markets. What is also interesting is the extent to which the mobility now involves skilled individuals who are citizens of other EU countries – the UK, Germany, France, Sweden, Finland and the Netherlands. The bulk of these immigrants are highly skilled, speaking good English (even with an American accent!) and their arrival has evoked little comment. A significant number of these immigrants are probably spouses or partners of returning Irish emigrants. In 1996, 28 per cent of all couples who were both long-term migrants consisted of one partner who was Irish and one partner who was foreign (Finneran and Punch 1999). However, many of the rest of those not born in Ireland, who are now coming to skilled jobs, have no traditional association with the country.

Looking to the future, the stock of Irish emigrants abroad is beginning to fall. Figure 4.11 shows an estimate of the stock of emigrants in 1996, classified by when they left Ireland (Fahey *et al.* 1998). The bulk of them were then in their early 30s, having left Ireland in the 1980s. However, with a reduced outflow in recent years, and with the existing stock who have not returned ageing, the likely inflow of returning emigrants in the future will be lower than in the 1990s. This means that for the future, the demands from the labour market are more likely to be met through an increase in numbers of foreign migrants than from returning Irish.

In the short term, because of the very high cost of accommodation, the returning emigrants, and the foreigners who are potential immigrants, are likely to fall in numbers. The cost of accommodation, and the potential cost of living for migrants, in Ireland is rising above that in many of its EU neighbours. This may see a temporary fall in net immigration until the constraint on housing supply is relaxed through increased investment in necessary support infrastructure.

A recent study by Barrett *et al.* (2000) indicates that the effect of the influx of skilled migrants, both Irish and foreign, has been to relax constraints on domestic production. In the four years ended 1999 skilled immigration is estimated to have contributed a cumulative additional 1.5 percentage points to the growth in GNP. In addition, by expanding the productive capacity of the economy, it has increased the demand for unskilled labour, resulting in a reduction in the unemployment rate of 0.7 percentage points.

This contrasts with the US experience, where unskilled immigration has also helped expand the productive capacity of the US economy and proved good for skilled labour (Borjas *et al.* 1997). However, it has also proved unfavourable for unskilled US citizens. For Ireland the availability of skilled labour from abroad has kept skilled wage rates from rising as rapidly as they would otherwise have done and has contributed to solving the problem of long-term unemployment. It has also moderated the tendency for the earnings of skilled labour to rise relative to earnings for unskilled.

Conclusions

The contrast between Ireland and the rest of Europe in the 1950s was a force for change pushing the country towards an opening up to the outside world. The contrast between the Ireland of the 1950s and the Ireland of today highlights the major economic benefits that have derived from the enthusiastic embrace of this process of globalisation.

However, this move to a more multicultural economy has also had a wide impact on Irish society and has been mirrored in a similar change elsewhere. The enthusiasm with which globalisation has been embraced has added to its success. The effects of opening up to the outside world have not been confined to economics. The wider social and cultural benefits have, if anything, strengthened the direct economic effects.

By opening up the economy to trade there have been clear long-term benefits. This has been particularly clear in the role that foreign direct investment has played. It has both enhanced the productive potential of the economy and has also produced indirect benefits through enhancing the skills of the domestic workforce. More recently the growth of Irish multinationals is adding to the resilience of the growing economy.

The tradition of emigration as a running sore must now be reinterpreted. The development of the phenomenon of 'homing pigeons' – the return of the emigrants, has played a vital role in making the current economic success possible. It has added directly to the labour supply and skills of the economy. The multicultural nature of the economy, if not of the wider society, has been part of the current Irish success story. Finally, globalisation and the reversal of the tradition of emigration have also helped create a more cosmopolitan and innovative society.

In terms of public policy the changing exposure of the economy has implications for future policy on Ireland's international relations. Whereas in the past Ireland was extremely dependent on the UK economy, it now has a substantial exposure to the US economy through the weight of foreign investment. The health of the US economy is probably more important to Ireland than to most of its EU neighbours. It is also very dependent on the EU economy and euro monetary policy. Even before EMU, the rise in EU interest rates as a result of German unification had a major negative impact on the Irish economy, probably postponing the boom, which would have happened in the early 1990s to today.

Developing policies to safeguard the current achievements in a rapidly changing international environment is the new task for Irish policy-makers. The future development of the European Union, which has been the key to the Irish economic success, will obviously be the central focus of economic policy over the coming decade.

Endnotes

1. Around 5 per cent each were employed in UK- and German-owned firms.
2. The *Irish Times* is one of the ten most widely read newspapers on the Internet precisely because of the volume of interest from emigrants.
3. Readers Digest (1964) *Atlas of the British Isles* (London: Readers Digest).
4. The Leaving Certificate is the examination taken in Ireland at the end of secondary school.
5. A wake is traditionally the gathering after a funeral to celebrate the life of the deceased. The 'American wake' was then the party to mark the departure for ever of the emigrant departing for North America.

References

Barrett, A. and O'Connell, P. (2000) 'Is there a wage premium for returning Irish migrants?', working paper No. 125 (Dublin: The Economic and Social Research Institute).

Barrett, A. and Trace, F. (1998) 'Who is coming back? The educational profile of returning migrants in the 1990s', *Irish Banking Review*, Summer, pp. 38–52.

Barrett, A., Fitz Gerald, J. and Nolan, B. (2000) 'Earnings inequality, returns to education and immigration into Ireland', working paper DP2493 (London: CEPR).

Barry, F., Bradley, J. and O'Malley, E. (1999) 'Indigenous and foreign industry: characteristics and performance', in F. Barry (ed.), *Understanding Ireland's Economic Growth* (Basingstoke: Macmillan Press).

Borjas, G., Freeman, R. and Katz, L. (1997) 'How much do immigration and trade affect labour market outcomes?', *Brookings Papers on Economic Activity*, 1, pp. 1–67.

Bradley, J., Fitz Gerald, J. and Storey, A. (1987) *Medium-Term Review 1987–1992* (Dublin: The Economic and Social Research Institute).

Fahey, T., Fitz Gerald, J. and Maître, B. (1998) 'The economic and social implications of population change', *Journal of the Statistical and Social Inquiry Society of Ireland 1997/1998*.

Finneran, C. and Punch, A. (1999) 'The demographic and socio-economic characteristics of migrants, 1986–1996', *Journal of the Statistical and Social Inquiry Society of Ireland 1998/1999*, pp. 213–64.

Kelleher, P. (1987) 'Familism in Irish capitalism in the 1950s', *The Economic and Social Review*, 18 (2), January.

Lee, J.J. (1989) *Ireland 1912–1985: Politics and Society* (Cambridge: Cambridge University Press).

Mjøset, L. (1993) *The Irish Economy in a Comparative Institutional Context*, Report No. 93 (Dublin: National Economic and Social Council).

O'Gorman, C., O'Malley, E. and Mooney, J. (1997) *Clusters in Ireland: the Irish Indigenous Software Industry*, Research Series No. 3 (Dublin: National Economic and Social Council).

O'Rourke, K. and Williamson, J. (1995) 'Around the European periphery 1870–1913: globalization, schooling and growth', working paper WP95/17 (University College Dublin).

Ruane, F. and Görg, H. (1997) 'The impact of foreign direct investment on sectoral adjustment in the Irish economy', *National Institute Economic Review*, No. 160, April, pp. 76–86.

Chapter 5

Ireland and the European Union

Brigid Laffan

Introduction

In January 1972, the Taoiseach Jack Lynch and his Foreign Minister, Dr Patrick Hillary, left Dublin airport for Luxembourg to sign Ireland's Treaty of Accession to the European Communities. Just over 50 years after the signing of the Anglo-Irish Treaty, a treaty that gave the people of 26 of the 32 counties of the island of Ireland the right to establish a state (the Irish Free State) separate from the United Kingdom, an Irish government negotiated membership of a Community that was altering the nature of statehood in Western Europe. The Taoiseach and his party were seen off at Dublin airport by the then President, de Valera. The television frame capturing the departing Taoiseach and the ageing president remains hugely symbolic. That *tableau* captured the ties but also the tensions between the Ireland of 1972 and the Ireland of 1916. Jack Lynch's departure to sign the Rome Treaties represented the end of the Ireland that de Valera would have had. Right up to the end of the 1950s, de Valera's idea or ideal of Ireland was that of a rural and preferably Gaelic-speaking society committed to spiritual rather than material values. The Ireland of the 1920s, 1930s, 1940s and 1950s was an Ireland fearful of the consequences of economic modernisation, urbanisation and growth. Consequently, in the post-war era, Ireland failed to participate in or benefit from a golden period of economic expansion in Western Europe.

Within the Irish civil service an acute battle was waged, in the 1950s, about the future direction of economic policy. The battle fought in well-crafted departmental memos and letters was a battle between protectionism and free trade, between economic conservatism and liberalisation and between Ireland's past and Ireland's future. At issue was whether or not the Irish state and its people would or could embrace the post-war political economy. The prevailing deep-seated political and economic conservatism was challenged by the clear evidence that Irish freedom had failed to deliver prosperity and well-being for its people. However, embracing international liberalisation carried with it the seeds of deep societal change and challenge. In the 1957 Organisation of European Economic Co-operation negotiations on a European-wide free-trade area, Ireland was categorised as a less developed country together with Greece, Iceland and Turkey. For the duration of the talks, these four states were collectively known as the 'peripherals'. Would Ireland remain a 'peripheral' or could it find the cultural and institutional capacity to fundamentally shift its 'policy paradigm' and find an alternative path of economic development? Was the Irish state capable of steering Irish society and the Irish economy in a new direction? Within the civil service, the Departments of the Taoiseach, Finance, Foreign Affairs, Agriculture, and Industry and Commerce attempted to craft an Irish response to developments in Europe. The debate revolved around the privileged position of Irish exports (both manufacturing and agricultural) in the UK market and the Irish response to trade liberalisation. In addition to the pervasive concern with dependency on the British market was the challenge of abandoning the autarchy of previous decades. Ken Whitaker, the secretary of the Finance ministry, was the main advocate of liberalisation in the public service. Throughout the 1950s he decried the policy of sheltering permanently behind tariff barriers and he sought to move the economy in the direction of free trade. The Departments of Industry and Commerce and Agriculture remained conservative on external economic policy, more concerned with protecting exports to Britain than exploring how Ireland might escape from dependency.

In 1958, Whitaker was responsible for penning *The Grey Book on Economic Development*, a report that set out the strategy Ireland would adopt in search of economic modernisation. The report strongly advocated the abandonment of protectionism and an acceptance of free trade and liberalisation. The strategy contained in the report together with its endorsement by the new Fianna Fáil Taoiseach, Sean Lemass, ensured that this policy shift was a critical juncture in Ireland's relations with the outside world. Sean Lemass proved capable of mediating between Ireland's past and its future. The desire for membership of the EU was a logical consequence of the change in the dominant policy paradigm. The EU could serve the dual objective of reducing Ireland's dependence on the British market and providing a large liberalising market for Irish products. In essence, the modernisers won the battle in the realm of both ideas and action in the period 1958–61. Although portrayed largely in economic terms, EU membership would have a profound impact on Irish society, economy and polity.

The Irish government made its first application for EU membership on 31 July 1961. It took 12 years to bring this key foreign policy goal to fruition largely because of events beyond the control of any Irish government. Throughout the 1960s, successive governments remained wedded to Ireland's eventual membership of the Union. The Taoiseach and key domestic ministers established contact with the emerging EU institutions and continued to prepare Ireland for membership of the Brussels club. Membership of the European Communities in 1973 would greatly increase the pressures of economic liberalisation begun by Sean Lemass in the 1960s. And it would herald a period of more intense involvement by successive Irish governments in the European arena. Irish taoisigh travel abroad with such frequency today to attend European Council meetings or to have bilateral meetings with their counterparts, that no president would see them off at the airport. The purpose of this chapter is to analyse the 'EU' dimension of Ireland's engagement with the wider world. Central to the analysis is the assumption that the EU straddles the boundary between the national and the international. EU membership internationalises domestic policy and domesticates foreign policy. EU membership in 1973 established a regional/continental framework for Ireland's engagement with the wider world. It changed the context of Anglo-Irish relations and diminished the importance of the UN as the central focus in Irish foreign policy. From 1973, Ireland would mediate its relations with the international system in the context of the Union. This short review of the EU component of Ireland's international engagement is developed in a number of sections. The first section analyses the compatibility of EU membership with Irish identity. The second section outlines how Irish negotiators work to promote and protect domestic space in the Union. The third section analyses how opt-outs and reservations are used in protecting domestic space. The fourth section examines the Irish approach to constitutional change in the Union as a small state. The fifth section provides a brief overview of the pressures on Ireland to re-position itself in the EU.

The EU – a place we belong

Membership of the European Union goes beyond the constraints of membership of a traditional international organisation in a number of important respects. First, the European Court of Justice (ECJ) has transformed the treaties of the EU into a constitutional framework that limits the legal sovereignty of the member states. The Irish state and its people operate within a dual constitutional framework – the national and the EU. Secondly, the decision-making processes of the EU are designed to foster collective decision-making by the sharing or pooling of member state sovereignty. The sharing of sovereignty ultimately transforms the exercise of sovereignty. Thirdly, membership of the EU implies a commitment to the EU as it evolves and not just as it is when a state joins the club. All three characteristics of the Union when taken together imply that the member states submit to a 'shared destiny', to a transformation of their statehood. To be a member state of the Union is to embrace membership of a densely institutionalised site of politics above the level of the state. It is to expose national policies, institutions, societies and economies to processes of Europeanisation. The ease with which state elites and the mass publics adjust to membership of the EU varies widely across the member states. Among the 'newcomers', Ireland's adjustment has been relatively smooth when compared to the United Kingdom and Denmark, the two other states that joined in 1973. Why should this be so?

Membership of the EU quickly became part of the cognitive frame of Ireland's state elite. The internalisation of the EU may be gleaned from the description of the EU as 'A Place We Belong' by the Taoiseach, Mr Bertie Ahern, in a speech delivered on 21 March 2000. It was underlined in the 1996 Government White Paper on Irish Foreign Policy, when it was stated:

> Irish people increasingly see the European Union not simply as an organisation to which Ireland belongs, but as an integral part of our future. We see ourselves increasingly as Europeans. (Government of Ireland 1996: 59)

Such a statement could not be made in a Danish or Swedish White Paper on foreign policy. The EU flag is habitually flown from public buildings with the Irish tricolour and the Taoiseach and ministers usually fly both flags in their offices. There was no opposition to the EU passport, driving licence or social security card in Ireland. There are three overlapping reasons for the relative compatibility between Ireland's state identity and membership of the EU.

1 EU membership was not just a foreign policy decision but was intrinsic to the national project of modernisation.
2 EU membership would help resolve Ireland's relationship with its significant 'other', the United Kingdom.
3 The renewed link with continental Europe resonated with Catholic Ireland. EU membership implied a re-joining of Europe in an important sense.

For these reasons, it could be argued that there was a high degree of compatibility between Ireland's national project and membership of the Union. EU membership appealed to the old concern of Irish nationalism – 'how to deal with Britain', and the new concern – how to make Ireland prosperous. Garvin captures the significance of the EU to Ireland in the following terms: 'In the Irish case, Europe offered a reality which had always been fantasised about: a powerful entity that was perceived as benign, was not English and was not controlled by England' (Garvin 2000: 39). Prior to 1973 successive Irish leaders had experience of the limits of formal sovereignty and were thus more than willing to embrace a pooling of sovereignty. The EU offered liberation not containment. An EU 'Top Decision Makers Survey' found that 98 per cent of Irish respondents felt that Ireland had benefited from EU membership and support for Ireland's membership was expressed by 95 per cent of respondents (EU Top Decision Makers Survey 1996). Notwithstanding these figures, only 40 per cent of respondents would support the concept of a European government. This suggests that the desire to protect national space remains strong among Irish officials and political leaders.

The Irish electorate has had to endorse the constitutional development of the Union in a number of referenda since the membership vote in 1972 when 83 per cent of the electorate voted in favour of membership. Since the Single European Act was negotiated in the mid-1980s, there have been three further referenda on the Single Act (1987), the Treaty on European Union (1992) and the Treaty of Amsterdam (1998). The size of the 'yes' vote has declined from the high of 83 per cent in 1972 to 62 per cent in 1998, although the Irish electorate, unlike its Danish counterpart, has never delivered a 'no' vote to an EU treaty. Acceptance of Ireland's involvement in European integration appears well rooted in the Irish body politic and, in surveys over many years, well over 80 per cent of respondents believe that membership has been good to Ireland. In Eurobarometer 48 (Autumn 1997), 88 per cent of Irish respondents felt that Ireland had benefited from membership. This was a far higher proportion than for any other member state. Support for Ireland's membership of the Union is not accompanied by a high level of knowledge about

EU affairs. Ireland ranks just above the Union average in knowledge of EU affairs, with 59 per cent of Irish respondents to Eurobarometer surveys displaying low or very low knowledge of the EU (Sinnott 1995: 34). Both the Irish state elite and the mass public appear comfortable with Ireland's place in the EU. However, the protection of national space remains important.

Promoting national preferences and protecting national space

There is remarkable consistency in the policy domains that are accorded a high priority by Ireland in the EU. Policy in the past was moulded by Ireland's low level of development relative to the core, by sustained high levels of employment and by its dependence on mobile foreign investment. The aim was thus to try to ensure that developments in social and economic governance at EU level could be accommodated by Ireland (see Coombes 1983; Drudy and McAleese 1984; Keatinge 1991; O'Donnell 2000). From an Irish perspective, the key policy areas have been:

- The EU's common agricultural policy that enabled Irish agriculture to escape from the traditional cheap food policies of the UK. The emphasis in relation to the CAP is to maintain or improve farm incomes. Ireland remains one of the key members together with France in the CAP supporters' club.
- To develop cohesion policies at EU level to assist Europe's peripheral areas catch up. Successive Irish governments deployed considerable diplomatic effort to ensuring that the EU would develop a cohesion policy and that Ireland would benefit from financial transfers from the EU budget. Following reform of the Structural Funds in 1988, Ireland experienced a significant increase in financial transfers from the EU budget. The volume of transfers will be reduced progressively to 2006 given Ireland's higher level of economic growth in the 1990s.
- Successive Irish governments have attempted to protect domestic space by carefully vetting sectoral policies and EU regulations that were likely to have an impact on Ireland's competitive position and on regulatory frameworks at national level. The internal market programme was thus accorded a high priority because of the weight of EC legislation and the need to prepare Irish industry and the service sector for the competitive shock of the 1992 programme. Irish administrations have been adamantly opposed to any harmonisation of taxation policy in Europe and fought a hard campaign to maintain low levels of corporation policy.
- The TEU marked a further deepening of integration with the inclusion of provisions on a single currency, the common foreign and security policy and pillar three. Rather than dislodging the high-ranking policies of the past, the TEU simply added additional priorities and concerns. Irish governments in the 1990s showed considerable commitment to the public debt philosophy and targets set out in the Maastricht Treaty and supported the full observance of the Maastricht criteria across Europe. In practice, the Irish

political and policy system was converted to the sound money/tight budget philosophy of the German Bundesbank.
- Successive Irish governments have endorsed EU social and environmental regulation provided such regulation does not impose an undue burden on Irish industry or the exchequer. Maintaining Ireland's attractiveness to foreign mobile investment, particularly American capital, runs through Irish policy.

In promoting domestic preferences and protecting national space, Irish politicians and administrators have had to engage in coalition building with like-minded states. Unlike other small states, such as the Nordics or the Benelux, Ireland does not have a natural grouping of like-minded states and must thus seek allies on a case-by-case basis – with the French on agriculture, the UK on taxation and the other cohesion countries on regional funds.

Domestic adaptation to the challenge of competition and Ireland's vulnerability as a small open economy were not unproblematic. Irish adjustment in the 1970s, notwithstanding the oil crises, was relatively smooth. However, by the end of the 1970s, Ireland entered a vicious circle of economic policy. Ireland had the worst economic performance in Europe during most of the 1980s, as a result of international recession, which was reinforced by a dramatic domestic adjustment to reduce public finance and balance of payments deficits and reduce inflation. By the mid-1980s, Ireland's economic and social strategy was in ruins and its hope of prospering in the EU was in considerable doubt. There was a widespread sense of Ireland's failure, not unlike the prevailing mood in the 1950s. The state and its society found itself at another critical juncture. Ireland had to find the institutional and cultural capacity to overcome the failure of the 1980s. Without this, the opportunities offered by the internal market and the deepening of integration would have been lost. Ireland would have reclaimed the title of peripheral, but this time inside the EU. Gradually there was a recognition by Government and the key representatives of the two sides of industry that 'membership of the Community does not reduce the need for clear Irish policy aims and methods. In particular, membership of the Community does not diminish the need for a national ability to identify solutions to national problems – even where these required Community policies or action' (NESC 1989: 218). Thus a key concern of this period was to ensure that Ireland's domestic policies were congruent with membership of a highly competitive market regime.

Irish efforts to manage Europeanisation and internationalisation, in this period, evolved through a form of neo-corporatism known as social partnership. This began in 1987 with the Programme for National Recovery (1987–90) and was followed by three subsequent programmes – the Programme for Economic and Social Progress (PESP 1990–93), the Programme for Competitiveness and Work (PCW 1994–96) and Partnership 2000 (1997–2000). The programmes involved agreement between employers, trade unions, farming interests and the Government on wage levels in the public and private sectors and on a wide range of economic and social policies. The content of all programmes was negotiated in the context of EU developments and the need to ensure that Ireland adjusted to the demands of economic integration.

Table 5.1 Ireland's economic performance

	1995	1996	1997	1998
Economic growth volume (GDP%)	10.1	7.7	10.7	9.0
Economic growth volume (GNP%)	7.3	7.2	6.9	8.1
Employment growth (%)	5.1	3.9	3.5	4.8
Debt/GDP ratio (%)	81.5	73.3	59.9	49.5

Source: Department of Finance, *Monthly Economic Bulletins*, August 1996, 1999.

The partnership approach together with an expansion of EU spending programmes in Ireland produced the much-needed recovery from the disastrous early and mid-1980s. From 1992 onwards, Ireland consistently out-performed its EU partners in terms of economic growth, employment creation and the growth of exports. As a result, per capita incomes in Ireland converged rapidly with the Union (see Table 5.1). EU finance was critical in helping Ireland create the human and physical infrastructure, which fuelled economic growth and recovery. Ireland is no longer the poor peripheral state that joined the Union in 1973. It is now a successful competitor for growth and employment creation with a distinctive model of economic governance. EU membership has fostered the Ireland of Lemass rather than the Ireland of de Valera.

Protecting domestic space through opt-outs/reservations

The senior officials that undertook the detailed assessment of Ireland's relationship with the EU in the period up to accession developed a sophisticated understanding of how the EU operated and how to position Ireland in the evolving Union. The strategy was summed up by Halligan when he claimed that Ireland 'would be a psychological insider within the integration process' (Halligan 2000: 29). Put simply, Ireland would attempt to go with the flow of integration and would help build the Union as a union of states and their peoples. Successive Irish governments sought to appear communautaire at least when seen from the perspective of the preferences of the Danes or the British. This was confirmed in 1985 at the Milan European Council, when Ireland was the only new member state to vote with the 'inner six' on the question of treaty change. Milan represented the re-launching of integration after the doldrums period of the early 1980s.

Notwithstanding the desire by Irish officials and political leaders to be at the core of the system, foreign policy cooperation and the Schengen system have been problematic. This reflects a statement on the Irish position made by Maire Geoghegan-Quinn, the then Minister of State for European Affairs, when she referred to Ireland as 'conditionally integrationist' (Geoghegan-Quinn 1990: 5). Ireland's traditional policy of non-membership of NATO and the continuing support in Irish public opinion for this position have meant that successive Irish governments have been cautious about the development of a security dimension in the EU. The collapse of communism in 1989 and the changing geo-politics of the continent have forced security issues up the EU agenda. The weak EU response to developments in the Balkans led to pressures for an enhancement of the EU's capacity. Ireland was much slower than the other EU neutral states to adjust its security policies to developments in Europe. It was the last EU state to join the Partnership for Peace and it is now faced with the rapid development of the EU's European Security and Defence Policy (ESDP). The other area that has proved difficult is the Schengen system and free movement of people. As a result of the common travel area with the United Kingdom, Ireland together with the UK sought opt-outs from the free movement provisions of the Treaty of Amsterdam and neither state is a member of the Schengen system. Schengen became part of the Union acquis in the form of a protocol that was added to the Treaty of Amsterdam. Since the Treaty of Amsterdam came into operation, both the UK and Ireland have sought to become party to parts of the Schengen system. Increasingly, the EU is the framework through which Ireland is attempting to deal with asylum and immigration control.

A small EU state

European integration provided small states with a strategy for managing 'smallness' and the presence of larger and more powerful neighbours. The continental order imposed by the development of the EU enabled small West European states to develop in the context of a stable and rule-bound external environment. It was essentially the capacity of European integration to take the sting out of ethnic nationalism, to tame large state power and the aggressive pursuit of national interest that made the Union so attractive to small European states. The EU as a strategy for managing size was embraced, at an early stage, by the Benelux and thereafter by many small states including Ireland. The EU consists of a range of large, medium and small states. In the power structures of the EU, small states carry less voice and influence than the larger states. Small states find it generally, although not always, harder to hold out against an emerging consensus in the Council of Ministers. Dr Garret Fitzgerald, former Irish Taoiseach, aptly summed up the case when he argued that: 'As a small country we must ensure that we do not create problems for our partners save in the case of issues that are of vital importance to us. Only when our case is so strong so overwhelmingly strong that in logic others should objectively accept it should we press our interests in a way that can create problems for other people. We must avoid pinpricking our partners and thus losing the good will that we need on certain relatively few crucial occasions' (Fitzgerald 1985: 23). In other words, small states must harness diplomatic good will in the EU, to be deployed on issues that are considered as key preferences or interests.

Size is not a good predictor of approaches to European integration. Some small states, notably the Benelux, have embraced a federalist view of the European project with zeal, whereas others, such as Denmark and Sweden, are among the most reticent about political integration. Moreover, size has little bearing on national approaches to substantive issues of EU policy which are formed by economic considerations, the attitude of domestic interests, national management of the issue in question and the proposed nature of the change. Nor are 'small states' likely to band together against the 'large states' in substantive policy discussions; their interests, just as those of the larger states, diverge. The coalition pattern in the Council of Ministers has always consisted of a mix of large and small states on particular policy issues. Small states do, however, have a combined interest in the institutional balance, the 'rules of the game' and their level of representation in the system. They have a shared interest in ensuring that small states have an adequate presence in the Union's governance structures and that the Union is not run by a club of the larger states.

During the 1990s, faced with the prospect of many more small states given the eastern enlargement, small state/large state tensions appeared in the Union. These tensions revolved around institutional reform, which remains the subject of member state negotiations on treaty change. The formal process by which the member states renegotiate the treaties is known as an intergovernmental conference (IGC). The key issues are a re-weighting of votes in the Council of Ministers, the size of the Commission and what is known as closer cooperation. These issues remain to be resolved before enlargement proceeds. The larger states signalled at an early stage in the 1996 IGC negotiations that they were concerned about the growing leverage of small states in the system. The Reflection Group Report which prepared the agenda for the 1996 IGC, drew attention to the fact that 'Several members point to a gradual deterioration in popular representation in the weighting of qualified-majority voting as a result of the under-representation of the people of the more populous States and the growing number of less populous States in the Union' (EU 1995: 28). The smaller states, including Ireland, have argued that it is unrealistic to consider that the smaller states would band together in the Council to outvote the larger states given the coalition patterns of the past. The former Irish Foreign Minister, Dick Spring, argued that:

> Votes in the Council never break down in terms of large states versus small states. The breakdown is determined by the issue under consideration. The suggestion that at some point in the distant future governments representing a minority of the population might outvote Governments representing a majority of the population depends on the very unlikely assumption that all of the smaller states both from the existing members and the new members would vote identically. (Dick Spring, Irish Foreign Minister, May 1995)

However well founded this argument is in empirical fact, the small states are going to have to make concessions to the larger states on voting. Agreement on changes to the voting system was not achieved at Amsterdam with the result that the issue is central to the agenda of IGC 2000, that should end in the Treaty of Nice in December 2000. Although the Taoiseach, Bertie Ahern, remains unconvinced that the current weights in the Council require revision, he has conceded that: 'We would be prepared to consider some limited re-weighting in the context envisaged at Amsterdam, that the larger Member States were prepared to five up their second Commissioner' (Ahern 2000: 13).

The Irish negotiators are clearly making a link between re-weighting of votes in the Council and the right to nominate a Commissioner. A well-established feature of Ireland's policy on EU institutions is support for the role of the Commission. Irish politicians and policy-makers regard the Commission as the key protector of the interests of small states in the Union. Experience since membership has supported this policy reference. The former Taoiseach, John Bruton, supported the Commission very forcefully in the lead-up to the 1996 IGC:

> The Commission's monopoly of the initiation of draft legislation and veto on subsequent amendment of that legislation by anything other than an unanimous vote of the Council ensure that the interests of all are safeguarded. That an autonomous institution devoted to the wider European interest has decisive control of the legislative agenda is very important. Were the Commission's powers in this regard diluted, the likelihood of the large states dominating the European agenda would be greatly increased. Such a development would inevitably lead to a significant diminution of the ability of small member states to protect their legitimate interests. (John Bruton, Taoiseach, 6 April 1995)

Maintaining an Irish Commissioner emerged as a central objective of Ireland's negotiating position at the 1996 IGC. The principle of one Commissioner per state was affirmed again and again as non-negotiable from an Irish perspective. The Taoiseach, Bertie Ahern, stated in March 2000 that he 'cannot envisage a situation whereby Ireland would forgo the right to nominate a Commissioner' (Ahern 2000). Without a full Commissioner, Ireland would have limited influence at the highest political level in this organisation.

A third issue, of interest to Ireland, in the negotiations of treaty change is the question of closer cooperation or flexibility. The Treaty of Amsterdam (1997) included a provision on closer cooperation that allowed a group of states (simple majority) to engage in closer cooperation within the institutions and legal framework of the Union. The purpose of this clause was to enable a group of states to pursue common interests and concerns and to avoid the blocking power of a small group of member states. Although the provision has never been used, the issue forms part of the agenda of the IGC 2000. The continental core states, especially the original member states, want to change the provisions so as to make it easier for sub-EU policy co-ordination. Irish negotiators have always been concerned about creating within the Union in-groups of states because of fears that Ireland might find itself in an outer ring. Given the pressures on enlargement, Ireland is likely to have to agree to changes in the existing provision on closer cooperation.

The overall approach of Irish negotiators in treaty negotiations is to protect, as far as possible, those elements of the institutional system that are central to the Union's institutional balances, notably: balances within institutions and between institutions; balances between larger and smaller member states; and balances between the interest of individual member states and the common interests advanced by the institutions. Faced with the concerns of the larger states, the small states, including Ireland, are faced with a trade-off between retaining the level of representation and voting power they have at present, or having a Union that functions effectively and binds the larger states. Europe's small states have an overwhelming interest in the preservation of the Union as a problem-solving arena and a source of order for the continent. Any return to balance of power politics, a fragmented Europe or national closure is not in their interests.

Re-positioning Ireland in the EU

Just over 25 years of membership of the Union and over 40 years since the Irish state altered its strategy of economic development, Ireland finds itself as a small prosperous West European state with per capita incomes that have converged with those of other wealthy EU states. The claim that Ireland is a 'nation caught on the hop between the traditional and the modern, between the Bishop of Rome and the Treaty of Rome' may no longer hold (Eagleton 1999: 177). The economic modernisation represented by the Treaty of Rome has prevailed. Ireland is the only poor EU state, to date, that has caught up with its European neighbours. The EU was critical to the catch-up for a number of inter-related reasons. First, it provided the Irish economy with a large and increasingly liberalising market. The European single market programme that commenced in the mid-1980s forced Irish economic actors to focus on competitiveness. Secondly, the Exchange Rate Mechanism (ERM) and later preparations for the Euro imposed strong disciplines on the Irish public finances. Monetary cooperation led to considerable learning by government, public service and economic actors. Thirdly, the Structural Funds provided a significant transfer of budgetary resources from the richer states to Ireland. More importantly, the Structural Funds imposed a multi-annual planning framework and a related evaluation culture on the Irish system. Fourth, EU regulation up-graded Irish law in the economic and social spheres. Fifth, the EU as an arena of governance demanded an internationalisation of the Irish public service.

The process of catching up placed considerable strain on Ireland's economic, institutional and social fabric. Ireland at the beginning of the second millennium is a country deeply engaged in the international political economy and in internationalised governance structures. Yet it continues to display, side by side, spheres of international excellence and deep-rooted incapacity. All the large multinational IT companies in the world have plants in Ireland and an indigenous IT sector has developed. The system of social partnership, although experiencing considerable strain as a result of prosperity, underlines the institutional capacity of the Irish system. That same system seems incapable of developing a functioning system of public transport, or of managing the industrial relations systems of its state companies or its health services. More significantly for the future of its democracy, it must find the political capacity to enhance accountability given the growing evidence of deep-rooted and systemic corruption emerging from a series of tribunals.

Within the EU, Ireland will find itself as one of over 20 small states in the decades ahead. It is no longer regarded as a deserving small and poor state in the EU. The leader of the Labour party, Deputy Quinn, captures the change in the following Dáil statement when he argued that:

> The European Council in Vienna (December 1998) was the first occasion on which it was apparent that Ireland's status as a favourite younger child or struggling participating member state, which was used by successive Governments to secure concessions, was at an end. (www.irlgov.ie/debates-98/17 dec98/sect3.htm)

This has implications for Ireland's participation in the Union's governance structures. Policy preferences are likely to change when Ireland becomes a net contributor to the EU budget. Irish officials will be expected to contribute more actively to EU debates rather than concentrate on the key issues of interest to Ireland. This will require a more strategic and co-ordinated approach to EU policy, more formal structures, and more intensive bilateral relationships with the growing number of member states. The informal pragmatism of the past must be complemented by careful scanning of the EU environment and system-wide assessment of the major policy developments in the Union. Given economic prosperity and sound public finances, the state is in a position to invest resources in managing its interaction with the wider European and international system.

References

Ahern, B. (2000) Irish Prime Minister, 'Ireland and the EU: future prospects', Address to the Institute of European Affairs, Dublin, 21 March.

Bruton, J. (1995) 'Robert Schuman Lecture', University College Cork, 6 April.

Coombes, D. (ed.) (1983) *Ireland and the European Communities: Ten Years of Membership* (Dublin: Gill and Macmillan).

Drudy, P.J. and McAleese, D. (eds) (1984) *Ireland and the European Community* (Cambridge: Cambridge University Press).

Eagleton, T. (1999) The *Truth About the Irish*, Dublin: New Island Books.

EU (1995) *Reflection Group Report*, 5 December.

EU (1996) *Top Decision Makers Survey: Summary Report* (Eurobarometer).

Fitzgerald, G. (1985) 'Ireland in Europe', Irish School of Ecumenics Lecture Series, Dublin, 25 February.

Garvin, T. (2000) 'The French are on the Sea', in O'Donnell (2000), pp. 35–43.

Geoghegan-Quinn, M. (1990) 'Ireland in a changing Europe', Patrick Magill Summer School, 12 August.

Government of Ireland (1996) *Challenges and Opportunities Abroad: White Paper on Foreign Policy* (Dublin: Government Publications).

Halligan, B. (2000) 'The political perspective in 1972', in O'Donnell (2000), pp. 18–34.

Keatinge, P. (ed.) (1991) *Ireland and EU Membership Evaluated* (London: Pinter).

NESC (1989) *Ireland in the European Community: Performance, Prospects, and Strategy*, no. 88 (Dublin: National Economic and Social Council).

O'Donnell, R. (ed.) (2000) *Europe: The Irish Experience* (Dublin: IEA).

Sinnott, R. (1995) 'Knowledge of the European Union: Irish public opinion sources and implications', occasional paper, no. 5 (Dublin: EEA).

Spring, D. (1995) 'The 1996 IGC and beyond: the future of the the European Union from an Irish perspective', IBEC Conference, 22 May.

Whitaker, K. (1958) 'Economic development' (Dublin: Government Publications).

Chapter 6

Irish–American relations

Richard B. Finnegan

To put things in perspective, Ireland's relationship with America hardly commanded the constant and diligent attention of the United States National Security Council. In the diplomatic realm Ireland has come on to the President's foreign policy agenda on only a handful of occasions. The most important was the period after World War I when the Irish movement for independence shook the relationship with Britain from 1916 to 1922. The second was during World War II when the neutrality of Ireland affected the potential strategy of the United States and Britain in the Battle of the Atlantic. The third was the achievement of the 1998 Good Friday Agreement, brokered by a former American Senator George Mitchell, and brought about in no small part because of the efforts of President Bill Clinton. While rarely breaking the diplomatic threshold of high international politics, the relationship of Ireland to the United States, however, is marked by wide and deep transnational networks and relationships. These relationships operate on the personal and familial level, on the economic level and on the political level. Successive administrations, for example, saw the problem of Northern Ireland as an internal matter for the United Kingdom and the issue was not treated as an independent foreign policy issue, yet at the transnational level a host of connections, activities and pressures were involving the FBI, the courts, members of Congress, state and local governments, the business community and labour unions. The transnational networks illuminate the influence of ethnic groups on international politics and Ireland is among the more illustrative cases of ethnic transnational pressures.

From the Famine to the Free State

Boats full of Irish people coming to America from the time of the Great Hunger set the pattern for successive waves of immigrants and shaped their politics with respect to Irish independence. Many observers have noted the 'Arcadian' romantic vision of Irish nationalism held by Irish Americans from the Famine to the Free State. The post-Famine migration from Ireland brought to the United States those who felt that they were not making a free choice to seek a new life in the new world but rather were in exile from their homeland as a result of British policy.[1] American Irish thus bore a deep and enduring hatred for the British that was in no way ameliorated by the events of the latter part of the 19th and early part of the 20th century when Britain reneged on the Home Rule Bill of 1912, crushed the Rebellion of 1916 and attempted to defeat Sinn Féin in the war from 1918 to 1921.

In the aftermath of the Civil War in the United States the tension between the United States and Britain created some political space for the American Fenian supporters of Irish independence to operate. Some Fenians, clearly devoid of a Clausewitz in their midst, urged the conquest of part of Canada to use in exchange for Irish freedom. In 1866 the Fenians attacked Canada and the American Government, rather than support them, took their arms and arrested them. Thereafter President Grant would not tolerate Fenian activities and Canadians could rest easier in their beds, spared the fear of this Fenian threat. Charles Stewart Parnell knew the strength of the Irish American when he visited the United States for 10 weeks in 1880 and sought money and political support for his Home Rule movement. Addressing a joint session of Congress Parnell urged support of his Land League. The more militant Irish Americans in Clan na Gael were supporting land agitation for rights into a paramilitary movement for home rule for Ireland. The amount of money raised for the Irish Parliamentary Party and Parnell was formidable but declined sharply when the Party split over the Parnell divorce scandal. The reconciliation of the two wings of the party was in part accomplished to reopen the coffers of Irish Americans in support of a singular effort to achieve home rule.

The support of Clan na Gael evaporated again, however, when John Redmond placed the Irish Parliamentary Party in support of the British war effort against the Germans. The American version of militant Irish nationalism could not brook any such collaboration with London and American Clan leaders were part of the planning of the 1916 rising. The support for Irish independence in the States was organised by the Friends of Irish Freedom which mobilised large numbers of Irish Americans and raised over $1 million. The Friends, reflecting their power at the transnational level, not only unified the Irish Americans on this issue, and raised large sums of money, but also succeeded in getting a resolution from the Senate in 1918 and the House of Representatives in 1919 in support of an Irish delegation at Versailles. At the diplomatic level the Friends sent a delegation to Versailles to persuade Woodrow Wilson that his support for self-determination expressed in his Fourteen Points should apply to Ireland. Though there appeared to be a slight possibility of approval of an Irish delegation to the League, Wilson, an anglophile, was unwilling to put that much pressure on his ally Britain. In addition the triumphalist actions of the Irish American delegation while visiting Ireland had inflamed British opinion and made any concession from Wilson unlikely.

Eamon de Valera's visit to the United States in 1919 exemplified the type of relationship the Irish Americans had with Ireland. De Valera provoked a major split in the Irish Americans over the use of the funds raised in America which de Valera wanted to spend on the Irish Republican Army and the war against Britain. When the Clan split de Valera founded his own organisation, the American

Association for the Recognition of the Irish Republic, which ballooned to 750,000 members. He raised millions of dollars from an Irish Bond 'Certificate' drive. Selling the ersatz bonds was in all likelihood illegal and put the United States in the position of having a revolutionary movement openly funding its efforts against a state with which the United States had friendly relations. The bond drive alone raised over $5 million and the overall amount raised in the States was over $10 million. Moreover de Valera was fêted at every sort of organisation and governmental body from local city councils to Congress. The split between de Valera's organisation and the Clan, however, undermined the opportunity to get resolutions supporting Irish independence into the platforms of the Republican and Democratic Parties in 1920.[2] Thus success for de Valera at the financial level was costly at the political level.

The Free State's neutrality in World War II

After the formation of the Free State in 1922, which the Irish Americans by and large favoured, their interest in Ireland dropped off sharply.[3] For most the Treaty was seen as the first step on the road to independence and Irish Americans became concerned with their own status at home. As the fault lines in Europe splintered under the tensions of German expansion in the 1930s, de Valera remembered the consequences of Redmond's actions. As long as the partition of Ireland existed he felt that the Irish people would not politically accept joining the British war effort. The practical realities of geography, political values, to say nothing of prudence, ruled out an alliance with the Germans. Neutrality, though seen negatively by the Allies in the war, was in many ways de Valera's only choice.

Recognising the repercussions, de Valera sought to ensure that Irish neutrality would be viewed favourably in the United States and formed the American Friends of Irish Neutrality in 1940. When Churchill, seeking Irish ports, considered invasion of Ireland, de Valera sought American help in dissuading him from doing so. After the United States entered the war, however, neutrality, of course, became decidedly less popular in America. De Valera's actions, protesting American troops being in Northern Ireland, refusing to expel Axis diplomats, and offering condolences to the German Ambassador on Hitler's death inflamed the wrath of the American Ambassador to Ireland, David Gray. Gray's pursuit of American interests was fuelled by the mutual loathing between him and de Valera. Gray became embroiled in the Northern Ireland issue as he sought to provide the ports for the American and British navies and did everything in his power to push Ireland into the war on the Allied side. He embarrassed de Valera with release in the United States of the exchange of their notes. Gray had requested that Ireland provide their ports for the war effort and de Valera had refused. Eventually as the tide of battle shifted the British dropped the issue, though Gray had succeeded in significantly discrediting Irish policy in American public opinion. In these events American-Irish relations reached the level of high wartime politics and diplomacy. For the United States the stakes were high as the Battle of the Atlantic and the alliance with Britain were central to the United States' war effort.

The Cold War years

The effects of neutrality, however much skewed toward the advantage of the British, spilled into the post-war years chilling relations with the United States. Neutrality had not endeared Ireland to the nations that had fought in what now all agreed was a necessary war against a profoundly evil regime. In addition Ireland was marginal to the centrepieces of post-war American diplomacy: the Marshall Plan and NATO. Ireland did receive Marshall Plan aid of $36 million in the form of loans but it was much less than other European states and considerably less than Ireland hoped to get. Discussion about entering NATO did not even reach the stage of a formal invitation. Dublin would not consider entry other than as a united Ireland, thus setting the end of Irish partition as a precondition of entry. Washington and, not surprisingly, London did not take this demand seriously.

Ireland in the United Nations took a neutralist, Third World approach to issues though in terms of anti-Communist values, and general direction in foreign affairs, Ireland fell in the Western camp. After the creation of the Free State prosperity did not come to the Irish but it did come to the Irish Americans. As Andrew Greeley has shown in his work the Irish Catholics became the most successful gentile group in the country.[4] The Irish Americans were assimilating so successfully that the situation in Ireland slipped down their political agenda to the point of invisibility. The election of John F. Kennedy to the Presidency in 1960 symbolically sealed the Irish Americans' place in the American social fabric, while his visit to Ireland symbolised the historical ethnic connection between the two countries, and the absence of any matter of diplomatic importance in his visit indicated the predominantly transnational ties between the two countries.

All nationalisms are, of course, a bouillabaisse of myths, historical facts and historical fiction, posited values and ascribed national characteristics and in this respect Irish nationalism did not differ from any other version. In America, however, Irish American nationalism was not subject to slow evolution engendered by the inexorable passage of time and events. Irish Americans held their nationalist myths antiseptically intact. That basically republican image of Ireland – Green, Gaelic, Catholic, and subject to British imperial exploitation – was preserved in older Irish American neighbourhoods, social clubs and civil service unions.

Irish–American relations in this period were predominantly at the familial level as there was a wave of immigration in the1950s. There were no matters of importance on the American foreign policy agenda concerning Ireland especially in light of the Irish elevation of neutrality from a pragmatic war-time decision to a principle of their foreign policy. The United States in the Cold War era was far more concerned with alliances in the 'Free World' than de Valera's fixation with partition.

The 'new troubles'

In 1969, in the immediate aftermath of the violence in Northern Ireland, Irish Americans were galvanised into action to help, directly at the transnational level, the Catholic nationalists of Northern Ireland. The response was from neighbourhoods and organisations which had preserved their Irish identity and the ideological garb available to put the Northern conflict into a political context was the well-worn cloak of Irish American nationalism. The irony was that the particular blend of American working class conservative attitudes coupled with traditionally militant Irish nationalism produced a group of Irish Americans, from dockworkers to retirees, who shared republicanism with Sinn Féin but certainly not their radicalism, and social conservatism with Ulster Protestants but certainly not their British identity. Irish American response to the Northern crisis was initially amorphous. Apart from the Ancient Order of Hibernians, which was founded in the 19th century, the first militant organisation was the Northern Aid Committee, formed in 1970 and known, of course, as NORAID. Support for Sinn Féin and the IRA by NORAID was explicit despite the fact that the Americans shared little of the left-wing, socialist, revolutionary ideology of the Official IRA and later the Provisional IRA. The Irish National Caucus followed in 1974 with the goal of lobbying Congress and mobilising public opinion on the Northern question.

What of Irish American elites? In the early 1970s their response was not unlike that of the grassroots with condemnation of British policy and calls for a united Ireland. Senator Edward M. 'Ted' Kennedy, for example, made frequent statements that compared the British in Ulster to the United States in Vietnam. In 1971 he introduced a Senate Resolution which called for a withdrawal of all British forces from Ulster and for a united Ireland, and in 1972 he held hearings on Northern Ireland in the Senate. In 1973 Senator Kennedy published an article in *Foreign Policy* in which he argued that Ulster was an international issue and warranted intervention by the international community (though by this time Kennedy's views were beginning to move beyond his 1969–71 positions).[5] Congressman Thomas P. 'Tip' O'Neill had collected the signatures of 100 members of Congress on a letter to President Nixon calling upon him to protest the discrimination against Catholics in Northern Ireland. O'Neill indicated to John Hume that he had been a contributor to NORAID during this period.[6] Then Congressman, and later Governor, Hugh Carey of New York called the British Army 'thugs' in 1971.[7] Sharing similar views at the time was Congressman Mario Biaggi, later to become the somewhat improbable herald of Sinn Féin ideology.

Irish American elites had, however, accumulated a new set of values as a result of their successful ascent up the socio-economic ladder. Calls for violence did not immediately trip to the tongues of politicians, business leaders, journalists, academics, doctors and lawyers. Nor were they in great sympathy with Official Sinn Féin and its anti-imperialist Third World revolutionary ideology, insofar as they were aware of the situation in Northern Ireland at all. The events of the early and mid-1970s brought about the slow mobilisation of this sector of the Irish American community such that by the end of the 1970s they had joined forces with the highly visible political leaders to shoulder aside the grassroots neighbourhood and labour union interests.

The political activity of the Irish American, even those of political clout, was at the level of contributions, political pressure and legislative resolutions and did not kick the issue of Northern Ireland onto the American foreign policy agenda of Presidents Nixon and Ford.[8]

In the first violent years of the conflict the voice of Irish Americans was essentially unified; by the late 1970s it was divided. What brought about the transformation in the attitudes of the Irish American elites in the early 1970s was a combination of John Hume and Sean Donlon. Each had concluded that the NORAID/Caucus perspective among Irish Americans was entirely too pervasive and encouraged the contribution of money which ended up in the hands of the IRA. John Hume had been contacted by Ted Kennedy in 1972 and began the relationship, both political and personal, which was to play an important part in the marginalisation of the NORAID/Caucus version of Irish American nationalism. Hume also was friendly with Speaker Thomas P. 'Tip' O'Neill. Garret FitzGerald, however, noted that 'Kennedy was more responsive to Hume, the Irish government had a better connection with O'Neill'. The influence of the Irish government on American politicians was clearly disproportionate to the place of Ireland and Irish interests on the United States' foreign policy agenda.

The central thrust of the message of Hume and the Irish government was that traditional Irish American nationalism was out-of-date in terms of the situation in Ulster. In fact, while not minimising their differences on security matters, the British and Irish governments had in common their opposition to the IRA, the quest for a devolved government in Ulster, and a peaceful solution to the violence based upon negotiation. The Irish American support of Sinn Féin and the IRA meant that they were extending and legitimising the violence. The transnational linkages between working-class Irish Americans and the republicans of the North were pressuring the Irish government at the diplomatic level to persuade Irish American political elites to offset these militant republican views.

Traditional Irish nationalism had never addressed the existence of 1 million Ulster Unionists, placing the onus for the political divisions of Ulster at the feet of London. Irish American nationalism was equivalently obtuse. As Garret FitzGerald observed: 'I was too impatient with Irish American groups and too willing to tell them to stop supporting violence in our country.' On the other hand FitzGerald noted: 'British efforts to condemn the violence in the North were counterproductive in the United States for it involved their justifying their presence.'[9] The importance of Hume and Donlon was to articulate these issues, with an Irish accent, and condemn the American grassroots support of the violence. The ironic twist of this policy was not lost on Congressman Brian Donnelly who later observed: 'the role of the Irish diplomats was to make the American Irish less green'.[10]

Events of the mid-1970s illuminate the diverging approaches of the political leaders to the Ulster crisis. Congressman Mario Biaggi for example, under the auspices of the Caucus, visited Ireland to meet with leaders of Sinn Féin and the IRA. The IRA, Biaggi asserted, focused attention on the problem of the North. But to the Irish government, as Jack Holland put it: 'the IRA did not focus attention on the problem–the IRA *was* the problem'.[11]

Speaker O'Neill, Senators Kennedy and Moynihan and Governor Carey began issuing annual statements on Northern Ireland on Saint Patrick's Day in 1977. The result was to undercut Irish American support for the violence in Northern Ireland, and by implication the groups that supported it. They did not neglect, however, to chide the British for their less than scintillating political initiatives on the North and the excesses of their security policy.

At the governmental level the Nixon and Ford administrations began, at the request of London, to investigate NORAID in order to discourage membership, curtail their fundraising efforts, and to see if the organisation was involved in the illegal exportation of arms. Thus the FBI became involved in the Northern issue in support of the traditional American position in support of the British. The FBI investigated the attempted gun-running to Ireland and the links to organised crime. Their investigation was to see if NORAID should be registered under the Foreign Agents Registration Act but was seen as a way to discourage their activities and was successful in doing so.

With the election of a Democratic President in 1976, Tip O'Neill emerges as the key figure on Irish issues for the next decade. His influence was felt on numerous developments. The first mark of his influence was the Carter statement on Northern Ireland in August of 1977 which began the process of moving the North from a transnational issue to a diplomatic one. Carter and his staff were not deeply familiar with the Ulster issue and there had been a long tradition of the United States having no foreign policy position on Northern Ireland. Ulster was seen as a domestic matter of the United Kingdom, one of the United States' major allies no less. O'Neill convinced Carter in the face of these difficulties to make a statement on Northern Ireland which had to meet the approval of so many constituencies that its most distinguished feature was its tepidity. The United States pledged to prosecute those who transferred money or guns illegally to groups in Ulster (an obligation it had anyway); called for a form of government acceptable to both communities (not very far out on a limb there), and promised job-creating investment to benefit all the people of Northern Ireland (making the assumption that the lack of jobs led to ethnic conflict). The letter was far more interesting for having been made than for what it said, for it was at the Presidential level and treated the Northern issue as an independent problem.

The Speaker had also blocked any effort to convene hearings on Northern Ireland after those of 1972 as he would not allow a forum for Sinn Féin's views. Mario Biaggi had pressed for hearings, which would include representatives from Sinn Féin, and revealed his frustration when he said: 'There is no question that the Irish government's representatives in Washington have been very close to Speaker O'Neill and as a result we have not been able to have hearings.'[12]

President Carter had, in fact, embarrassed the British government by including the United Kingdom on the annual list of states that had violated human rights based upon their treatment of prisoners in Northern Ireland. Biaggi proposed an amendment to the State Department's Appropriations Bill which forbade the granting of the export licence from allowing the sale of the guns to Northern Ireland. O'Neill let the amendment go forward. Biaggi later agreed to withdraw the amendment in exchange for hearings which would further embarrass the British government for they would bring out the reports by Amnesty International and the decision of the European Court of Human Rights on the treatment of prisoners in the Maze, the prisoners 'on the blanket' and like events. O'Neill caused a rumpus in London by declaring that London had treated Northern Ireland like a 'political football', and had been reviled in the British press for interfering in a British election and not understanding the situation in Ulster. Thus by July of 1979 the Speaker was in no mood to be accommodating to the British and, to calm his ire and avoid high-profile hearings on security policy and human rights abuses in Northern Ireland, the State Department suspended the sale of weapons to the Royal Ulster Constabulary. Adrian Guelke in assessing the results saw a 'tremendous boost for the Ad Hoc Committee and its associate the Irish National Caucus'.[13] We should not assume, however, that Mario Biaggi and Speaker O'Neill had equivalent influence over the events that took place within the House of Representatives, the Congress as a whole, or the executive branch. The record was clear. In Congress Biaggi's group could not move without the Speaker's willingness to cooperate.

At the grassroots level the efforts by Irish American Republican groups to delegitimise the British presence in Ulster were made easier by British policy in Ulster during these years. Republican groups provided a constant stream of information about the British abuses in the prisons, the legal system and police procedures. British policy produced a cascade of such abuses of individual rights and threats of violence that the message was not all that difficult to convey. The police in Ulster searched homes with brutality; used plastic bullets for the control of demonstrations; shot unarmed demonstrators; used juryless trials; convicted on the uncorroborated word of a single police officer; used physical abuse to obtain confessions; fabricated or suppressed evidence as suited their case; closed off investigations of their own police abuses; and, apparently, adopted a police policy of 'shoot to kill' when encountering suspected IRA types.[14]

Irish American militant republicans were numerous and both visible and invisible. During the 1970s guns were being run into Northern Ireland on a consistent basis but not so much by NORAID as by George Harrison. Jack Holland indicated that throughout the 1970s Harrison, not a member of Sinn Féin or the IRA, moved more arms to Ireland than any other source. When he was arrested and tried, with four others, what appeared to be a rather simple case of illegal arms exporting turned into a complicated defence in which the CIA was implicated. The question hinged on whether George De Meo, a person involved with Harrison, was in the CIA or not. The evidence was mixed with the government denying any connection and the defence pointing out evidence of De Meo's connections to the government. The story was ambiguous enough for the jury to acquit all five men. If the CIA connection is true, and the denials are at the least up for discussion, then another layer of governmental involvement along with the FBI was coming from the Executive branch operating against the gun running.[15] Suffice it to say the efforts to stop the movement of arms were successful and, though there are isolated cases after that, the FBI and Bureau of Alcohol, Firearms and Tobacco stemmed the major flow from the United States to Ireland by the mid-1980s.

The role of Tip O'Neill over Irish matters was further illuminated in the case of the dismissal of Sean Donlon, the Irish Ambassador to the United States. Garret

FitzGerald, Prime Minister of Ireland at the time, stated: 'Sean Donlon was the most important connection to the Irish American Congressmen.'[16] He lobbied the O'Neill group to pressure the British government to adopt policies in the North that would involve support of power sharing and justice for the Nationalist community, and at the same time mount attacks on the NORAID/Caucus groups of Irish Americans for supporting the IRA. Donlon had thus alienated a variety of Irish American groups who felt that their legitimate viewpoints about Sinn Féin and the British record in Ulster were being dismissed. Dealing with the perspective of some of these groups and their monocausal view of Ireland could be less than delightful.[17] In Ireland those who inhabited the republican edge of constitutional politics listened with greater favour to the Biaggi/NORAID/Caucus viewpoint. Not surprisingly such republicans were in Fianna Fáil and when Charles Haughey took power in 1980 the Caucus and others saw it as an opportunity to amplify the voice of the more republican-oriented groups in the United States.

At the end of June Haughey called Donlon back to Dublin to be told he was moving to a post at the United Nations. Within the week the press were reporting Tip's anger with the decision. He indicated that there would be no new initiatives on Ireland and cooperation with the Haughey government would not be forthcoming. Haughey bowed to the pressure and announced that Donlon was not being moved. The whole affair was an embarrassment to Haughey and indicated the power of O'Neill and Senator Kennedy. At the Congressional level Irish American politicians were dictating to Dublin the choice of the Irish Ambassador to the United States.

The Reagan years

In 1981 a loose network of Congressmen and Senators, who shared the O'Neill–Kennedy approach to Northern Ireland and Irish matters in general, became the 'Friends of Ireland' with O'Neill as leader. After Margaret Thatcher's rejection of the Forum for a New Ireland Report in 1983, Sean Donlon contacted the Speaker and asked that he request of President Reagan an intervention with the Prime Minister on the Irish question. Thatcher had been sharply criticised by the Congressional Friends of Ireland who had written to the President that: 'The destructive alienation and violence that plague the people of that land are also unfortunately becoming an increasing source of contention between the United States and Great Britain.'[18] President Reagan did bring up the matter in December of 1984 and prompted a bevy of denials from Thatcher that there was any breakdown between the Irish government and London on Ulster. Though President Reagan was willing to bring up the issue it was clear that it was not high on his diplomatic agenda and was not going to interfere with his relationship with Margaret Thatcher.[19] The Congressional leaders could influence the choice of an ambassador but could not push Northern Ireland higher on the foreign policy agenda.

In February of 1985 Speaker O'Neill met with Prime Minister Thatcher personally to express his concerns and to pledge his support for reconstruction efforts should there be a breakthrough on the Northern question.[20] It would be presumptuous to think that the American interventions in these negotiations made all the difference but it also would be erroneous to think that they made no difference at all. The Anglo-Irish Agreement was signed in November of 1985, and that day found Speaker O'Neill in the Oval Office with President Reagan promising to implement the promise of aid to Northern Ireland made by his predecessor Jimmy Carter. It represented, no doubt, the only time Reagan came to praise Carter rather than to blame him. Fulfilling the promise that O'Neill had given to Garret FitzGerald in May of 1985, a bill went through the House by Saint Patrick's Day of 1986. When the Senate approved the bill it was for one year for $50 million, the same amount as the House bill. It was subsequently extended for two more years at $35 million a year.

While Irish foreign policy was focused on the United States during the Reagan years it could make an impact only at the Congressional level. President Reagan, rather than challenging British policy, was in fact being accommodating to London's views on the extradition of 'terrorists' by trying to eliminate the federal courts from the process and letting the State Department make the determination on political asylum. The effect would be decisions more politically sensitive to the administration and would allow the disposition of terrorists to be in the hands of State and not the courts. It would thus allow the return of IRA members to Britain.

Tip and Senator Kennedy balanced the dissatisfaction with British policy and pressure to change it without endorsing the violence of the IRA and the blood of Irish people the IRA shed in the name of a united Ireland. The groups that clustered around that Republican orientation in the United States, and their counterparts in Ireland and Ulster, were excluded from framing the issue in republican terms as a British 'occupation' of the North and disingenuously excluding the rights and wishes of one million Unionists who lived there. This was an undeniable success of Irish foreign policy at the elite level though the grassroots support for Sinn Féin and the IRA among AOH, NORAID and Caucus supporters was dented but not destroyed.

The Clinton years

By far the most important intervention into Northern Ireland was that of President Clinton. Clinton's decision to involve himself in the Northern Ireland conflict is itself puzzling given the history of the issue and the panoply of problems that confront any President. His choice has been seen as part of his overall strategy of 'democratic enlargement'. Joseph O'Grady asserts that the President was responding to the Irish American constituency in the critical states as a ploy to get Irish American votes, but the evidence suggests that only his initial response in the New York State primary was designed to get votes.[21] Clinton had been a Rhodes Scholar, had studied in Britain and had both an in-depth knowledge of the problem and a personal interest in Northern Ireland. His increasing commitment emerged from a constellation of voices including his close connection to Senator Kennedy and the pressure brought by a group of prominent Irish Americans, Americans for a New Irish Agenda (ANIA). The serendipitous timing of events in Northern Ireland helped as did Clinton's willingness to pay the price of British ire for not following the usual path which treated the North as a domestic matter in British politics.

To promote the issue of Ulster on to his foreign policy agenda from its place on the transnational and Congressional agenda required that the President take the risk that his actions would not produce any results, while at the same time alienating London. Clinton took office in January of 1993, the year of the culmination of the Hume–Adams talks, the arrival of Albert Reynolds as Prime Minister of Ireland with Dick Spring as his Foreign Minister and of John Major's agreement to the Downing Street Declaration. That Declaration appeared to be the breakthrough that convinced the President that the risk of putting Ulster on his agenda was worth taking. In 1993 Clinton had twice turned down requests for visas from Gerry Adams to visit the United States.[22] In January of 1994 the President considered allowing Gerry Adams to visit the United States on a visa to attend a conference in New York. Policy Adviser Nancy Soderberg said of the President's decision: 'He weighed the pros and cons of taking a risk for peace or missing what might have been a historic opportunity. He decided it was worth the risk of reaching out to Adams a little bit in the hopes he would then help deliver on the cease-fire.'[23] President Clinton's decision was opposed by his own key advisers. The Attorney General Janet Reno, Secretary of State Warren Christopher, the FBI, the CIA and the United States Ambassador to Britain all thought issuing the visa to Adams would appear to be an endorsement of international terrorism. London was of course angered by the President's choice and subsequent acts such as Adams meeting National Security Adviser Anthony Lake at the White House in October of 1994. Yet the President was unwilling to concede to the British on this issue, at the risk of cooperation on others, because he believed that the fundamentals of the situation in Ulster had been realigned. Clinton wanted the United States to be on the positive side of the movement for peace.[24] As it turns out the President's judgement was correct, though in casting the weight of the United States into the equation it, in fact, changed the equation itself and facilitated the peace process. From the visa in 1994; the President's visit in 1995; the appointment of Senator George Mitchell as the Chair of the Northern Ireland talks; the President's phone calls at critical moments during the April 1998 negotiations; to Mitchell's return to Belfast in 1999, the United States and the President became key players in the outcome.

Senator Kennedy's sister Jean Kennedy Smith, the United States Ambassador to Ireland, had aligned herself in Ireland with those who thought there was a possibility of traversing the Northern impasse.[25] She persuaded her brother, now the most influential Congressional figure in Irish matters, to support the President's decision to issue a visa to Gerry Adams in January of 1994.[26] Hume had also been trying to convince the Irish government to give Adams more room for manoeuvre and told Senator Kennedy the same.[27] The ANIA was composed of figures such as former Congressman Bruce Morrison, Naill O'Dowd, the editor of the *Irish Voice*, Joe Jamison, a trade union executive, and Charles Feeney and William Flynn, both successful businessmen. This group convinced both Sinn Féin and the White House that they had credibility with the other group. Sinn Féin was convinced of the importance of the United States' support in gaining a political settlement and getting concrete benefits for the North, and the White House was convinced that the word of Sinn Féin was good on promises to take actions toward a peaceful settlement.

The visa was a signal that the United States had changed its role from the tradition of support for the British position. In August of 1994 the IRA declared a cease-fire followed shortly by a similar declaration by the Loyalist paramilitaries.[28] The opening for talks was, however, stymied by the (now painfully familiar) demand by London and the Unionists that there be a connection between the decommissioning of arms by the IRA and the inclusion of Sinn Féin in the talks around the Framework document. The ritual dance continued to the point where again an initiative was needed and it was produced by President Clinton. He allowed Sinn Féin to raise funds in the United States and had Gerry Adams at the White House in March of 1995. While further enraging London (editorials announced the end of the 'special relationship' between the United States and the United Kingdom) these actions were accompanied by promises from Adams to put all the issues on the table and accept the outcome of the negotiations.

The visit to Northern Ireland by President Clinton in November of 1995, the first by an American President, was an enormous success, with crowds gathered everywhere and speeches proclaiming the advent of a new day of peace, and brought pressure on London to move forward. Clinton's visit, however, came at a low ebb in the peace process as the IRA had already secretly decided to break the cease-fire, the British and Irish governments were incapable of moving the process forward and the Unionists were intransigent on the talks. The most formidable barrier to progress was that the parties would not talk while the IRA still had their guns. The problem was solved, in that most enduring bureaucratic fashion, by appointing a commission. The International Commission was chaired by former Senator Mitchell. Mitchell was joined by former Finnish Prime Minister Harri Holkeri and retired Canadian General John de Chastelain.

Mitchell was already involved in Northern Ireland as he had helped President Clinton set up investment conferences in the United States in May of 1995 to show the players in the Northern drama that there could be an economic reward for peace in the province. The three-member Commission was endorsed by President Clinton creating some pressure to accept its findings. In the final Report the Commission called for the initiation of talks before decommissioning arms if all parties agreed to six principles, which in effect committed them to ultimately decommissioning their arms, to verification of the process, to peaceful negotiation and to acceptance of the outcome without resort to violence.

The talks would proceed on two tracks: the issue of arms and the issues from the three strands. Senator Mitchell would chair the key negotiations of party leaders on the institutions and procedures of a devolved government in Ulster. Mitchell's appointment raised suspicions among the Unionists that he was biased toward the Nationalists. It took some time before Mitchell gained their trust. Unionists perceived all American officials, politicians and citizens as pro-nationalist. Nancy Soderberg, the President's adviser on Irish matters, indicated that the Unionists always felt the United States had a hidden agenda of a united Ireland while the President's policy was that the outcome should be determined by the negotiations. The President's visit to Northern Ireland, and the recommendation of the International Commission, were unable to pressure London to begin the twin-track all-party talks.

The Commission had in effect rejected Prime Minister Major's position and Major countered with a call for elections in May of 1996 to a Forum in Northern Ireland as a 'confidence building measure' before negotiations could begin.

On 9 February 1996 the IRA set off a bomb at Canary Wharf in London that killed two people and injured 36. The cease-fire was over and the peace process derailed. The election took place and the Forum began its deliberation. Senator Mitchell was adroit in handling the various crises in the talks that occurred among groups so mistrustful of one another. David Trimble of the Unionists would not meet face to face with Gerry Adams of Sinn Féin and Mitchell acted as a go-between. It was months before the negotiators would stand around the table with the coffee on it and engage in small talk. Setting preconditions to start the talks, which were elements to be decided by the negotiations, constantly produced impasses which Senator Mitchell would have to resolve. The talks were grinding down and appeared to be another failed attempt at settlement in the North when Tony Blair was elected Prime Minister of Britain in May of 1997. At the same time an election in Ireland produced a new Fianna Fáil Prime Minister, Bertie Ahern, who had somewhat more credibility than John Bruton in the negotiations. The openness of Blair to new conditions in the North, his appointment of Mo Mowlam as Northern Ireland Secretary of State and her blunt but adroit handling of the Irish Americans, Unionists and Nationalists were as a breath of fresh air to the peace process.

The discussion went on for months until Senator Mitchell concluded: 'It had become obvious to me that the longer the negotiations dragged on the better the chance those outside the process had to ruin them.'[29] Mitchell set a deadline which was essentially arbitrary but he felt would move the negotiations toward resolution on a number of issues such as human rights, prisoners, the police and the powers of government. President Clinton spent that week and especially the night before the announcement on the phone persuading Trimble and Adams to compromise and produce an agreement.

On 10 April 1998 the Agreement was signed. Only days before it appeared to have collapsed. As momentous as the Good Friday Agreement was, the negotiations to deal with the decommissioning of arms, or the lack thereof, caused the talks to stall. The Unionists held that Sinn Féin negotiated with an army at their back and had no commitment to democratic processes as long as the IRA held their weapons. Like an old fire horse answering the bell, Senator Mitchell went to Belfast in the autumn of 1999 to once again get the talks moving. He indicated that this was the last time he would do so and that the parties to the Agreement would have to work their way out of dead ends in the future without his counsel. As his brother had died during the original negotiations, his baby had been born back in the States, and he had spent over a year on the task, one could understand his reluctance to be perpetually on call. He also recognised that the future of Northern Ireland depended on the ability of the parties to reach agreement without the pattern of persistent impasses being resolved only by interventions of outside figures.

As the circumstances change in Northern Ireland and as new administrations take power the place of Ireland on the United States agenda will again be marked by the relative unimportance of high-level diplomatic exchange. The Bush administration taking office in 2001 will not have the interest in Northern Ireland that Clinton had. In the longer term, the more Ireland integrates into the European Union the more matters of foreign affairs will find Dublin's interests subsumed into negotiations with Brussels.

Those changes will not diminish the importance of transnational linkages between the United States and Ireland in the realm of economic investment, cultural exchange and political pressure on the Ulster question. In many ways Ireland and Irish culture are more present in the United States than they ever were even at the apex of the immigration tide. The experience of the earlier generations of Irish immigrants with their political and familial linkages to Ireland has been replaced by the presence of the new Irish immigrants. The burgeoning 'Celtic Tiger' has extended the expansion of economic linkages to the United States and the world, the explosion of Irish culture in a second Irish Renaissance has made Irish music, dance, films and literature pervasive on the American cultural scene. The advent of the internet and e-mail, low-cost flights, fax machines and phones make the transnational connection to Ireland more dense. Yet the generational change of Irish Americans, political developments in the North and the bond of Dublin to Brussels make the foreign policy connection less substantial. We can expect more Presidents going to Ireland to find their roots; let us hope none will have to go again to facilitate peace in Ulster.

Endnotes

1. See Kerby Miller, *Emigrants and Exiles* (Oxford: Oxford University Press, 1985).
2. For a detailed treatment of this era see Francis M. Carroll, *American Opinion and the Irish Question 1910–1923* (Dublin: Gill and Macmillan, 1978).
3. John P. McCarthy, 'Northern Ireland: Irish American responses', *The Recorder* (Winter, 1986), pp. 43–52.
4. Andrew M. Greeley, *The Irish Americans* (New York, 1981), pp. 3–4.
5. Edward M. Kennedy, 'Ulster is an international issue', *Foreign Policy*, 57 (Summer, 1973), pp. 57–71.
6. Barry White, *John Hume: Statesman of the Troubles* (Belfast: Blackstaff Press, 1984), p. 188.
7. Jack Holland, *The American Connection: U.S. Guns, Money and Influence in Northern Ireland* (New York: Viking Press, 1987), p. 116.
8. Henry Kissinger in his memoirs describes Nixon's visit to Ireland in 1970 as 'frankly a domestic political one' to establish his Irish American roots and pay off a contributor to his campaign. Kissinger's briefing book on Ireland noted: 'The Irish stop has no great international significance . . .' (*White House Years* (Boston: Little Brown, 1979), p. 935).
9. Garret FitzGerald, interview, 12 January 1991.
10. Congressman Brian Donnelly, interview, 12 July 1991.
11. Jack Holland (1987), p. 120.
12. *New York Times*, 21 April 1979, p. 4.
13. Adrian Guelke, *Northern Ireland: The International Perspective* (Dublin: Gill and Macmillan, 1988), p. 141.

14. See Padraig O'Malley, *The Uncivil Wars: Ireland Today* (Boston: Houghton Mifflin, 1983); J. Bowyer Bell, *The Irish Troubles* (New York: St. Martins Press, 1993); J. Stalker, *Stalker* (London: Harrap Press, 1988).
15. Holland (1987), pp. 63–113.
16. Garret FitzGerald, interview, 1991.
17. An example would be John J. Finucane, Editor of the *American Irish Political Education Newsletter*, who wrote in December of 1990: 'Britain's record, often condemned by the Soviet Union, would have shamed the likes of Hitler and Stalin. She has resorted to mass murder, torture censorship, shoot to kill, juryless courts, politics of exclusion, discrimination of every sort. Britain has even attempted genocide. Worst of all she has done this in the name of democracy.' To parse this statement so as to bring it in any way in line with the events that actually happened in Northern Ireland would require so many pages as to run the risk of deforesting Canada. It exemplifies a particular, and peculiar, world view of some militant Irish Americans. This view is so locked into its own construal of reality that it cites the testimony of the former Soviet Union (with its renowned commitment to historical fidelity) as evidence in a statement that compares Britain's behaviour with that of Stalin. It is a world view which bludgeons the capacity of words to provide distinctions in meaning, however fragile those meanings may be in this post-modernist age.
18. Sean Cronin, *Washington's Irish Policy: 1916–1986, Independence, Partition and Neutrality* (Dublin: Anvil Books, 1989), p. 322.
19. Reagan would raise the issue of Ulster with Prime Minister Thatcher but challenging her was another matter. He was an anglophile whose visit to Ballyporeen in Ireland as President was another symbolic presidential 'roots' journey. His great-great-grandfather came from that town and allowed Reagan to display enough Irishness as he thought to be politically advantageous.
20. Holland (1987), p. 146 and Garret FitzGerald, *All in a Life* (Dublin: Gill and Macmillan, 1991), p. 535.
21. Joseph O'Grady, 'An Irish Policy Born in the U.S.A.', *Foreign Policy*, 75 (May–June, 1996), pp. 2–7; and Andrew J. Wilson, 'From the Beltway to Belfast: The Clinton Administration, Sinn Féin and the Northern Ireland Peace Process', *New Hibernian Review*, 1(3) (Autumn 1997), pp. 23–39.
22. Gerry Adams was not being singled out in this instance as the State Department from the mid-1970s had excluded all Sinn Féin and Republican figures from visiting the United States.
23. Quoted in Wilson (1997), p. 31.
24. The fact that the British Conservative Party had sent representatives to help the George Bush campaign in the waning days of the 1992 election, and that the British government had searched their intelligence files for information deleterious to Clinton, no doubt dulled Clinton's sensitivities to the concerns of John Major and the Conservative Party. The end of the Cold War also allowed more 'wiggle room' even between major allies as the sense of threat from the Soviet Union diminished.
25. Her appointment, in fact, had been made by President Clinton as a favour to Senator Kennedy as there were many people well qualified by experience and connections for the position.
26. Speaker O'Neill had retired from Congress. Brian Donnelly from Massachusetts, who became the Head of the Friends of Ireland in the Congress after Tip, had also retired from the House. Bruce Morrison of Connecticut, who had been very influential in getting visas for Irish immigrants to the United States, had also left Congress. Representative Biaggi had got into some legal difficulties. Senator Moynihan had taken a step back as a high-profile figure on Irish issues, thus Senator Kennedy was far and away the most visible and powerful figure.
27. As events developed Kennedy's foreign policy adviser, Trina Vargo, could communicate with Sinn Féin through the Americans for a New Irish Agenda and in turn communicate with Nancy Soderberg of the National Security Council and in turn with Anthony Lake, the

President's National Security Adviser in the White House; Wilson (1997), p. 30.

28. After the State Department had quietly issued a visa to Joe Cahill, a widely known IRA veteran, who was to come to America to shore up support among Irish American militants for the cease-fire.

29. Quoted by Kevin Cullen in the *Boston Globe*, 19 April 1998, p. A37.

Bibliography

Davis, Troy, *Dublin's American Policy: Irish American Diplomatic Relations 1945–1952* (Washington, DC: Catholic University of America Press, 1998).

Holland, Jack, *The American Connection: U.S. Guns Money and Influence in Northern Ireland* (New York: Viking Press, 1999).

Mitchell, George J., *Making Peace* (New York: Knopf, 1999).

O' Clery, Conor, *The Greening of the White House* (Dublin: Gill and Macmillan, 1996).

Wilson, Andrew J., *Irish America and the Ulster Conflict* (Washington, DC: Catholic University of America Press, 1995).

Chapter 7

The Northern Ireland conflict and the impact of globalisation

Joseph Ruane and Jennifer Todd

Introduction

Globalisation has been described as 'the widening, deepening and speeding up of worldwide interconnectedness in all areas of contemporary social life' (Held *et al.* 1999: 2). It is manifested in flows of money, goods, peoples, ideas, images, messages (Appadurai 1990) and in new transnational political institutions. It is often identified as involving a 'post-modern' change in identification, value-orientation and national identity (Waters 1995; Jameson 1998). In this chapter we examine the very uneven impact of globalising processes on a particular social situation – Northern Ireland. We show how its impact has been mediated by state action as well as by the particular culture and institutions of Northern Ireland. We conclude that globalisation does not necessarily override the more specific logics embedded in local, regional or national situations. It has brought a complex, changing environment which opens a range of new political possibilities. It has provided the arena in which political leaders have forged a peace process and the Good Friday Agreement. It by no means guarantees the continuation or success of the Agreement. If it gives space for radical political initiatives, it also generates tendencies that challenge their success. It demands continuing political effort to maintain and amplify the political achievements of the 1990s in Northern Ireland in this – newly uncertain – environment.

We take globalisation not as a new configuration with totalising effects throughout social life (Albrow 1996), but rather as a new level of socio-political organisation, pursued and brought further by a multitude of actors and social forces in a wide range of areas (Held *et al.* 1999). As such, it is a level of organisation alongside other levels. On the economic level, globalisation includes a reorganisation and dispersal of production units, trade, finance and consumption on a global scale. It involves the emergence of global capital markets and financial systems, global trade and production networks, and global regulatory organisations, e.g. GATT, IMF, G7, the World Bank. Communication becomes a core sector of production, while tourism and consumption more generally take on new economic importance. It involves a refiguring of class relations and centre and periphery in the new economic system and a spatial reshaping of the environment. Politically, it involves the emergence of transnational institutions, organisations and political practices (including regional organisations such as the European Union (EU) and changing styles and relations of international politics in the post-Cold War period. Culturally, it involves global communication systems and population movements. These changes tend to weaken community formation, and bring changes in modes of perception, norms and identity formation, conceived variously as greater cosmopolitanism, individualism, reflective-ness and choice, or as greater hybridity, situationism, fragmentation, shallowness and lack of affect (Baudrillard 1993; Waters 1995).

How does globalisation, as thus understood, impact on particular situations? We structure our analysis of Northern Ireland around two sets of questions:

1 What are the parameters of globalisation in Northern Ireland? In what sectors have globalising trends been most apparent? How has their impact been mediated by state action?
2 How have globalising processes affected the Northern Ireland conflict? What is the direction of their effect? In particular, what role did globalising processes play in laying the foundations for the Good Friday Agreement of 10 April 1998?

The parameters of globalisation in Northern Ireland

Economics

Economic profile

Economically, Northern Ireland is a periphery at once in the British and in the global market economy. It was an early industrialiser and participant in the global economy, its old heavy industry and textile industry have declined, and it has failed successfully to restructure and to find a niche in the new global economy. In 1950, manufacturing took up 36 per cent of the workforce; in 1990 only 18 per cent (Borooah 1993: 2). The most dramatic fall was in FDI: the employment it generated fell from 53 per cent to 39 per cent of total manufacturing employment between 1973 and 1990. Participation in the global, as opposed to the British-centred, market has not been strong: in 1990, over half of FDI was from British-owned multinationals (Hamilton 1993: 197) and much manufacturing production is for mainly Northern Ireland or Great Britain markets (Bew *et al.* 1997: 104). Unemployment has been the highest in the United Kingdom, and is augmented by a growing population: unlike comparable regions in the North of England or France which have experienced population decline due to out-migration, Northern Ireland has seen population growth and also growth in participation in the workforce (Lovering 1991; Borooah 1993; Reitel 1994). Living standards and wages are the lowest in the UK (Borooah 1993: 2; Bew *et al.* 1997: 110).

The 1990s saw a beginning of a reversal of this economic decline (Gudgin 1994). The economic resurgence of the 1990s has, however, largely been in retailing and the hotel/catering industry with a growth in the low-paid, high-turnover sector of the labour force (Bew *et al.* 1997: 109ff.). The underlying prospects became more positive after the Good Friday Agreement. In 1999, for example, inward foreign investment rose dramatically by 57 per cent, with 80 per cent of the new jobs in high-tech industries (*Irish Times*, 19 May 2000). Even then, the forecast growth rate of GNP in Northern Ireland (3 per cent) is only half that of the Republic, from which it may suffer in competition (*Irish Times*, 17 December 1999; *Sunday Business Post*, 19 March 2000). Unemployment figures have decreased to about 7 per cent in 1999, although the mode of assessment (in terms of claimants) tends to underestimate numbers, and long-term unemployment remains a serious problem.

The social effects of this economic peripheralisation have been cushioned by state subventions. The political conflict generated and sustained a high level of public sector service positions: 42 per cent of total employment in the mid-1980s, which fell back to 37 per cent in the 1990s, included over 13,000 officers in the police service alone (Bew *et al.* 1997: 92; Patten 1999). The policies of the Thatcher age in Britain – deregulation, recommodification, cuts in the public sector – were not applied to the same degree in Northern Ireland because of the conflict there. In the late 1980s, direct per capita state assistance to Northern Ireland industry was three times higher than in assisted areas of Scotland and seven times higher than in England and also considerably higher than most areas of the EU (Ryan and O'Dowd 1991: 196). International funding, arising from and attempting to address the conflict, was also available: in the 1980s, the International Fund for Ireland, the generous EU cross-border funding; in the 1990s, the peace process and GFA saw an increased pace of inward investment, some promoted explicitly as part of the 'peace dividend'. In short, living standards in Northern Ireland have been much more closely tied to British government policies and to international political decisions than to market success. It has to a large extent been shielded by state policies from the full impact of economic globalisation. In purely economic terms, Northern Ireland is a marginalised European region, subject to but not fully participating in or benefiting from global economic developments: however, the associated economic hardship has been cushioned by political subsidies and politically motivated investment.

Class structure

The result in Northern Ireland, abstracting for the moment from the community division, is a social division not atypical of the new 'global' economy. Baumann (1998) points out that globalisation makes for a new brutal class distinction, distinguishing the active global participants, open to global travel, living in secure (secured) homes, privately insured against illness, the subjects of consumer activity, from the excluded and marginalised, unemployed or in low-skill, high-turnover occupations, increasingly seen as threats, criminalised, dependent on an increasingly run-down public welfare and health system. There is at once a new cultural tendency to stigmatise and exclude failure, and a concomitant anxiety and insecurity in the 'working' populations: will their jobs survive, are they financially secure if they fall ill?

There is a comparable distinction in Northern Ireland, complicated by the community division and the opportunities which arise specifically from the political conflict. On the one hand there is a relatively highly paid sector able to take advantage of the expanding opportunities for consumption. The numbers of 'active global participants' have also increased, although less because of increasing wealth and economic contacts than because of the global interest in the political conflict in Northern Ireland: political parties and non-governmental organisations (NGOs) have web pages, and even relatively minor political actors and commentators enjoy frequent global travel. On the other hand there is a serious problem of long-term unemployment and low-paid unskilled employment, and high levels of poverty (Bew *et al.* 1997: 109–12). The situation is likely to worsen when the UK subvention, appropriate to a war economy, is decreased. Unemployment is disproportionately Catholic (Cormack *et al.* 1993), but within each community the division between the relatively highly paid and the excluded exists. Middle-class Protestants in particular feel insecure for themselves and their families, vulnerable to the effects of fair employment policy and fearful of downward mobility (Dunn and Morgan 1994).

Consumption and the reconstitution of space

Global economic trends are towards an increasing economic importance of retailing and consumption. The new shopping malls and stores have constituted the outskirts, and to an extent the centres, of cities as 'non-places', empty contractual spaces like airports or motorways where individuals are outside of communal relations (Augé 1995). The new means of communication are refiguring the relations of centre and periphery. Many commentators have noted the declining importance of community, the increasing privatisation and the social depthlessness which this brings (Adamson 1991; Ritzer 1997: ch. 11).

The particular economic profile of Northern Ireland – with living standards cushioned by state subsidies – means that retailing and consumption have increased in importance, in line with global trends. Moreover the spatial reconfiguration of Northern Ireland – the substitution of non-places for traditional communities – was already well under way before the recent retailing boom. It was exemplified in the motorway construction and redevelopment of Belfast: the ring road cuts through central areas which once housed local communities, and necessitated a major redevelopment of housing. However, these developments take on a very specific meaning in Northern Ireland where the reconfiguration of space was in large part a product of state planning. Urban redevelopment was explicitly politically motivated: the aim was to rid parts of the city of their sectarian communal character, to separate communally defined areas of the city one from another, and to create an architecture of new housing estates that would ease surveillance and preclude either sectarian attack or escape routes for paramilitaries. It was a modernist, state-initiated, Haussmannesque attempt to reform the city in the context of conflict rather than a global consumerist transformation of space. Its unintended result, however, was to refigure the spatial boundaries of communities, rather than to dissolve them (Cormack *et al.* 1993: section 2). Non-places – shopping malls, motorways – are juxtaposed with strongly local and communal environments. Commuting and shopping practices are conditioned by concern for communal safety: does the route to work or to the shopping centre pass through the territory of the other? (Eversley 1989: chs 10, 11).

Moreover, consumerism itself is mediated by Northern Ireland's place in the United Kingdom and by the communal division. In some spheres – car sales – the full global range of manufacturers and models is apparent. For other items, the main stores are British multinationals, and the dominant style a regional British, rather than a variegated, globalised one. Consumption, in at least some areas, follows a local rather than a global logic. There is considerable evidence, for example, that the construction of the body (involving a wide range of consumption activity from clothes to make-up to hairstyles) differs between Protestant and Catholic (Burton 1978). In this respect, what Henry Patterson has called 'the rush of middle Ulster to the shopping malls' may be providing new modes of distinction in communal as well as class terms.

The new modes of communication and transport have refigured Northern Ireland's relation to outside centres. Movement, either emigration or on business, from Northern Ireland to Great Britain, is common: with direct rule it became more symbolically important as the new British political elite and journalists imported the concept of 'the mainland' to Northern Ireland. In more recent years, the USA has also become closer, funding frequent trips for politicians, and the venue of business activity. The EU's presence, too, has become evident in border communities. In important respects, Derry is no longer a periphery given its political and business contacts with the US and its involvement in EU cross-border programmes.

Politics

Global and transnational political linkages are of prime and growing importance in contemporary Northern Ireland. The various forms of political interdependence into which Northern Ireland is now linked, mean that the distinctions between external and internal political concerns are no longer clear-cut (e.g. Holton 1998: ch. 5; Held *et al.* 1999: 81).

Supranational institutions, organisations and models of politics

Political globalisation is associated with the creation of new institutions and models of political activity: supranational institutions and organisations, and models of politics and citizenship that go beyond the nation state (Held *et al.* 1999). Such institutions have impacted strongly on Northern Ireland, which participates in a dense network of linkages with such organisations; only some of these linkages are state-initiated or state-sustained.

Despite the fact that Northern Ireland participates in the EU simply as a region of the United Kingdom, its linkages are more than those of other British regions. The

EU has taken a special interest in Northern Ireland, giving generous economic and political provisions as a mode of helping resolve the conflict: as well as generous allocation of Structural Funds (despite the fact that on the conventional economic indicators, Northern Ireland was not a qualifying region) and Interreg II funds, there was the EU Special Support Programme for Peace and Reconciliation in Northern Ireland and the Border Counties of the Republic of Ireland which was set up in 1995 as a peace dividend. A Northern Ireland Centre in Brussels was set up in 1991, from initiatives by business groups and the political parties (Arthur 1999). Northern Ireland representation in the European Parliament is more than proportional to population, and the European Parliament has researched and debated Northern Ireland issues.

The Council of Europe has been especially important through the European Convention on Human Rights and the European Court of Human Rights, to which individuals have taken cases against the British state. International NGOs – Amnesty International, Human Rights Watch – have played a crucial role in publicising and giving independent corroboration of breaches of human rights in Northern Ireland. Indeed one of the important provisions of the Good Friday Agreement was to ensure that the European Convention on Human Rights would be incorporated in both British and Northern Ireland legislation (Human Rights Act, 1998).

These institutions have been equally important in providing new models of politics. The EU inspired models of supranational governance and of changing notions of sovereignty were particularly important in the makings of the Anglo-Irish Agreement of 1985 and the Good Friday Agreement of 1998 (see below, also Kennedy 1994). Notions of citizenship which meet international norms of human and civil rights are now broadly accepted by all political parties. A new language of pluralism, self-determination by agreement, and the need for consent of all significant groups to the political order have given the possibility of negotiation and agreement between political opponents (McCall 1999; Ruane and Todd 1999a).

International relations and conflict mediation

Northern Ireland has been one of the core arenas in which the art of 'soft diplomacy' has flourished (Arthur 1999). This form of informal international mediation of conflict has become important in the post-Cold War world where the major powers (particularly the United States) are concerned to find new modes to prevent the outbreak of destabilising regional conflicts which in recent decades – as the example of ex-Yugoslavia suggests – have become at once more prevalent and internationally difficult or impossible to manage. Since the 1980s, the US has become an increasingly important actor in the conflict, aiding the peace process by formal and informal interventions, providing American money and investment for peace and providing experienced and high-status mediators, most notably Senator George Mitchell who chaired the Multi-Party Negotiations which led to the Good Friday Agreement of 1998 (Arthur 1999; McGinty 1997). Northern Ireland has been considered a foreign policy success of American soft diplomacy (Doyle 1999: 210). South African negotiators have also become more deeply involved since the GFA.

Culture and identity

Globalisation is associated with a culture of consumption and advertising, focusing on youth, and ever new areas of commodification – from leisure and travel to the remaking of the human body. It is promoted through the mass media, by way of fast, ever-changing and distracting images. The result is said to be a weakening of traditional and communal cultures and authorities, individualisation, choice and fragmentation of experience (Jameson 1991; Waters 1995). It is associated with a shrinkage of the content of political culture. As more and more issues are beyond the power of citizens or even governments to control, politics becomes divorced from power and constituted as spectacle – a politics of 'simulacra' rather than of substance (Baudrillard 1993).

Some evidence of these changes exists in Northern Ireland which is open to all the global trends in the mass media and advertising. Global trends in youth culture are clearly visible, for example in resistance towards traditional and community authorities often manifested as general lawlessness, joy riding, or the extreme and relatively unstructured sectarianism of youth culture (Bell 1990). Equally acceptance of church authority has decreased, as has the willingness to affirm a religious identity, although secularising tendencies in Northern Ireland are slower than in other parts of the United Kingdom (Bruce and Alderdice 1993). New global discourses – 'pluralism', 'citizenship', 'peace' and 'democracy' – are quickly adopted by the local media and political parties. Magazines like the high-profile *Fortnight*, and publications of the Cultural Traditions Group, highlight issues of cultural hybridisation, the ability and value of 'picking and mixing' elements of culture and identity.

The particular social and political context, however, frames these cultural changes. Rather than simply an effect of globalisation, they are to an important extent products of state policy. The British state – directly or indirectly through the Arts Council – funds many of the institutions and media which emphasise cultural hybridity and new globalising ideas, as part of its programme of cultural renovation of Northern Ireland. Where new themes and ideas are accepted, they are often assimilated within existing traditional categories: youth culture in Northern Ireland rejects communal authority while remaining within communal boundaries (Bell 1990). Concepts – democracy or pluralism – that elsewhere are used in increasingly empty ways are used in Northern Ireland to express the substantive – and different and oppositional – meanings and aims of the different parties (Ruane and Todd 1996: ch. 4; Nairn 2000). Indeed it could be argued that it is the unwillingness of Northern Irish actors to accept the substitution of simulacra for the substance of communal power or equality that prevents the compromises and policies worked out in London, or between London and Dublin, from being easily accepted there.

Moreover, the new cultural trends do not signify any radical change in identity. The weight of evidence points to an increase in strong communal identification within Northern Ireland: there are now more people who claim to be at once Protestant, British and Unionist, or Catholic, Irish and Nationalist than before, and fewer 'hybrids' (Hayes and McAllister 1999). What is new, however, is the affirmation of new global ideas by many such 'traditional' identifiers: in the last decade, 'extreme' loyalists and republicans have embraced such changes while retaining strong communal and national identifications. Rather than simply reactions against globalisation, in Northern Ireland (as in some parts of the Muslim world) strong fundamentalist and nationalist ideas are vehicles of globalisation (Axtmann 1996: 129).

The impact of globalisation

In summary, Northern Ireland has experienced the impact of globalisation in all spheres, although economically and culturally the impact has been strongly mediated by the role of the British state and of the communal conflict. As we have seen, while Northern Ireland participates in many global processes – for example, the restructuring of class, consumption and space – the causes of these processes in Northern Ireland are in important ways specific to the society and state there. Rather than a totalising logic of globalisation which produces these effects, existing social relations or state action mediate the impact of globalising processes, creating institutions and practices which are – in terms of the logic of their action – more local than global. Moreover the cultural effects of such processes – from consumption to individuation – are also specific, producing reconfigurations of communal distinction as much as transformations of cultural identities or aspirations. The impact of globalisation appears to be strongest and most direct in the political sphere. In the next section we look more closely at the specific impact of globalisation on the political conflict in Northern Ireland.

The Good Friday Agreement: the mode of interaction of globalising processes, state strategies and the logic of conflict

How does globalisation impact on the political process in Northern Ireland? In particular, how did it impact on the peace process and the making of the Good Friday Agreement of 1998? The course of the political conflict in Northern Ireland is complexly and multiply determined; causes of political conflict exist at many different levels, from the historical system of relations linking the communities in Northern Ireland with power structures in the British Isles as a whole (Ruane and Todd 1996) to the conjunctural events which may provoke immediate political reactions. Global forces and processes impact at each level, from the immediate and conjunctural to the restructuring of the historic system of relations. In what follows we look at four modes of impact of globalisation on the making of the Good Friday Agreement. The four modes are complementary, not competing. Each details one level of change in the social system, from the strategic and conjunctural to the more profound restructuring of the very conditions of conflict. Together they show the multi-levelled determinants which went into the making of the Agreement.

Globalisation, the balance of power and changes in political strategy

The Agreement was made possible by the strategic reassessments of each of the main political parties. These strategic shifts were reactions to changes in the power-balance in Northern Ireland, and globalising processes played a part both in producing these changes and in clarifying their nature.

The crucial factor was a change in nationalist strategy. John Hume and the SDLP had early adopted the EU as a context and a model for change within Northern Ireland, within Ireland and between Ireland and Britain. After the Ulster Workers Council Strike of 1974, when it became clear that unionists retained the power to veto reform, Hume's strategy was to mobilise international alliances in support of reform. He won strong support within the Republic of Ireland, the European Parliament and the US for a modified constitutional nationalism, appealing to notions of pluralism and justice, and accepting the principle of no constitutional change without majority consent in Northern Ireland. His success in doing so secured a counter-balance to unionist power, and eventually led to the Anglo-Irish Agreement (AIA) of 1985.

The AIA proved to unionists that the power-balance had changed. After 1985, the Irish role in the government of Northern Ireland increased, the reform process within Northern Ireland accelerated and the relative demographic, economic and cultural position of Catholics improved. The unionist strategy of relying on the British government had proven ineffectual. Increasingly unionists – at least those represented by the majority Ulster Unionist Party (UUP) and the small loyalist parties – came to realise that it was only by negotiation with Northern nationalists and acceptance of wide-ranging reforms within Northern Ireland and partnership government with Northern nationalists that the Union could be secured. Once it emerged, the new proactive unionism, open to negotiation and reform, won a receptive and supportive audience in the US, at the cost of opening itself in turn to US influence and pressure to compromise (Doyle 1999).

Republicans exploited the international situation to aid their terrorist campaign; the 1980s importation of arms from Libya increased their military strength and the widespread sense that they could not be defeated by the British. However, the closure of the Libyan link, together with stalemate in the military struggle, also showed the limits of terrorism. Moreover the fear of political marginalisation after the AIA, the example of the increasing Irish role in Northern Ireland that the AIA provided, and the possibilities of electoral success, North and South, all gave an incentive for a reconsideration of military strategy. At the same time, new opportunities and alliances were opened to them – in the US as well as within Ireland – on the condition that they adopt a peaceful political strategy. A few key international actions – in particular the US visa granted to Gerry Adams against British wishes and the possibility of fundraising in the US – showed the potential benefits of an alternative peaceful strategy. Moreover such a strategy also promised to accelerate the changes and reforms already under way within Northern Ireland. The possibilities of a gradual, step-by-step move towards a united Ireland began to be explored.

The international community not only gave incentives to strategic change, it also provided a context in which realistic strategic thinking became possible. By the 1990s, the ground-rules for politics in Northern Ireland – equality, an Irish dimension, no constitutional change without majority consent in Northern Ireland – were guaranteed by the British and Irish governments and re-emphasised and reinforced by the European Union and the United States. The increasing role of informal and soft diplomacy, the increasing interaction of Northern Ireland politicians with politicians in the USA, in South Africa and with the international chairmen of the talks process of 1996–98, all served to reinforce a realistic sense of the limits of what could be politically achieved in the short term (Arthur 1999). With it came an awareness among all political groups of the potential strategic benefits of a compromise settlement which would give a new political arena in which they could pursue their long-term aims. The active involvement of political leaders – including President Clinton – gave added pressure and incentive to each side to compromise.

In short, strategic reassessments – provoked in large part by changes in the balance of power – allowed for the negotiation of the Good Friday Agreement. Within this process, globalising political processes – and in particular EU and US involvement – were crucial. But globalisation, in this sense, led to a change in political strategy, not in the structure of opposition between the communities. It had an important role in forging an agreement, without, however, changing the character or structure of the underlying conflict (cf. Doyle 1999: 214; Ruane 1999).

Global institutions and institutionalised practices

Emergent global or supranational institutions and institutionalised practices have introduced new elements into the politics of Northern Ireland, providing arenas in which the parties to the conflict could develop new and more cooperative forms of action, practice and ideas.

EU institutions provided opportunities and incentives for British–Irish cooperation. This was especially important in the late 1970s and early 1980s before British–Irish cooperation was itself institutionalised in the AIA. EU funding provides for cross-border economic initiatives in Ireland which themselves provide the arena for cross-border debate and cooperation and development of 'local micro-economies' encompassing communities on both sides of the border (McCall 1999: 78–9). The new informal diplomacy which became important in the last decade provided venues and opportunities for Northern Ireland politicians to meet and discuss informally issues which could not publicly be broached (Arthur 1999). After the GFA, the economic opportunities which opened in the USA provided new incentives and opportunities for political cooperation in securing American investment. The European Convention on Human Rights and the United Nations Declaration on the Rights of Persons belonging to National, Ethnic, Religious and Linguistic Minorities give internationally accepted norms and the European Court of Human Rights an international judicial arena for critique of government policy and institutions in Northern Ireland. These multiple international forums in which Northern

Ireland parties act require them to argue their case in terms of universalisable and universally justifiable norms.

Taking the examples one by one, it is possible to argue that none gave rise to strong enough tendencies to counter the entrenched tendency towards conflict (Opsahl 1993; Ruane and Todd 1996: ch. 10; Arthur 1999). Even a commentator keen to emphasise the importance of the EU for ameliorating conflict in Northern Ireland can speak only of the 'intimations of postmodernity' (McCall 1999) which it brings. Yet the cumulative effect of participation in transnational institutions may well have been to create some acceptance of the norms of those institutions: cooperation, negotiation, pluralism. In this sense, globalisation helped create a political climate in which meaningful negotiation became possible, in which the parties spoke a language comprehensible one to another, and in which each was able, and at times willing, to anticipate and take account of the others' concerns in their own proposals (cf. Arthur 1999). If globalisation in this sense did not change the content of the conflict, nor guarantee any eventual compromise settlement, it at least ameliorated the cultural oppositions between the parties sufficiently to allow for meaningful negotiation.

The use of global models to transform the nature of conflict

More profoundly again, the creative use of political models derived from transnational institutions has provided much of the content of governmental strategy since the 1980s and much of the substance of the Good Friday Agreement.

We have already mentioned the crucial role of the Anglo-Irish Agreement of 1985 in preparing the ground for the Good Friday Agreement. It was inspired (at least on the Irish side) by models of European integration and cooperation which could provide strong and institutionalised Irish influence on British policy in Northern Ireland short of sovereignty or even legal authority. Equally, later intergovernmental statements (the Downing Street Declaration of 1993, the joint British–Irish Framework Document of 1995) which played a crucial role in the peace process were based on models of politics which diverged from a simple state-nation-sovereignty model. The GFA itself can be seen as a sophisticated attempt institutionally to distinguish the various aspects of the state's role – sovereignty, decision-making, cultural presence, administrative integration, citizenship rights – and to redistribute them more evenly between the sovereign British state, regional Northern Irish institutions, the Irish state, and new North–South institutions (Ruane and Todd 2000). In this sense it is a clear break with the model of a sovereign and indivisible nation state.

In each case the political models used were inspired by the new interrelations of the state in a global political environment. Yet they are far from mere copies of European or international models. The Anglo-Irish Agreement was a creative re-modelling (critics have said misreading (Kennedy 1994)) of European models to fit the Irish case. The Downing Street Declaration, the joint Framework Document and the Good Friday Agreement were carefully drafted documents designed to help resolve a specific conflict, rather than philosophical blueprints applied to the case.

Yet each broke with older paradigms of state sovereignty and nation-state identity in ways that would have been inconceivable before the political globalisation of the past decades. Even conceptually, the North–South bodies of the joint Framework Document and the GFA gain their political meaning by association with the process and discourse of European integration. Equally, the benefits which nationalists sense in the GFA can be perceived only via a break with the state sovereignty model (Todd 1999).

In this sense we can see the adaptation of global political models as a conscious attempt by state and party political actors to begin to break out of the structures which for so long defined conflict in Northern Ireland. In the process, both Irish and British states redefined their own relationship so as to break from the older oppositional structure of national difference. Such conscious adoption and adaption of global models to change the particular social structure which generates conflict in Northern Ireland exemplifies a reflexive mode of globalisation.

Global restructuring of the conditions of conflict?

Globalising processes have an even more profound impact in restructuring the conditions of conflict in Northern Ireland. We have outlined above the broad changes in conditions in Northern Ireland associated with globalisation. These have impacted on the conditions of conflict. Changes in the balance of power between the communities brought by de-industrialisation, increasing economic dependence on the British state, and the changing economic and political resources of the Irish state, have radically changed the balance of power between the communities. British strategic interests have changed in the post-Cold War age, allowing the development of convergent British–Irish strategies to undo the relations of power and inequality between the communities in Northern Ireland and in their relation to the states. Wider cultural and social changes and the decline of the older modes of communal bonding endogamy, church attendance – have begun to restructure communal divisions (Whyte 1990; Coulter 1996).

Some have hoped that these changes may signal a dissolution of the conditions of conflict – as fewer people have reasons for conflict, and as those reasons become less pressing, the incentives for cooperation generated by the new institutions and international system may triumph over the tendencies for conflict. The process still has far to go, but the fact that it has begun may explain the vision and hope that was apparent at the time of the Good Friday Agreement.

But if globalisation, in the sense of the broad political and cultural trends noted above, is restructuring the system of relations in Northern Ireland, it is not necessarily destroying its conflict-generating capacity. As we have seen, many of the cultural changes – the dominance of consumption, the restructuring of space – are reabsorbed within a structure of communal opposition. While reasons for conflict remain, the new institutions may be absorbed into the conflictual system and become resources in communal struggle. So the new Assembly in Northern Ireland might function not as a vehicle of reconciliation but as an 'Assembly of

Antagonisms', and the new institutions – rather than providing an incentive for cooperation – simply form a new arena for conflict (Aughey 1999).

The limits to globalisation and the persistence of conflict

Globalisation has affected political development in Northern Ireland in all the ways discussed above. It affected political strategy by changing the balance of power, but strategic changes alone do not explain the Agreement. Without some diminishing of the acute oppositions between the parties, fear of the other's potential to mould the Agreement to their purpose would have triumphed over the faith that the institutions could constitute a balanced settlement. Globalising processes also contributed to a diminution of oppositions, by providing new opportunities and modes of interaction (see the section on global institutions, pp. 120–1 above) and by affecting identities and ideologies (see the section on global restructuring, pp. 121–2 above). Globalisation has not, however, dissolved the conditions of conflict: despite some changes and restructuring, national oppositions remain. Indeed the GFA, rather than signalling a dissolution of national conflict, fully recognises the importance and political substance of the national conflict in all its aspects: its novelty lies in disaggregating the nation-state problematic into its several parts (sovereignty, equality, citizenship, institutional integration, decision-making, etc.) and allowing processual change in each. Here, global models have been used creatively in an attempt to transform, rather than dissolve, the structure of conflict (see the section on global models, p. 121 above). Whether or not this attempt succeeds, whether, once the institutions are implemented, they function to create a dynamic of co-operation or whether they are absorbed into a dynamic of conflict remains at time of writing as yet unclear.

We have suggested that all of these modes of globalisation came together to help produce the Good Friday Agreement. For a brief period, strategic and idealistic, self-interested and transformist motivations coincided and diverse processes with potentially contradictory implications together pointed in the direction of agreement. Since April 1998, gaps between party strategy, political opportunity and future vision have reopened. What is increasingly clear is that globalisation, while affecting the conflict in Northern Ireland, does not affect it simply or benignly: rather, conflicting, perhaps contradictory, currents are set up which give windows of opportunity, but also limits, to political progress (Ruane 1999).

Conclusion: the impact of globalisation on Northern Ireland

In this chapter we have argued that globalisation is a multiple set of processes with uncertain and potentially contradictory effects. Globalising processes do not necessarily override the more specific logics embedded in local, regional or national situations but rather interact with them. As we have seen, globalising processes have already impacted on Northern Ireland and have helped to create the conditions for the Good Friday Agreement. But their impact on the structure of the conflict itself has been less certain. Global elements have been incorporated within the existing structure of conflict, provoking changes in political strategy but reproducing communal opposition within a changed political arena. At the same time there is the tendency – although by no means yet realised – that global processes may come to dissolve the conflictual system of relations, rendering irrelevant older cultural and communal divisions and prioritising different inequalities. The contradictory tendencies – towards reproduction and dissolution of the conflict – give a sense of openness of the future. These windows of opportunity are grasped by actors (primarily, but not exclusively, the British and Irish states) who use global models and processes in order to transform the particular social system: so, in the Good Friday Agreement, the British and Irish states, with the Northern Ireland political parties, agreed institutions which promised to transform the logic of conflict. But the older conflict-generating system retains the capacity to reassert itself and the transformative potential of the Good Friday is not certain to be fulfilled. If globalisation gives new possibilities for conflict management and resolution, it also requires continued political creativity to grasp and realise those possibilities.

References

Adamson, David (1991) 'Lived experience, social consumption and political change: Welsh politics into the 1990s', in Graham Day and Gareth Rees (eds), *Regions, Nations and European Integration: Remaking the Celtic Periphery* (Cardiff: University of Wales).

Albrow, Martin (1996) *The Global Age* (Cambridge: Polity Press).

Appadurai, Arjun (1990) 'Disjuncture and difference in the global cultural economy', in Mike Featherstone (ed.), *Global Culture: Nationalism, Globalization and Modernity* (London: Sage).

Arthur, Paul (1999) '"Quiet diplomacy and personal conversation": Track Two diplomacy and the search for a settlement in Northern Ireland', in Ruane and Todd (1999a), pp. 71–95.

Augé, Marc (1995) *Non-places: introduction to an anthropology of supermodernity*, trans. by John Howe (London: Verso).

Aughey, Arthur (1999) 'A new beginning?: the prospects for a politics of civility in Northern Ireland', in Ruane and Todd (1999a), pp. 122–44.

Axtmann, Roland (1996) *Liberal Democracy in the Twenty-First Century: Globalization, Integration and the Nation State* (Manchester: Manchester University Press).

Baudrillard, Jean (1993) *Symbolic Exchange and Death*, trans. by Ian Hamilton Grant (London: Sage).

Baumann, Zygmunt (1998) *Work, Consumerism and the New Poor* (Buckingham: Open University Press).

Bell, Desmond (1990) *Youth Culture and Sectarianism in Northern Ireland* (London: Macmillan).

Bew, Paul, Henry Patterson and Paul Teague (1997) *Beyond War and Peace: the Political Future of Northern Ireland* (London: Lawrence and Wishart).

Borooah, Vani K. (1993) 'Northern Ireland – typology of a regional economy', in Paul Teague (ed.), *The Economy of Northern Ireland: Perspectives for Structural Change* (London: Lawrence and Wishart).

Bruce, Steve and Fiona Alderdice (1993) 'Religious belief and behavior', in Peter Stringer and Gillian Robinson (eds), *Social Attitudes in Northern Ireland: the Third Report* (Belfast: Blackstaff).

Burton, Frank (1978) *The Politics of Legitimacy: Struggles in a Belfast Community* (London: Routledge and Kegan Paul).

Cormack, R.J., Gallagher, A.M. and Osborne, R.D. (1993) *Fair Enough: Religion and the 1991 Population Census* (Belfast: FEC).

Coulter, Colin (1996) 'Direct rule and the unionist middle classes', in Richard English and Graham Walker (eds), *Unionism in Modern Ireland: New Perspectives on Politics and Culture* (London: Macmillan).

Doyle, John (1999) 'Governance and citizenship in contested states: the Northern Ireland Peace Agreement as internationalised governance', *Irish Studies in International Relations*, 10: 201–19.

Dunn, Seamus and Valerie Morgan (1994) *Protestant Alienation in Northern Ireland: a Preliminary Survey* (Coleraine: Centre for the Study of Conflict).

Eversley, David (1989) *Religion and Employment in Northern Ireland* (London: Sage).

Gudgin, Graham (1994) 'Pulling ahead: industrial growth in Northern Ireland', *Irish Banking Review*, summer.

Hamilton, Douglas (1993) 'Foreign investment and industrial development in Northern Ireland', in Paul Teague (ed.), *The Economy of Northern Ireland: Perspectives for Structural Change* (London: Lawrence and Wishart).

Hayes, Bernadette C. and Ian McAllister (1999) 'Ethnonationalism, public opinion and the Good Friday Agreement', in Ruane and Todd (1999a).

Held, David, Anthony McGrew, David Goldblatt and Jonathan Perraton (1999) *Global Transformations: Politics, Economics and Culture* (Cambridge: Polity Press).

Holton, Robert J. (1998) *Globalization and the Nation State* (London: Macmillan).

Jameson, Fredric (1991) *Postmodernism, or, The Cultural Logic of Late Capitalism* (London: Verso).

Jameson, Fredric (1998) 'Notes on globalization as a philosophical issue', in Fredric Jameson and Masao Miyoshi (eds), *The Cultures of Globalization* (London: Duke University Press).

Kennedy, Dennis (1994) 'The European Union and the Northern Ireland question', in Brian Barton and Patrick J. Roche (eds), *The Northern Ireland Question: Perspectives and Policies* (Aldershot: Avebury).

Lovering, John (1991) 'Southbound again: the peripheralization of Britain', in Graham Day and Gareth Rees (eds), *Regions, Nations and European Integration: Remaking the Celtic Periphery* (Cardiff: University of Wales Press).

McCall, Cathal (1999) *Identity in Northern Ireland: Communities, Politics and Change* (London: Macmillan).

McGarry, John and Brendan O'Leary (1995) *Explaining Northern Ireland: Broken Images* (Oxford: Basil Blackwell).

McGinty, Roger (1997) 'American influences on the Northern Ireland peace process', *The Journal of Confiict Studies*, Fall, pp. 31–50.

Nairn, Tom (2000) *After Britain: New Labour and the Return of Scotland* (London: Granta).

Opsahl, Torkel (1993) 'Some comments on Kevin Boyle's contribution', in Harald Olav Skar and Bjorn Lydersen (eds), *Northern Ireland: a Crucial Test for a Europe of Peaceful Regions*, Norwegian Foreign Policy Studies no. 80 (Norwegian Institute of International Affairs).

[Patten] (1999) *A New Beginning: Policing in Northern Ireland: The Report of the Independent Commission on Policing for Northern Ireland.*

Reitel, François (1994) 'Lorraine', in André Gamblin (ed.), pilote, *La France dans ses Regions*, 1 (Paris: Sedes).

Ritzer, George (1997) *Postmodern Social Theory* (New York: McGraw-Hill).
Ruane, Joseph (1999) 'The end of (Irish) history? Three readings of the current conjuncture', in Ruane and Todd (1999a).
Ruane, Joseph and Jennifer Todd (1996) *The Dynamics of Conflict in Northern Ireland* (Cambridge: Cambridge University Press).
Ruane, Joseph and Jennifer Todd (1999a) *After the Good Friday Agreement: Analysing Political Change in Northern Ireland* (Dublin: University College Dublin Press).
Ruane, Joseph and Jennifer Todd (1999b) 'The Belfast Agreement: content, context, consequences', in Ruane and Todd (1999a).
Ruane, Joseph and Jennifer Todd (2000) 'The Good Friday Agreement: a new constitutional beginning in Northern Ireland?', *Civitas Europas*.
Ryan, Colm and Liam O'Dowd (1991) 'Restructuring the periphery: state, region and locality in Northern Ireland', in Graham Day and Gareth Rees (eds), *Regions, Nations and European Integration: Remaking the Celtic Periphery* (Cardiff: University of Wales Press).
Todd, Jennifer (1999) 'Nationalism, republicanism and the Good Friday Agreement', in Ruane and Todd (1999a).
Waters, Malcolm (1995) *Globalization* (London: Routledge).
Whyte, John (1990) *Interpreting Northern Ireland* (Oxford: Clarendon).

Chapter 8

Northern Ireland and the international system

Adrian Guelke

The onset of Northern Ireland's troubles in the late 1960s coincided with the beginnings of the post-colonial era, while the troubles started to peter out with the end of the Cold War. It is argued that the correspondence was not accidental, but that the different assumptions of the two eras profoundly influenced events in Northern Ireland, notwithstanding claims that what set Northern Ireland apart from other places was its resistance to external trends. In particular, changing interpretations of international norms have made a profound difference to the course of the conflict. At the start of the troubles, the prevailing interpretation of self-determination was territorial and the world appeared to be heading towards an international political system composed entirely of sovereign independent states with permanently fixed boundaries.

By contrast, by the end of the troubles not merely had the interpretation of self-determination become problematic, but the process of globalisation was eroding the concept of sovereignty with the consequence that the notion of the modern international political system as being based on the principles established by the Peace Treaty of Westphalia in 1648 was being widely challenged. Similarly, at the beginning of the troubles the emphasis on individual human rights undercut the notion that minorities should enjoy special rights. By the end of the troubles, the notion of minority rights was firmly embedded in a number of international conventions. This chapter charts these changes and their effects on the parties in Northern Ireland. At the same time, the stark statement of the argument given above will be qualified in important respects since there were contradictory tendencies in the two eras that reduce the differences between them.

Decolonisation

During the process of decolonisation the principle of self-determination was interpreted as a right of peoples, and 'people' was defined in territorial terms as simply being the inhabitants of a political entity with pre-existing boundaries. Colonies, generally speaking, were administered as separate political entities by colonial powers so that treating the self entitled to self-determination as the majority of people within any given territory facilitated the transfer of power to nationalist movements with a minimum of disruption to the international political system. However, this political revolution was not achieved universally without violence. This was because in some instances there was conflict among nationalists over the spoils of independence and because in other cases there was resistance by the colonial power in question to ending its rule for strategic, economic or ideological reasons. Thus, it was only after the transfer of power had been completed in most parts of the world that the principle of self-determination as outlined above was incorporated in pronouncements of the United Nations, most notably in the 1960 *Declaration on the Granting of Independence to Colonial Countries and Peoples* and in the 1970 *Declaration of Principles of International Law Concerning Friendly Relations and Cooperation among States in Accordance with the Charter of the United Nations*.

The resistance of some colonial powers, particularly Portugal and France, to decolonisation took the form of the integration of overseas territories into the metropolitan country. Thus Lisbon claimed that Angola and Mozambique were overseas provinces of Portugal. However, as a dictatorship the Portuguese government was poorly placed to convince the outside world that this proposition enjoyed popular support either in mainland Portugal or in the overseas territories themselves. Paris likewise gave some of its overseas territories the status of departments of France, with the inhabitants electing representatives to France's national parliament and participating in French presidential elections. Integration has proved workable in France's case in respect of a number of territories with small populations. However, it has by no means gained universal acceptance. In particular, the location of these departments outside of Europe has tended to militate against acceptance of the proposition that these territories can legitimately be regarded as extensions of France.

But at the end of the 1960s and the beginning of the 1970s, the much more serious question was where the line should be drawn in the unfolding process of decolonisation. In particular, did 'peoples' of regions of former colonies have a right to secede from a newly established independent state? And did 'peoples' of regions of the former European colonial powers themselves possess any right to self-determination? In particular, were such regions entitled to secede if a majority of the people in the region supported such a step? And would a bare majority in a referendum suffice? One of the reasons for the adoption of the 1970 *Declaration* was the desire of most members of the international community to provide definitive answers to these questions. It was seen as a way both of underpinning the legitimacy of the new post-colonial order in Asia and Africa and of drawing a line as to where the process of decolonisation should stop.

Thus, the strongest element in the 1970 *Declaration* was its anathema against secession, though some room for argument was left by the reference to 'sovereign and independent States conducting themselves in compliance with the principle of equal rights and self-determination and thus possessed of a government representing the whole state belonging to the territory without distinction as to race, creed, or colour' (Cassese 1995: 306). The main purpose of restricting protection against secession to such states was to prevent colonial powers which integrated territories administratively without extending full citizenship rights to their population from invoking the anathema against secession to resist decolonisation. The hostility of the international community towards secession was reflected in practice in the response of most states to the two principal African conflicts of the 1960s, the Congo crisis and the Nigerian civil war. In particular, they refused to recognise the governments of Katanga and Biafra, the two secessionist entities created in the course of the conflicts. That contributed to the failure of both secessions.

First World nationalisms

Northern Ireland was one of a number of places within the First World of Western states where conflict erupted in the late 1960s and early 1970s that challenged attempts to limit the geographical scope of decolonisation. Acts of violence by groups demanding decolonisation in some shape or form occurred in Quebec, Corsica and the Basque country, to name some of the most prominent cases, as well as in Northern Ireland. The violence in Quebec spluttered out quickly, but not the challenge to the existence of Canada from Quebec nationalists, which continues to this day in the form of a powerful separatist party seeking to achieve its ends by constitutional means. In the cases of Corsica and the Basque country, as in that of Northern Ireland, nationalists have been divided between those pursuing separatist objectives exclusively by constitutional means and those regarding violence as a legitimate means in the pursuit of self-determination. In Quebec the nationalists have hitherto failed to win a majority in a referendum on the issue of the province's constitutional status, but the central government supported by the country's supreme court disputes the right of Quebec to secede from Canada unilaterally on the basis of a bare majority obtained in a referendum (Seymour 2000: 250).

In Corsica, nationalists currently constitute well under a quarter of the electorate, hence the prospect of a fundamental clash between the central government and political institutions of the region over who has a legitimate right to rule the island is unlikely in the foreseeable future. However, not merely does France not acknowledge any right of secession by majorities in any region of France, even the symbolic gesture made by the government of according recognition to the Corsican people (while stressing that they were a component part of the people of France) was struck down by the country's constitutional council on the grounds that such symbolic recognition might be taken to imply that the Corsican 'people' had a right to self-determination separately from the right enjoyed by the people of France. Spain likewise does not accept a right of secession by any of the country's autonomous regions. A complicating factor for Basque nationalists is that the autonomous region consists of only three of the seven historic provinces of the Basque country. Excluded are the three provinces of the Basque country that lie in France and a fourth Spanish province.

In Northern Ireland, the case of the nationalists at the onset of the troubles was not that they were even potentially a majority within the province or that the British government illegitimately refused to recognise the right of Northern Ireland to secede. Indeed, what set Northern Ireland apart in this period from other regions in the First World was precisely the conditional nature of Northern Ireland's membership of the United Kingdom and London's resistance to the full integration of Northern Ireland into the British polity. The nationalist argument was that Northern Ireland was a gerrymandered political entity constructed on the basis of covering the largest part of the north-east of the island as was compatible with the maintenance within it of a secure and permanent Unionist majority. Nationalists rejected the legitimacy of partition, which was imposed unilaterally by the British government under the Government of Ireland Act of 1920 and which, significantly, preceded the negotiations with Sinn Féin to end the Anglo-Irish war. The fact that the southern leader, John Redmond, had reluctantly agreed to this division of the island during the war on an unfulfilled promise that it would lead to the speedy implementation of home rule counted for little in this context.

However, more problematic for nationalists in sustaining their view of partition as illegitimate, particularly from a legal perspective, was the confirmation of the border by the government of the Irish Free State in an agreement with the government of Northern Ireland in 1925. The agreement followed the leaking to an English newspaper of the recommendations of the Boundary Commission set up under the Anglo-Irish Treaty of 1922. Nationalist expectations had been that the Boundary Commission would propose substantial changes to the existing border, transferring to the Irish Free State contiguous areas where Catholics constituted a majority of the population. In the event, the Commission gave economic reasons for overriding the wishes of local communities and recommended only very minor changes to the border. Furthermore, their recommendations entailed the transfer of territory from the Irish Free State to Northern Ireland as well as the other way round. It was the unacceptability of this prospect that persuaded the Irish government to pre-empt the Commission's report by opting for the status quo. As the Unionists had campaigned against the Boundary Commission under the slogan 'not an inch', securing the agreement of the government of Northern Ireland to set aside the report was little more than a formality.

A weakness of the case for partition from a political perspective was that dividing of the island between entities comprising respectively 26 counties and six was difficult to defend on the basis of the pre-existing administrative divisions of colonial Ireland. The opt-out of the province of Ulster, comprising nine counties, might have been justified on the grounds of the opposition of a majority of the inhabitants of the province to rule from Dublin. Alternatively, the exclusion of four counties from rule by Dublin might have been justified on the basis of the opt-out of individual counties with Unionist majorities. The actual exclusion of six counties entailed including in Northern Ireland two counties with nationalist majorities. After World War I, the principle that boundaries between the newly created states in Eastern Europe should be determined, at least in part, by the wishes of the population in disputed areas, enjoyed considerable legitimacy. Thus, the principle of the partition of Ireland could be defended as compatible with the interpretation of national self-determination that prevailed at that time. But the border between

Ireland's two political entities could not, even if it might be argued that by ensuring the relative homogeneity of the Southern entity, where the border was drawn had the effect of helping to consolidate the South's political independence.

Arguments over the genesis of partition were almost certainly less important to members of the international community at the start of the troubles than the simple argument that the division of an island under more than one sovereignty was a violation of the principle of territorial integrity. Political acceptance of the notion of the wholeness of islands was reflected in political practice. The division of islands under more than one sovereignty was comparatively rare and in the small number of cases where it occurred it was often the product of establishment of settlements by rival colonial powers and the partition of the island could be justified as corresponding to this division, as in the case of the island of Hispaniola, divided between Haiti and the Dominican Republic. A topical case is that of the island of Timor. Further, the dominance of the territorial criterion in the interpretation of the principle of self-determination undercut arguments that proposed the existence of two nations on the island of Ireland, each entitled to self-determination.

A number of factors contributed to the perception of Northern Ireland as an illegitimate political entity at the onset of the troubles. The peculiar status of Northern Ireland within the United Kingdom was one factor. Northern Ireland was the only part of the United Kingdom then to have a devolved government of its own. It was the only part of the country where elections were not contested by Britain's main national political parties. It was also the only part of the United Kingdom where membership of the United Kingdom was explicitly stated to depend on the continuing support of a majority of its electorate or, to put it another way, to be accorded the right of secession from the union. The corollary of the constitutional guarantee that Northern Ireland would remain part of the United Kingdom as long as that was the wish of its parliament at Stormont and, after its suspension, that of the Northern Irish electorate as expressed in a referendum, was that it would cease to remain part of the United Kingdom if that condition was not met. The outbreak of disturbances in the province itself put a question mark over its legitimacy by the visible demonstration of the disaffection from the polity of a sizeable minority of the population. Further, in the context of the completion of the process of decolonisation, it seemed to provide an answer to the questions, where next and what is left?

Admittedly, the demand of the Northern Ireland Civil Rights Association for equality within the province implied that Northern Ireland's political ills might be curable through reform of the province's institutions rather than the dissolution of Northern Ireland as a political entity. Further, even if it is accepted that Northern Ireland's conditional status appeared anomalous in a post-colonial world, it could be argued that a united Ireland was not the only way of resolving its position in accordance with the principle of self-determination. Other ways of ending its anomalous status included the full integration of Northern Ireland into the British political system, the creation of an independent Northern Ireland, and the re-establishment of the whole archipelago of the British Isles as a single political system. The last of these implied that the partition of Ireland had been the product of the secession of

Southern Ireland and that the system could be made whole again by the reversal of that step. The enhancement of the status of the Republic of Ireland as a result of the country's entry into the European Community in 1973 made that seem a highly improbable eventuality. However, in an attenuated form it attracted advocates during the course of the troubles, as did the other options. Advocates of an independent Northern Ireland argued that it would provide a context in which there would be no winners and no losers in the conflict between Unionism and nationalism. Opponents questioned the economic viability of an independent Northern Ireland. Integration became a popular option among Unionists in Northern Ireland. The weakness of this option was the lack of enthusiasm for it in the rest of the United Kingdom.

The difficulty of addressing the question of Northern Ireland's place in the world and at the same time devising political arrangements capable of securing widespread support across the province's sectarian divide contributed to the intractability of the Northern Ireland problem through the course of the 1970s. The either/or basis on which the issue of sovereignty was perceived during this era was reflected in the attitudes of both the politicians and the paramilitaries. The interpretation of existing international norms underpinned the zero/sum approach taken by Republicans and most Unionists. The prevailing emphasis on individual human rights and the lack of any special provision for the rights of minority groups gave Republicans little incentive to accept the framework of the six counties. Republicans had a stronger case in terms of world opinion by pressing their claim to self-determination as part of a territorial majority on the island of Ireland. Even constitutional nationalists seeking a political accommodation with Unionists rejected the notion of a wholly internal settlement, insisting that there had to be an Irish dimension to the resolution of the Northern Ireland problem. Republican and nationalist attacks on the legitimacy of Northern Ireland as a political entity had the effect of reinforcing the siege mentality of Unionists. Compromise was seen by most Unionists as entailing a slippery slope to a united Ireland. At the same time, the contrast between the principles underlying proposals for the governance of Northern Ireland and those underpinning the status quo in the rest of the United Kingdom provided a ready justification for Unionist opposition to change.

National liberation

At the time of Northern Ireland's experiment in power-sharing in 1974, Third World states were pressing for the creation of a New International Economic Order, which was designed to enhance the economic sovereignty of states by increasing the power of governments to control and to regulate the activities of multinational companies. The context of the debate in the United Nations General Assembly on a New International Economic Order was the threat that the quadrupling of oil prices posed to the economies of Western states. The use of the oil weapon was intended to put pressure on the West in relation to the Israeli–Arab dispute, but it also gave the Third World majority in the General Assembly a measure of leverage to press for changes to the organisation of the world economy in line with prevailing ideology in economic matters among Third World states, which was nationalist in its assumptions.

One way of interpreting the attitude of Third World states on economic issues was as a defensive reaction to growing economic interdependence, a process that was attracting the attention of international relations scholars and providing a challenge to the dominance of the realist perspective in the discipline. But it could also be presented as a logical extension to the economic sphere of the quest of Third World states for independence. Thus, it was commonly argued that the continuing dependence of Third World states on the West amounted to a system of neo-colonialism. Those fighting against this system saw themselves as engaged in a common anti-imperialist struggle. The aspiration to combine economic and political independence – often allied to a radical programme for the transformation of society through measures such as land reform – was encapsulated in the concept of national liberation. Through the 1970s the example of Vietnam provided inspiration to revolutionary movements throughout the world, while the popularity of the concept of national liberation was reflected in the inclusion of the term in a variety of languages in the names of numerous violent organisations that emerged in the 1970s in both the Third World and regions of the First World. These points were exemplified in Ireland by frequent references by Republicans to Northern Ireland as Britain's Vietnam and the formation of the Irish National Liberation Army (INLA) in 1975.

From the vantage point of the beginning of the 21st century, it seems that these ideas reached the peak of their influence in the mid-1970s. Despite declarations from the United Nations General Assembly, a New International Economic Order was not adopted. The threat posed to Western economies by the rise in oil prices was met by the recycling of petro-dollars through the Western banking system and not by a new deal for the Third World. The significance of this outcome tended to be masked at the time by political developments, particularly the collapse of authoritarian right-wing governments in Southern Europe, which seemed to provide a further boost for left-wing forces. Moreover, the overthrow of the Shah of Iran in 1979, the revolution in Nicaragua in the same year and the victory of guerrilla forces in Rhodesia culminating in the emergence of Zimbabwe in 1980 hardly suggested that anti-imperialist forces were in retreat and concerns over these and other challenges to Western influence were a factor in the victories of conservatives in elections in Britain and the United States in 1979 and 1980. However, none of these political developments actually enhanced the credibility of an economically nationalist alternative to the rejuvenation of the capitalist system through measures of economic liberalisation.

The long war

By the end of the 1970s, the Provisional IRA had abandoned its expectations of a quick victory achieved as a result of the withdrawal of British forces. A new strategy was adopted, that of the long war, in the expectation that only sustained pressure over a long period would secure the Republicans' objective of a British declaration of intent to withdraw from Ireland. During the 1970s Republicans had set great store by opinion polls that showed that a large majority of the British electorate wanted the troops withdrawn. The failure of public opinion to change policy led to a reassessment of British intentions. Republicans explained the reluctance of Britain to withdraw in terms of strategic and economic interests in the maintenance of partition. The political boost to the position of the Republican movement as a result of the 1981 hunger-strike crisis in the prisons ensured that for almost a decade these propositions were not subjected to critical scrutiny. In addition, the revival of the Cold War in the first half of the 1980s lent verisimilitude to strategic arguments, even though a major source of arms for the Provisional IRA was the United States and not the Soviet Union, though Libyan involvement enabled the proponents of the notion of a terror network to fit the Irish case into their construction of a global conspiracy directed at the West (Sterling 1981: 161). In 1983 the then Secretary of State for Northern Ireland, James Prior, invoked the notion of an Irish Cuba if Sinn Féin was not stopped, giving instant credibility to Republican claims that Britain was motivated in its policy towards Northern Ireland by strategic considerations.

The proposition that Britain had an economic stake in partition was only possible to sustain on the basis that autarky was a viable economic strategy in the context of a united Ireland. This was not immediately undermined by the entry of the United Kingdom and the Republic of Ireland into the European Community, since on the left in both countries there was considerable support for the view that entry had been a mistake because the rules of the Community, particularly in relation to free movement of capital and economic competition, prevented the adoption of socialist policies. When a referendum was held in the United Kingdom in 1975 on whether the country should remain in the Community on the terms re-negotiated by the Labour government, the Social Democratic and Labour Party (SDLP) was split on the issue, with both Gerry Fitt and Paddy Devlin opposed to Britain remaining in for just this reason. By the 1980s the party was strongly identified with support for the European Community. Indeed, its leader, John Hume, presented the success of the Community in bringing about reconciliation between France and Germany as a model for reconciliation between the two parts of Ireland.

The hostility of the Republican movement towards the European Community proved more durable. Thus, in the 1992 referendum on the Maastricht Treaty in the Republic of Ireland, Sinn Féin advocated a 'no' vote. It did not affect the outcome of a large majority in favour of the Treaty, reflecting the electorate's acceptance of the argument that European integration had played a significant role in the substantial growth of the Irish economy. However, despite the negative stance taken by Sinn Féin on the issue of the ratification of the Maastricht Treaty, it was evident in a number of policy documents that Sinn Féin's view of the impact of European integration on the Irish Question was gradually changing. In particular, in an interview with Michael Cox in 1996, a leading figure in Sinn Féin, Mitchel McLaughlin, identified as one of the factors behind the peace process 'the Single European Act and the dominance of the EU on the island of Ireland' (Cox 1998:

83). By this point, the model which had once been central to Republican thinking of a socialist, economically self-sufficient, united Ireland seemed a pipe-dream, even to Republicans.

The credibility of the Republican movement's revolutionary project for Ireland began to be eroded at least as far back as the signing of the Anglo-Irish Agreement. The British government's readiness to enter into an agreement with the Irish government over the governance of Northern Ireland was a reflection of London's recognition of the damage the conflict in Northern Ireland was doing to Britain's reputation, particularly in the wake of the hunger-strike crisis. It also stemmed from the importance that the British government attached to relations with the Irish government because of the Republic of Ireland's membership of the European Community. The furious Unionist reaction to the Agreement undercut the notion of a strong British commitment to the union. The political effect of the Agreement was to shore up the position of the SDLP in its electoral competition with Sinn Féin. Sinn Féin leaders gravitated between denunciation of the Agreement as copper-fastening partition and claiming the credit for the benefits that accrued to nationalists under the Agreement. The SDLP leader, John Hume, tried to persuade the Sinn Féin leadership that the Agreement meant that the British government was now neutral on the question of the union and that there was therefore no justification whatsoever for the continuance of the Provisional IRA's campaign of violence. He did not succeed largely because the Republican movement remained wedded to the view that inclusion of Northern Ireland in NATO was still an important objective of British policy.

With the fall of the Berlin Wall and the end of the Cold War, this last prop of the Republican analysis of British policy in Northern Ireland disintegrated. In November 1990, the Secretary of State for Northern Ireland, Peter Brooke made an important speech in which he declared that 'the British government has no selfish strategic or economic interest in Northern Ireland' (Mallie and McKittrick 1996: 107). (In fact, Brooke had wanted to make the speech a year earlier. It was delayed by Cold War strategic concerns of the Prime Minister, Margaret Thatcher.) The speech had a profound effect on Republican perceptions. Brooke's declaration was a core element in the discussions between John Hume and Gerry Adams on the peace initiative that paved the way to the Joint Declaration by the British and Irish governments in December 1993. This restated Brooke's words (HMSO 1993: 3). While Sinn Féin actually rejected the Joint Declaration because of its incorporation of the principle of consent that Northern Ireland would not cease to be part of the United Kingdom without the consent of a majority of its electorate, the declaration satisfied the Republican movement sufficiently to bring about a cease-fire by the Provisional IRA in August 1994.

Other changes in the external environment played a part in the Republican movement's abandonment of the long war. During the 1980s the Republican movement made wide use of comparison of the Provisional IRA's campaign of violence with the 'armed struggle' of the African National Congress (ANC) in South Africa and that of the Palestine Liberation Organisation (PLO) against the state of Israel and its continuing occupation of territories captured in 1967. It was reflected in the murals in West Belfast highlighting connections among the different campaigns, as well as in the writings of the Sinn Féin President, Gerry Adams (Adams 1986: 5, 27, 28, 113, 118 and Rolston 1992: 49–50). The need for the Republican movement to find external reference points to legitimise IRA violence was linked to the adoption of the long war strategy which assumed the continuation of the campaign into the 21st century. Inevitably, President de Klerk's liberalisation of the South African polity in February 1990 and the decision of the ANC to suspend its armed struggle in August of that year had a profound impact on the Republican movement. If fundamental change was achievable in South Africa of all places through negotiation, then how could Republicans sustain the position that Northern Ireland was irreformable? Agreement between Israel and the PLO in September 1993 simply added to the pressure on Sinn Féin to come up with a peace strategy to sustain the credibility of the comparisons it had come to rely upon.

A further source of external pressure on Sinn Féin was evolution in the attitudes of the various elements of the Irish American lobby. Influential in changing the reactive basis of the lobby's engagement with the conflict was a new organisation, Americans for a New Irish Agenda (ANIA). While sympathetic to the Republican movement, it subtly changed the objective of American involvement from the achievement of Irish unity to the ending of the conflict without prejudging the shape of a settlement. At the beginning of 1994 ANIA persuaded President Clinton to admit Adams on a 48-hour visa to attend a conference, on the understanding that such a development would facilitate its efforts to bring about a cease-fire by the Provisional IRA. (It is worth noting in parenthesis that an American President would hardly have contemplated taking such a step during the Cold War, since it was entirely predictable that it would anger the British government, despite its ultimately pacific intent.)

The Good Friday Agreement

The declaration by the Provisional IRA of a cease-fire in August 1994 did not lead directly or quickly to a political settlement. The Republican movement's dissatisfaction with the pace of political developments after the cease-fire led to its breaking down in February 1996. The cease-fire was reinstated in July 1997. It took a further nine months for agreement to be reached in the multi-party talks. Further, the Good Friday Agreement of 10 April 1998 fell far short of the political objectives of the Republican movement, leading to Sinn Féin's qualified endorsement of the Agreement on the basis that it would facilitate a transition to a united Ireland. The Agreement was far closer to the objectives of its nationalist rival, the SDLP, in its emphasis on political accommodation. It also bore a sufficiently close resemblance to the power-sharing experiment in 1974, which the SDLP had participated in but which the Republican movement had denounced, that the Deputy Leader of the SDLP was moved to describe the Agreement as 'Sunningdale for slow learners'. The same basic elements of power-sharing in a devolved government for Northern Ireland and an Irish dimension were present in both Agreements.

However, both the external environment and the ideological climate of opinion surrounding the Agreements were very different. In particular, by 1998 globalisation and rapid technological change through the information revolution had discredited policies of economic nationalism. The progress of European integration had reached the point of agreement on the creation of a single currency, though, admittedly, without Britain's participation. The demise of Communism had led to a decline in politics based on class as parties aspiring to government found themselves driven by market forces to operate within the prevailing neo-liberal consensus on economic policy. Identity politics had tended to displace class politics, facilitating – and facilitated by – an increasing focus on the rights of minority groups. The prospect of the devolution of power to Scotland and Wales created the context of the innovative proposal for a British–Irish Council to balance the enhancement of North–South ties within Ireland, thereby ameliorating Unionist fears that closer ties between the two parts of Ireland would automatically distance Northern Ireland further from the rest of the United Kingdom.

In addition, the interpretation of both self-determination and sovereignty was undergoing considerable change in the wake of the collapse of Communism in Eastern Europe and the Soviet Union. The international community's anathema against secession had been considerably weakened as a result of the break-up of Yugoslavia. Admittedly, the independence of Slovenia and Croatia and their recognition by the international community have yet to prompt the United Nations General Assembly to rewrite the 1970 *Declaration*, but these two cases clearly set a precedent for the unilateral secession of regions from existing sovereign states. At the same time, cases of genocide and other atrocities in the post-Cold War world have led to the view that intervention in the affairs of sovereign states may be justifiable if gross violations of human rights are occurring. This has taken the world further away from the Westphalian ideal of the international political system as being made up of sovereign, territorial states not penetrated by external authority; an ideal which had been supported by most members of the international community as recently as the 1970s.

These changes in the interpretation of both self-determination and sovereignty have been reflected in a remarkable transformation in perceptions of Northern Ireland's conditional status. At the start of the troubles it was viewed as an indication of the province's semi-colonial status, detracting from its legitimacy as a political entity. Enshrined as the consent principle in the Good Friday Agreement, it has been hailed by regional nationalists and ethno-nationalists in other parts of Europe, such as the Basque country and Corsica, as providing a model for their situations. However, in part, the change has come about because the implications of the province's conditional status appear in a different light as a result of demographic change. Thus, at the start of the troubles there seemed no prospect whatever that the principle of consent might facilitate any change to its constitutional position. The prospect that it might, has played a very large role in nationalist acceptance of the principle. The facilitation of cross-boundary links under the Good Friday Agreement, the soft sovereignty which that implies, the emphasis on minority rights and the explicit provision for the transfer of sovereignty if that is a wish of a majority are aspects of the Agreement that have attracted interest as possible elements in the resolution of ethnic conflicts elsewhere.

International interest in the Good Friday Agreement is a good indication of how much more favourable both the external environment and the ideological climate have become to a political settlement in Northern Ireland than was the case at the time of the Sunningdale Agreement. Of course, this is by no means the only reason why the prospects for the success of the Good Friday Agreement seem so much better than those of its ill-fated predecessor. The more inclusive nature of the Good Friday Agreement and the much greater level of popular support for the settlement are also important factors in improving its chances of survival. In this context, the most important factor has been the change in Unionist attitudes, brought about in part by demographic change which has made the case for accommodation with the Catholic community more compelling, but in part also by changes in the external environment which have reduced their fear of the consequences of compromise. However, as the difficulties that have been encountered in the implementation of the Agreement have underlined, the survival of the Good Friday Agreement is by no means assured.

Further, some aspects of the Good Friday Agreement actually run counter to current trends in world opinion. The most significant of these trends is the evolving consensus that the perpetrators of serious human rights violations should in no circumstances enjoy impunity, regardless both of the political context of their crimes and whether they were acting as the agents of an existing state or not. The release of members of paramilitary organisations, including individuals with convictions for more than one murder, under the Good Friday Agreement clearly runs counter to the spirit of this consensus. At the same time, the difficulties that the inquiry into the Bloody Sunday massacre in Derry in January 1972 has encountered have underlined the improbability that agents of the state will willingly provide a full account of their actions during the troubles. Further, the current emphasis on not forgetting the victims of conflict has become an obstacle to closing the chapter on the troubles in Northern Ireland while forging a new relationship between the communities has been made more difficult by the arguments generated by their differing interpretations of the past.

It is also possible to envisage changes in Northern Ireland's external environment that would undermine the Good Friday Agreement. The dissolution of the United Kingdom would be one such change. The most likely context of such a development would be Scottish independence, which has become a realistic possibility as a result of the growth of the popularity of the Scottish National Party since the establishment of devolved government in Scotland. Of course, it is conceivable that Scottish independence might be accommodated within the framework of the British–Irish Council, but there would be a substantial danger that such a process would be overwhelmed by an English backlash following Scottish repudiation of the union. Anything that fundamentally disturbed the basis of the participation of the United Kingdom or of the Republic of Ireland in European integration would also present a difficulty for the Good Friday Agreement, given the incentive provided by the two countries' membership of the European Union to their cooperation over

Northern Ireland. That might happen either if the European project failed due to the overload of expansion eastwards and the single currency or if Britain withdrew from the European Union when eventually faced with the choice between the adoption of the single currency or an end to its membership.

Global trends are more difficult to predict but might also have a strong bearing on the durability of the Good Friday Agreement. Thus, it is conceivable that a downturn in the world economy might exacerbate hostility towards globalisation sufficiently to undermine the current neo-liberal consensus on economic matters. In such circumstances a revival of class politics could occur and the recognition accorded to ethnic identities in the Good Friday Agreement might come to be seen as an obstacle to the transcending of sectarian divisions in class alliances. The codification of a new global consensus on the principle of self-determination would also be likely to have implications for the viability of the Good Friday Agreement, though continuing confusion and drift over this issue seems a much more likely eventuality, at least in the medium term.

Bibliography

Adams, G. (1986) *The Politics of Irish Freedom* (Dingle: Brandon).

Alford, J. (1986) 'North's strategic value is a non-issue', *The Irish Times*, 31 January.

Cassese, A. (1995) *Self-Determination of Peoples: a Legal Appraisal* (Cambridge: Cambridge University Press).

Coogan, T.P. (1995) *The Troubles: Ireland's Ordeal 1966–1995 and the Search for Peace* (London: Hutchinson).

Cox, M. (1998) 'Northern Ireland: the war that came in from the cold', *Irish Studies in International Affairs*, 9: 73–84.

Gillespie, P. (1999) 'NI accord is EU-style sovereignty pooling to optimise influence', *Irish Times*, 4 December.

HMSO (1993) *Joint Declaration: Downing Street, 15 December 1973* (Belfast).

HMSO (1995) *A New Framework for Agreement: a Shared Understanding between the British and Irish Governments to Assist Discussion and Negotiation Involving the Northern Ireland Parties* (Belfast).

Kelley, K. (1982) *The Longest War: Northern Ireland and the IRA* (Dingle: Brandon).

Mallie, E. and McKittrick, D. (1996) *The Fight for Peace: the Secret Story behind the Irish Peace Process* (London: Heinemann).

Munck, R. (1995) 'Irish Republicanism: containment or new departure', in A. O'Day (ed.), *Terrorism's Laboratory: the Case of Northern Ireland* (Aldershot: Dartmouth).

Oliver, Q. (1998) *Working for 'YES': the Story of the May 1998 Referendum in Northern Ireland* (Belfast: The 'Yes' Campaign).

Rolston, B. (1992) *Drawing Support: Murals in Northern Ireland* (Belfast: Beyond the Pale Publications).

Seitz, R. (1998) *Over Here* (London: Weidenfeld and Nicolson).

Seymour, M. (2000) 'Quebec and Canada at the crossroads: a nation within a nation', *Nations and Nationalism*, 6 (2): 227–55.

Sinn Féin (1987) *A Scenario for Peace* (Dublin).

Sinn Féin (1992) *Towards a Lasting Peace in Ireland* (Dublin).

Sterling, C. (1981) *The Terror Network: the Secret War of International Terrorism* (New York: Holt, Rinehart and Winston).

Whyte, J. (1990) *Interpreting Northern Ireland* (Oxford: Clarendon Press).

Chapter 9

Ireland and the international security environment: changing police and military roles

Eunan O'Halpin

Introduction

This chapter discusses Ireland's external defence, security and police engagements at the turn of the 21st century. These reflect significant developments in recent years in Ireland's commitments and policy outlook as a member both of the UN and of the EU. While these have taken place in the context of the collapse of Soviet power, it would be a mistake to ascribe them entirely to the end of the Cold War. Major changes in policing and security cooperation were an inevitable and expected consequence of increasing EU integration, even if the Iron Curtain had remained in place. Similarly, the manifest inadequacies of the UN's various essays in politico-military intervention in the cause of peace would surely have prompted radical change in the way that such operations were mandated and carried out. That in turn would have had major implications for the Irish army, whose operational *raison d'être* has since 1960 lain largely in international peacekeeping rather than in conventional external defence.

The changing climate has been reflected *inter alia* in the appearance and content of the state's first-ever White Papers on Foreign Policy (1996) and on Defence (2000), both documents which are intended to chart a path for Ireland in international affairs in the post-Cold War era, as well as in the uncontentious passage of far-reaching measures such as the Europol Act of 1997.

The visible internationalisation of Irish life in matters of security, defence and criminal affairs is nicely illustrated in a single issue of Ireland's daily journal of record, the *Irish Times*. On 29 July 2000 the newspaper carried the following major stories:

1 The arrest of a number of Irishmen and the seizure of a large quantity of weapons in the Croatian city of Split, action which followed the tracking by Irish and foreign police services of Irish republican suspects as they travelled across Europe. These were on an arms purchasing mission for two breakaway IRA groups, the 'Real IRA' and the 'Continuity IRA', which are opposed to the Good Friday Agreement to which the Provisional republican movement is a party.

2 A call by the Northern Ireland First Minister David Trimble for continued vigilance and intensified north/south cooperation, as it was 'vital for the two governments to work together to fight dissident republican groups . . . the fact that many attempted operations by dissidents had been frustrated proved that when the two jurisdictions co-operated they were effective in preventing paramilitary attacks'.
3 A profile of Major General Colm Mangan, whose appointment as chief of staff of the Irish Defence Forces from September 2000 had just been announced by the government. Under the heading 'New Chief of Staff prepared for EU role', the newspaper lays stress not only on General Mangan's extensive domestic and UN service, but on his periods of study and service with the German army and on his commitment to preparing the Irish army for operations as part of an integrated European Union force.
4 A report of Supreme Court hearings on the constitutionality of provisions of the Illegal Immigrants (Trafficking) Bill, a piece of legislation intended to provide an effective deportation process for persons denied asylum.
   The bill was introduced amidst much controversy about the large number of asylum seekers reaching Ireland, a state which until the late 1990s was virtually immune from non-EU immigration.
5 The conviction of an Englishman and three Nigerians for operating an elaborate multi-million-dollar fraud scheme from a Dublin base. The paper reported that an officer of the 'international operations branch of the US Secret Service' was on hand to liaise with the Garda about the case.

On the same day, although too late for that morning's newspapers, Customs officers searched a car which had arrived by ferry from France and found 250 kilos of cannabis, estimated to be worth IR2,500,000. The drugs were believed to have been brought up from Morocco through Spain, and the shipment was reportedly the work of an Irish drug dealer who had fled to Spain some time previously (*Irish Times*, 31 July 2000).

It will be seen that times have changed considerably in the last decade. We should, however, note the persistence of one enduringly sensitive theme in Irish public discourse about the state's external defence and security engagements, that of military neutrality (Keatinge 1984, 1996; Salmon 1989). This is despite changes in the post-Cold War European security environment which have seen Cold War neutrals such as Austria, Finland and Sweden combine in urging the EU towards collective security arrangements, and which have seen even ultra-neutral Switzerland enthusiastically embrace Partnership for Peace (PfP), the NATO-organised training and standards network. Despite Ireland's recent and much debated accession to PfP, military neutrality remains a sacred cow for most Irish politicians, resulting in fantastic linguistic contortions as ministers seek to reconcile that aspiration with the imperatives of deepening EU integration and the transformation seen in the 1990s in the nature of international military interventions sanctioned by the UN. The White Paper on Defence argues that:

> the State's long-standing policy of military neutrality has never been a limiting factor in the use of defence as an appropriate tool of international policy in the UN context and in the context of European Union (EU) membership having regard to the provisions of the Treaty of Amsterdam. (para. 1.3.7)

but the reality is that the issue remains very sensitive domestically. This is so even in an era when the state has finally seized the economic and social opportunities offered by European integration, and when the public have accepted the corollary of the increased Europeanisation not only of law making but of law enforcement without a qualm despite the dilution of national sovereignty involved.

Irish defence and the new Europe

For two decades after Irish accession to the EU, the conflicting views of member states, and the existence of NATO as the guarantor of Western European security against Eastern bloc attack, meant that no progress was made on the question of the desirability of framing defence and security arrangements covering the entire Union. After 1990 the collapse of Soviet power, the fragmentation of the Soviet Union itself, the violent disintegration of Yugoslavia, and the inevitability of EU expansion eastwards, provided a completely new security environment. Under the Treaty of Amsterdam of 1997, the EU accepted proposals from Sweden and Finland, two Cold War neutrals, for the adoption of the 'Petersberg Tasks', defined as 'humanitarian and rescue tasks, peacekeeping tasks and tasks of combat forces in crisis management' (McDonagh 1998: 117–19). These had considerable implications for individual EU states, particularly non-NATO members, because participation would necessitate a high degree of interoperability with the forces of other members. In December 1999 the EU's Helsinki summit advanced the matter considerably by adopting detailed proposals aimed at developing the Union's 'military and non-military crisis management capability as part of a strengthened common European policy on security and defence'. These measures include the development of

> an autonomous capacity to take decisions and, where NATO as a whole is not engaged, to launch and conduct EU-led military operations in response to international crises. This process will avoid unnecessary duplication and does not imply the creation of a European army . . . the European Council has agreed in particular the following: cooperating voluntarily in EU-led operations, Member States must be able, by 2003, to deploy within 60 days and sustain for at least 1 year military forces of up to 50,000–60,000 persons capable of the full range of Petersberg tasks. (European Council 1999)

To facilitate this, 'modalities will be developed for full consultation, cooperation and transparency between the EU and NATO, taking into account the needs of all EU Member States', and methods will be devised which would allow for non-EU NATO members 'and other interested States' to contribute to EU military crisis management, whilst 'respecting the Union's decision-making autonomy' (European Council 1999).

These developments have profound implications for the Irish defence forces, whose current international commitments to the UN, the Organisation for Security and Cooperation in Europe (OSCE) and other peacekeeping and confidence building bodies account for about 10 per cent of its active strength. They offer the prospect of international service within a coherent European military framework, and they provide the rationale for a fundamental reorientation of defence policy and practice. The Defence White Paper is at pains to argue that:

> participation in Petersberg Tasks will not affect our long-standing policy of military neutrality. Proposals for the development of European military forces which would be available to the EU to undertake Petersberg operations are indicative of the recognition of both the indivisibility of European security and the need for a collective response by Europeans to these challenges. The EU member states have set an agreed, voluntary target, known as a Headline Goal, to improve capabilities for Petersberg Tasks which they aim to meet by the year 2003. Ireland will maintain the sovereign decision over whether, when and how to commit Irish personnel to a Petersberg Task or to any overseas peacekeeping or crisis management operation. The EU have identified the capabilities to ensure effective performance in peace support and crisis management. These include: deployability, sustainability, interoperability, flexibility, mobility, survivability and command and control. The qualitative importance of these capabilities is borne out by Ireland's experience of peacekeeping and crisis management over many years. (3.2.7)

That statement requires further exploration, in the light both of the origins of Irish defence policy and of Ireland's international military engagements to date.

The origins of Irish defence policy

After 1922 Irish defence policy was theoretically based on the promise of collective security offered by the League of Nations (Kennedy 1996). The League's failures in the 1930s meant that this promise was never put to the test, although we should note that Ireland did offer to contribute troops to a League of Nations supervisory force in the Saarland in 1935 (O'Halpin 1999: 35). Because of the issue of partition, the new state would not countenance discussions with the United Kingdom on the collective defence of the British Isles. This was despite the fact that under the 1921 Anglo-Irish treaty, Britain retained extensive rights in independent Ireland in respect of naval operations, of airfields for Atlantic defence, and of war communications. In 1938, however, Britain relinquished these rights as part of a wider Anglo-Irish settlement. This made Irish neutrality, or at any rate non-belligerency, possible even if the United Kingdom, including Northern Ireland, were at war (O'Halpin 1999: 140–5), because Ireland was sheltered from all likely strategic threats by Great Britain, and Britain's strategic interests dictated that she control the seas and airspace around independent Ireland. In addition, Britain retained sovereignty over Northern Ireland, where land, air and sea forces were stationed. From a military point of view, independent Ireland was utterly incapable of defending herself. External defence was entirely in the hands of very limited land forces – when World War II broke out the army had less than 7,000 regular soldiers with virtually no equipment or modern weapons. After the German invasion of France and the Low Countries in the summer of 1940, detailed discussions were held and secret plans drawn up for combined Anglo-Irish defence against a German air or seaborne assault, but it is extremely doubtful whether, even with British help from troops in Northern Ireland, the state could have repelled a serious German attack. In the event, the danger of invasion passed by the autumn of 1941. From then until the end of the war in 1945 the biggest threat to Irish neutrality came from Britain and the United States, where Roosevelt was particularly unsympathetic to Ireland's refusal to provide naval facilities for Atlantic defence. The Irish softened the blow somewhat, at least as far as Britain was concerned, by very extensive covert cooperation in naval and air matters, as well as on security and counter-intelligence, although such unneutral activities remained highly secret and could not be publicly acknowledged in diplomatic debate.

Neutralist sentiment derives from a number of factors, some generational and some ideological. For the first generation of Irish leaders, neutrality in World War II was the final proof of the state's claim to sovereignty. The domestic political success of neutrality was, however, qualified by other results. Although it had little long-term impact on Anglo-Irish relations, it arguably deepened the gulf between the state and Northern Ireland, and it undoubtedly offended the American foreign policy elite which – the United States' own neutrality until December 1941 notwithstanding – regarded Irish neutrality as a wilful and cowardly policy which reaped all the benefits of Allied protection while incurring none of the costs, and which seriously threatened Allied security interests (Fanning 2000: 315–22; O'Halpin 2000). Irish isolation was compounded after World War II, when the state's application to join the United Nations was blocked due to Soviet objections. In 1949, furthermore, the government declined an American invitation to join the North Atlantic pact. This was done solely on the grounds of the existence of partition: indeed Sean MacBride, the minister who engineered the refusal, was at the time rabidly anti-Soviet, and publicly fearful for the future of western European democracy and Christianity. He afterwards made overtures to the United States for a bilateral defence pact, and for a time he appeared enthusiastic for a European defence community which he felt Ireland could join without compromising its stance against partition. He was also an enthusiastic advocate of Irish membership of the Council of Europe, which he portrayed as a bulwark against Soviet aggression. This was scarcely the viewpoint of an ideological neutral (Kennedy and O'Halpin 2000: 30). When Ireland finally succeeded in securing admission to the UN in 1955, the state pursued a distinctive line which was at once stridently anti-Communist, critical of the arms race and particularly of nuclear weapons, and quite strongly anti-colonial. These policies reflected the twin threads of Ireland's self-image as a small newly independent ex-colonial state with no axe to grind (except, of course, its differences with its nearest neighbour the United Kingdom, whose claim to Northern Ireland the state still termed illegitimate), and its attachment to Western political values (Skelly 1996).

Ireland's international military involvements since 1955

Ireland was particularly attracted by the prospect of military service under the UN, as it was generally accepted that such service was not inconsistent with neutrality. From 1958, when 50 officers took up duty as UN observers in the Sinai, UN operations for 40 years provided the main opportunity for Irish soldiers to serve abroad. This is reflected in the fact that cumulatively Ireland remains the sixth largest contributor of troops to UN operations (Defence Forces).

The initial Sinai commitment was followed two years later by participation in the UN peacekeeping mission in the Congo, where from 1960 to 1964 Ireland provided a succession of composite battalions to support the UN's attempts to hold the country together in the face of a secessionist war. This proved domestically popular, as the engagement fitted Ireland's self-image as a non-aligned European state, untarnished by an imperial past and sympathetic to the difficulties faced by the emerging post-colonial states of Africa and Asia (Skelly 1996). The Congo proved an exotic, challenging and sometimes costly engagement. It was Ireland's first exposure to the problems of mandate, command, intelligence provision, logistics and operational cooperation between foreign forces of widely varying competence, skill, commitment and military outlook which were to characterise the UN operations in which Ireland participated thereafter. Despite the extra-ordinary difficulties encountered, the experience was crucial in building the army's self-esteem, because it allowed troops to measure themselves against other forces in terms of training, doctrines and discipline. It also provided a compelling reason for some overdue improvements in equipment which had previously been refused on grounds of cost. Despite the confused purpose and outcome of the UN's intervention, and the loss of 26 Irish soldiers on operations, the Congo transformed the army from being *de facto* simply a lightly armed gendarmerie expected to provide domestic security and a ceremonial presence into an instrument of Irish foreign policy. That development outweighed the fact that Irish lives were undoubtedly lost because of inadequate weapons and equipment, confused rules of engagement, poor communications and the absence of common operating procedures amongst the various national contingents in the UN force.

The Congo operation ended in 1964, leaving the army with nowhere to go beyond the state's borders. However, in the same year the government took the decision to provide troops for the UN force in Cyprus, after initial hesitation because of fear that they would be accused of contributing to the partition of the island. For almost a decade thereafter Cyprus was the main overseas theatre of operations for the army, with a battalion forming part of the UN force on a six-month rotation. The primacy of national security considerations was, however, demonstrated in the summer of 1974 as the major Cyprus engagement ended, when an Irish battalion was withdrawn from Sinai following bombings by Northern Ireland loyalist paramilitaries which left 31 people dead in Dublin and Monaghan. This period was regarded as the Irish army's darkest hour because it denied officers and men the chance of overseas service. By 1978, the domestic security situation had improved sufficiently to persuade the government to despatch a battalion for service with the UN in Southern Lebanon (UNIFIL). This, one of the eleven UN missions in which the army is currently involved, remains its major overseas commitment, although there are some doubts about its long-term suitability. Those serving in Lebanon are components of a lightly armed, poorly protected and widely dispersed force in the middle of what remained a war zone until the Israeli withdrawal of May 2000, and their safety depends in part on other national detachments, some of which are poorly organised and trained.

This problem of military standards and interoperability has become increasingly salient in the 1990s, as other opportunities for service in Europe have arisen through the OSCE, the EU (notably through the European Communities Monitoring Mission in Yugoslavia in the early 1990s), and in UN-mandated but NATO-led operations in the Balkans. The defence forces currently participate in eleven such missions, the largest contributions being in Bosnia (SFOR) and Kosovo (KFOR) (Defence Forces). After the collapse of the Soviet Union Irish observers found it instructive to see how quickly other European neutrals such as Finland, Sweden and Austria, which like Ireland had been mainstays of UN peacekeeping operations during the Cold War, began to seek a common European approach to security questions and to reorient their armed forces accordingly. By the mid-1990s a serious dialogue was underway within the EU on a future security framework as an element in a common foreign and security policy, and this eventually resulted in the adoption of the 'Petersberg tasks' in 1997 (White Paper on Foreign Policy, paras 7.1–18). In the post-Cold War era of the 1990s, furthermore, the UN's own view of its military role evolved significantly. The old conception of lightly armed 'blue helmet' operations bringing calm and confidence in the aftermath of conflict – never an accurate picture of UN operations – was discredited by experience in Somalia, Yugoslavia and Rwanda. Initially under Boutros Boutros Ghalli and subsequently under Kofe Annan, UN headquarters' attitude to peace operations shifted markedly, with a move away from direct organisation and control towards reliance on existing regional security organisations, operating under UN mandate, as the most effective providers of armed interventions.

In parallel with this change in peacekeeping philosophy at UN headquarters came developments in European and EU security doctrine, most importantly the iteration of the 'Petersberg tasks' in the Treaty of Amsterdam. The Petersberg tasks require a degree of military sophistication well beyond what was achievable in traditional multinational UN missions. These have been particularly welcome to the Irish defence forces, because they mean that the era of symbolic contributions independent of effectiveness is over, and that participating states will have to be able to provide functionally efficient units which can play their part as integrated elements of larger formations. While the basic training of Irish soldiers has generally been regarded as good, in the past there were acute difficulties in providing sufficient collective training at unit level because of the nature of Irish military service, with soldiers constantly being assigned to a miscellany of secondary tasks, and units continually losing officers to UN and other international service. The need for interoperability with other forces requires the standardisation of operational procedures and of equipment, which in effect means a levelling up for the

Irish particularly in matters such as communications and infantry transport. The army has already begun to adjust to this new environment, as the practice of providing composite infantry battalions and smaller groups drawn from across the defence forces has gradually been replaced by that of sending functional units carrying out the same basic tasks as they do in Ireland: thus the main Irish contribution to IFOR and SFOR in Sarajevo came from the military police corps, while a heavy transport company was assigned to KFOR in Kosovo and, most strikingly, a detachment of the special forces Ranger Wing were sent to join the INTERFET mission in East Timor. Lastly, in December 1999 Ireland finally joined the PfP network, after much political dithering and well-publicised opposition from peace groups. The military reasons for doing so were obvious: PfP is the best vehicle for training and development, enabling participating states to learn from each other (the Irish army sees its long experience of UN peacekeeping operations as a crucial area where it has much to offer other European armies which hitherto have been organised and trained overwhelmingly to fight wars). The political reasons were also fairly clear: while a NATO construct, PfP embraces almost every European state, including Switzerland and Russia, and this was a powerful argument against the simplistic charge that it was simply an ante-room for states wishing to join NATO. Irish membership of PfP sent an important message to the other neutral states in the EU, a number of which were very impatient at what they saw as Irish particularism bordering on irresponsibility about the security dimension of European integration.

The attractiveness of these European developments for a professional military establishment is obvious: it means that soldiers abroad in the planned Rapid Reaction Force will carry out much the same military tasks for which they have been trained at home, in the same unit and with the same equipment, and as functioning elements of an integrated multinational military organisation. This contrasts with earlier UN operations, where Irish soldiers would form one mixed unit, in a patchwork of national detachments of very varied quality and training. Consequently the new approach facilitates a synthesis of training and organisation for both national and international tasks. This is supported in principle by the development programme outlined in the state's first-ever and long-delayed Defence White Paper. This envisages a properly armed light infantry force of sufficient strength and 'capabilities to meet needs at home and to make a significant contribution abroad', in itself a tacit admission of how ill-equipped the army currently is for service overseas. Some doubts persist on whether the requisite money will be forthcoming to achieve the aim of having an appropriately armed and equipped infantry battalion constantly in readiness to operate as part of a European force for Petersberg tasks purposes, while there is little evidence that the Department of Defence takes seriously the need to change its approach to civilian control of the defence forces. The army's way of coping with these uncertainties is to engage as quickly and as deeply as possible in European security arrangements so that the state will have no option but to provide the necessary resources which it has promised.

Public perception of this new style of military involvement has generally been positive, yet hesitations remain. The influential and vociferous Irish development and justice NGO sector in particular remains suspicious of anything that smacks of military cooperation with the traditional western powers and especially with NATO. From the invasion of Kuwait to the despoliation of Kosovo, such groups have argued that the use of military force – even when sanctioned by the UN – is never justified because such action also serves the interests of the United States and other western powers (see e.g. *Examiner*, 10 April 1999). Yet the same groups which argued against outside interference in Kosovo and later criticised Irish involvement in KFOR in 1999 on the grounds, *inter alia*, that these operations drew on NATO resources and were under NATO command, demanded, in much the same sharp tones, international military intervention to prevent an ethnic catastrophe in East Timor. Indeed, pro-East Timorese feeling was so strong within the Irish development lobby that no public protest was raised at the despatch of Ireland's least pacific soldiers, a special forces unit. These were sent not to wear the blue helmet but, in conjunction with Australian and New Zealand special forces, to carry out border reconnaissance and to provide an aggressive and credible deterrent to Indonesian-backed infiltration from West Timor.

Cumulatively, recent developments in Irish participation in UN, EU and international security networks have overcome some of the taboos about military neutrality which have long impeded serious discussion of Ireland's defence and security needs and responsibilities. Yet, as the debate on PfP indicates, many politicians continue to run scared of the charge that they are simply NATO stooges. They remain diffident about making a pragmatic, an ideological or a moral case for Irish military involvement in an EU regional security organisation, and instead take refuge in generalities or in silence.

The internationalisation of Irish policing and law enforcement

Since 1922 Ireland has habitually dealt with problems of non-political criminal activity with an external dimension through informal bilateral dialogue with friendly countries. Although Ireland was a party to various conventions negotiated through the League of Nations dealing with problems such as trafficking in women and drugs, the state's geographic isolation and the fact that it was shielded from Europe by Britain meant that until the 1970s it had little experience of these or of other varieties of international crime. Since 1973 the Garda Siochana have, however, seen a marked internationalisation of their activities, in parallel with the expansion in the transnational activities of terrorist and particularly of criminal organisations. This internationalisation has taken three forms: increased bilateral dealings with foreign police forces, most importantly those of the state's nearest neighbour the United Kingdom; involvement through the UN and other international bodies in the development or restoration of efficient police services in divided communities; and, since the 1970s, increasing collaborative work against transnational crime under the aegis of the EU. We will examine these in turn.

The Garda's most important and long-standing bilateral links are those with United Kingdom police forces, most importantly the RUC and the Metropolitan Police Special Branch. The main focus is on republican terrorism related to partition, together with intelligence on Northern Irish loyalist terrorism directed against the Irish state. Although these links have operated to a greater or lesser degree since the foundation of the state, their political sensitivity was such that they were explicitly acknowledged only in 1973 as part of the abortive Sunningdale Agreement. Since then the deepening of these links has been publicly referred to from time to time, notably at the signing of the Anglo-Irish agreement of 1985. They are now a familiar element of Anglo-Irish dialogue, despite occasional controversies and accusations of breaches of faith and lapses in security on both sides of the Irish border (*Irish Independent*, 29 July 2000). There have also been increased exchanges on non-political crime (see, e.g., the Garda Press Office note on a visit of the Commissioner of the Metropolitan Police, 14 January 1999 at http://www.garda.ie).

Since the 1950s the Garda have also had some bilateral dealings with United States, Canadian and other Western police and security agencies, in respect of both non-political crime and international terrorism. Until the collapse of the Soviet Union, there was also liaison relating to Cold War security, espionage and subversion (matters which were also the subject of dialogue between Irish army intelligence and agencies such as the United States' CIA and Britain's MI5). Nowadays problems such as intelligence on Islamic terrorism are dealt with through these channels. Irish willingness to cooperate with Western governments in such spheres reflects long-standing policy, which reached its apogee in the extensive security liaison operated with Britain and the United States during the Second World War, of diluting the impact of military neutrality through covert cooperation with the Allies (O'Halpin 1999: 225–37).

In addition to such bilateral links, the work of the Garda has been profoundly affected by the evolution of the EU. There, new frameworks for police cooperation have evolved, initially outside the formal frameworks of the community but now incorporated as the 'third pillar' covering justice and home affairs issues under article 30 of the 1997 Treaty of Amsterdam. The establishment of Europol as a criminal intelligence clearing house, analytical and coordinating agency has seen a significant increment in Irish collaboration with other EU states as well as the pooling of much information. There are now Garda officers stationed at Europol headquarters in The Hague and in Madrid. Europol's brief extends beyond the exchange of information: the organisation also aims to provide support expertise for investigations conducted by police forces, and like other Brussels institutions seeks to promote the harmonisation of forensic and other investigative techniques across the Union. In its 15–16 October 1999 meeting at Tampere in Finland the European Council endorsed further developments in Europol's role, encouraging the formation of cross-national task forces of law enforcement officers and enhancing Europol's planning role in relation to combined operations against transnational organised crime (Europol, 26 July 2000). If not on course to become the EU's equivalent of the FBI, the organisation is already far more than an information clearing house. In December 1999, furthermore, the EU summit at Helsinki approved the establishment of an Anti-Fraud Office (OLAF), and it signalled additional future moves to combat white-collar crime at Union level which various authorities have identified as necessary to increase effectiveness (Notre Europe, 2000). We should also note an increase in the Garda's bilateral dealings with non-EU states, illustrated not only in the recent Croatian police action against Irish arms smuggling but in the 'Memorandum of Understanding' with the Russian Interior Ministry which the Garda Commissioner signed in Moscow in February 2000 to 'develop international cooperation in the field of law enforcement with a view to establishing and strengthening the co-operation between both countries' in matters including training and the exchange of criminal intelligence (Garda 2000).

Such developments, the logical corollary of the principle of the free movement of goods and people upon which the EU is based, have taken place largely without comment in Ireland. This is in part perhaps because the public case for intensified cooperation is presented largely in terms of the manifest need to combat the transnational drugs trade, as well as the other kinds of criminal activity which fall within Europol's scope including the operation of clandestine immigration networks; illicit vehicle trafficking; trafficking in people including child pornography; various kinds of monetary and financial crime; trafficking in radioactive and nuclear substances; and terrorism (White Paper on Foreign Policy, paras 3.90–96). Public acquiescence in the evident Europeanisation of significant elements of law enforcement also reflects an enduring propensity in Irish public attitudes since the 1970s to accept from Brussels what would never be tolerated if emanating from the national government.

A final aspect of the internationalisation of policing which has impacted on the Garda is that of overseas service for international organisations operating in post-conflict situations. Since the 1970s Garda officers have served in places such as Namibia, Cambodia, the Western Sahara, Cyprus and Bosnia–Herzegovina, helping to develop communally acceptable policing in divided societies. At present about fifty members of the force, representing about 0.5 per cent of strength, are engaged on such work. Despite the strong case against systematic interstate police cooperation which could be made on grounds both of sovereignty and of civil liberties, problems of drug-related crime have made international cooperation both inevitable and politically acceptable; the 1996 White Paper on Foreign Policy made a virtue of coordinated EU action in this area, and such arguments undoubtedly simplified the matter of Irish membership of Europol. While not a fully fledged EU criminal investigation bureau, this is a complex and sophisticated organisation and its role is bound to increase in respect not only of drugs and terrorism but of trafficking in people, of internationally organised theft and of financial crime.

Conclusion

The 1990s have seen a marked shift in Ireland's external security, defence and law enforcement relationships. It is now taken for granted that the development of the EU, and the political and economic liberalisation in central and eastern Europe since the end of the Cold War, mean that it is no longer possible publicly to separate issues of foreign policy entirely from those of security, defence and law enforcement. Across the political spectrum it is taken as axiomatic that drug smuggling, trafficking in humans, and a range of white-collar crimes which feed off the freedom of movement offered by the wider European space can only be combated effectively through international police and judicial action. The late 1990s has seen not simply the intensification but the codification of relationships in relation to law enforcement throughout the EU. While the statutory frameworks for Irish participation are couched in EU terms, it is abundantly clear that bilateral dealings with non-EU states will also increase.

In the realms of defence and security, there have been both continuity and change. Since its establishment the state has worked quite closely though discreetly with Britain and to a lesser extent the United States on questions of external subversion, of espionage and in recent years of Irish and foreign terrorism. Since joining the EU, interaction with other European countries on such matters has also grown considerably. The last years of the 20th century have also seen some redefinition of what Irish military neutrality does and does not mean. The UN has moved away from the direct organisation of peacekeeping operations towards reliance on regional security networks, while a genuine security dimension in EU activities has emerged with the Petersberg tasks. This has prompted an overdue reorientation of the Irish defence forces designed to enable them to play an integrated part in future regional security operations, a development which is likely to be militarily more challenging, and probably safer for individual soldiers, than traditional blue helmet operations such as those in the Congo or the Lebanon. Discussion of Ireland's role in future EU and UN security operations, and of the threat which these do or do not pose to the powerful if ahistorical ideal of genuine Irish neutrality will, however, remain dogged by the timidity of the Irish political elite.

References

Sources

(a) Newspapers

Irish Times
Examiner
Irish Independent

(b) Books and articles

Department of Defence (2000) *White Paper on Defence* (Dublin: Department of Defence).

Department of Foreign Affairs (1996) *Challenges and Opportunities Abroad: White Paper on Foreign Policy* (Dublin: Department of Foreign Affairs).

Fanning, R. (2000) 'Raison d'Etat and the evolution of Irish foreign policy', in Kennedy, M. and Skelly, J.M. (eds), *Irish Foreign Policy, 1919–1966: from Independence to Internationalism* (Dublin: Four Courts Press).

Keatinge, P. (1984) *A Singular Stance: Irish Neutrality in the 1980s* (Dublin: Institute of Public Administration).

Keatinge, P. (1996) *European Security: Ireland's Choices* (Dublin: Institute of European Affairs).

Kennedy, M. (1996) *Ireland and the League of Nations, 1919–1946: International Relations, Diplomacy and Politics* (Dublin: Irish Academic Press).

Kennedy, M. and O'Halpin, E. (2000) *Ireland and the Council of Europe: from Isolation Towards Integration* (Strasbourg: Council of Europe).
McDonagh, Bobby (1998) *Original Sin in a Brave New World* (Dublin: Institute of European Affairs).
Notre Europe (2000) *Protecting European Citizens Against International Crime* (Paris: Notre Europe).
O'Halpin, E. (1999) *Defending Ireland: the Irish State and Its Enemies since 1922* (Oxford: Oxford University Press).
O'Halpin, E. (2000) 'Irish–Allied security relations and the "American note" crisis: new evidence from British records', *Irish Studies in International Affairs*, 9, pp. 103–18.
Salmon, T. (1989) *Unneutral Ireland an Ambivalent and Unique Security Policy* (Oxford: Clarendon Press).
Skelly, J.M. (1996) *Irish Diplomacy at the United Nations, 1945–1965: National Interests and the International Order* (Dublin: Irish Academic Press).

(c) Websites
Defence Forces (http://www.military.ie)
Garda Siochana (http://www.garda.ie)

Chapter 10

Ireland and human rights

Eilís Ward

Introduction

The collapse of the former Soviet Union eased a path through the biggest barrier to effective application of human rights in international relations – the Cold War divide (Donnelly 1993). Now, the pursuit of human rights by a state no longer runs the risk of collapsing under East–West divisions. Ireland is not alone as a state that endorses human rights as a central component of its foreign policy framework (Department of Foreign Affairs 1996). The type of language used to address human rights in Ireland's foreign policy manifesto – the White Paper on Foreign Policy – would not be out of place in the meeting chambers of international organisations such as the OSCE and the UN bodies.

However, at the same time, there have been several developments in the structure and processing of Irish foreign policy in recent years that point to a fresh orientation towards a foreign policy that concerns itself with human rights beyond the rhetoric of international diplomacy. Perhaps echoing the international trend or, perhaps, reflecting some internal changes, human rights considerations have formed a significant part of the state's discourse on its foreign policy over the last decade.

As Ireland took over the Presidency of the Council of Europe in 1999 then Minister of Foreign Affairs, David Andrews, stressed the ethical values to which Ireland was committed in the framing of foreign policy issues. Minister of State for Foreign Affairs, Liz O'Donnell, with special responsibility for human rights, regularly refers to the defining nature of human rights in the development of Irish foreign policy (O'Donnell 1998).

At an institutional level, three significant developments have underscored positive change. First, arising from White Paper recommendations, the government established a human rights unit within the Department of Foreign Affairs (DFA) in 1996. Secondly, a joint Department of Foreign Affairs/NGO Standing Committee on Human Rights was subsequently established to formalise the ongoing dialogue between officials and the many Irish NGOs campaigning on human rights and related issues. A third departure was the establishment of an inter-departmental committee, hosted by DFA, to discuss the wider implications of human rights across government policy.

The appointment of the former Irish President, Mary Robinson to the position of UN High Commission for Human Rights, while not connected to any state policy (the appointment was on personal merit) appeared to strengthen a perceived relationship between Irish foreign policy and human rights. A student of Irish foreign policy history would not be surprised by such a perception. Within the chambers of the League of Nations and of the UN, an audit of Ireland's participation would reveal a concern for the pre-eminence of international law. From the late 1980s onwards Ireland's record of ratifying international rights regimes improved (Swift 1995).

The true test of a human rights policy is, however, the pursuit of rhetoric through policy implementation into the realm of actions. Ritual condemnation of human rights abuses comes with little cost. This chapter will argue that while Ireland has a good record in supporting the construction of human rights institutions and has begun to build its own internal structure to raise human rights as a central concern of Iveagh House, there is little evidence to suggest, so far, that human rights are a defining theme of foreign policy (Holmes *et al.* 1993).

Such a conclusion must be attenuated by a recognition of the real constraints on what we call 'Irish' foreign policy. It is somewhat difficult to talk about a coherent, not to mention sovereign, 'Irish' foreign policy in the context of the Common Foreign and Security Policy (CFSP) of the EU. Not only does the CFSP process require internal agreement within the EU and therefore a log-rolling of positions towards one consensus posture, but the restraints of the CFSP dictate, generally, how EU members behave in other multi-lateral forums such as the UN and with other regional actors such as the Association of South East Asian Nations (ASEAN). However, EU policy is not the sum total of Irish policy.

This chapter will take a focused case study on the evolution of Ireland's position on East Timor – an issue that raised many sensitive human rights issues and challenged the world community's commitment to those rights. However, taking a focused case study as the centre of an exploration of Irish foreign policy and human rights prompts one question: can we extrapolate from one very particular case? Indeed, it might be suggested that the case of East Timor is remarkable because it was highly unusual. Ireland had nothing to 'lose' in taking a stance against the Indonesian regime. There was no national interest, be it political or economic, at stake. The extent and consistency in human rights violations within East Timor by the Indonesian government made the case fairly straightforward. Organisations such as Amnesty International and Human Rights Watch provided regular information on abuses such as arbitrary detention and execution of political prisoners, torture and violations of labour rights. Indonesia's legitimacy as a target for criticism arising from human rights violations was found in, *inter alia*, its adoption of the Vienna Declaration on Human Rights in 1993 which reaffirmed its signatories to the purposes and principles laid down in the Universal Declaration of Human Rights (Glasius 1999: 9).

This case study allows us to trace the manner in which a human rights issue evolved within the Irish system. Furthermore, the case of East Timor was rarely far from Ireland's domestic and international agenda in the 1990s. More specifically, this case study allows us to explore two salient aspects to Ireland's human rights policies.

First, is the issue of the role of organised civil society. Secondly, the case study underlines the complex relationship between the Irish foreign policy process and the greater foreign policy institutions and process of the EU.

The study reveals the manner in which the state negotiated, over a long time, a path between the domestic consensus on East Timor and its extra-national obligations to the process of consensus building in the EU. Like the case of South Africa, it is highly unlikely that the state would have initiated this dialogue over its policy position without that domestic pressure from below. Thus the study underlines the critical lead role taken by public opinion and civil society in Ireland's policy in relation to the human rights dimensions of the case of East Timor.

The chapter is organised into three sections. The first section presents a brief history of the human rights dimensions of Irish foreign policy up to and including the recent institutions development referred to above. The second section will present the issue of East Timor, focusing particularly on the period from 1992 to 1996 when Ireland took over the EU Presidency at a time when East Timor was high on the agenda of the CFSP. The third section will draw conclusions.

Human rights: issues and mechanisms

While it is difficult to speak coherently of 'human rights' in international relations terms prior to the foundation of the UN, Ireland's participation in international forums in the post-independence period did exhibit a commitment to the same pool of ideas from whence human rights responsibilities evolved – the supreme importance of international law the many dimensions of the post-colonial experience and the ethical dimensions of international relations itself.

Ireland was a key articulator of the ideals of the League of Nations and a keen defender of the importance of non-violent resolution of conflict (Kennedy 1996: 19–29). In other words, it could not be considered to take a position in defence of power politics or the politics of domination or control. These ideas were reflected during Ireland's 'golden period' of membership of the UN (Skelly 1997). During the 1950s and into the 1960s Ireland, while pursuing national protectionism at home, was defending internationalism abroad. The external orientation altered, however, with the EU membership process in the 1960s and the UN became a less important focus of activity (Keatinge 1973). The 1970s saw an increase in economic pragmatism reflected in support for the process of integration in Europe. At this stage of the EU's development, external action on human rights was not on the agenda for discussion. The rise of Irish bilateral aid programmes at this time linked Ireland's increasing confidence as an international actor with its growing domestic wealth and its historical orientation towards the developing world.

A general trend towards humanitarianism marked, for instance, Ireland's negotiations through the EC on the round of Lomé negotiations that began in 1988 and were completed in December 1990 (Holmes *et al.* 1993: 128–32). This overall perspective was reflected in Ireland's participation in regional EC negotiations with Central and South America during the 1970s and 1980s (Holmes *et al.* 1993: 132–8). It would not be controversial to argue, however, that Ireland did not begin to formally acknowledge the human rights dimensions to its own domestic policy process and institutions until the late 1980s. While siding with institutional arrangements (such as in Lomé or the EU San José Process) that supported the inclusion of human rights, the absence of policies that actively pursued these arrangements has been noted (Kirby 1992: 137–41).

Taking a broad sweep of Ireland's human rights history, the issue that immediately stands out is undoubtedly that of Ireland's position on apartheid in South Africa during the 1980s. For Ireland, the South African case impinged on both economic concerns and ethical considerations arising from human rights commitments – the latter impact particularly led Ireland to become a constant critic of South Africa in the UN and the then EC (Laffan 1988: 24–5). The public abhorrence of apartheid and domestic condemnation came to a dramatic head when, following a strike of a group of workers in a Dublin chain store over the handling of South African fruit in 1984, the government agreed to unilaterally impose sanctions on the importation of certain South African products. The ban was imposed following protracted debate between governmental departments and the cabinet in December 1985.

A key to understanding why Ireland took this measure, alone of its fellow EU members, was the strength of public opinion and the positions of organised interest groups within the state. The Irish Anti-Apartheid Movement (IAAM) had been first established in 1964 and became a significant force within the Irish polity. Traditional Irish missionary links to Africa had created a sympathy for African development issues, maintained by the fundraising activities of missionary groups. The Catholic Church, the major trade unions and other organised interest groups had been engaged in lobbying and public activism on the issue of apartheid for some time. The combined effect was to create a powerful bloc of public opinion that the government could not ignore.

The debate on South Africa can also be understood within a period of change in Irish society within which, *inter alia*, we can locate the rise of civil society activism on issues of peace and justice in foreign policy. From the late 1960s on, the church-linked aid agencies became a feature of Irish society and, inspired by the liberation of Vatican Two on Catholicism, they brought a more political dimension to aid debates than had existed before. The church's engagement in foreign policy politics is illustrated by the request from Catholic Bishop Eamon Casey, acting as Chairperson of Trócaire (the church's aid agency), that Ireland should break off relations with the United States because of the latter's policies in Central America (Kirby 1992: 154).

The first generation of groups founded to promote international solidarity can be traced to this time. As Ireland's multilateralism increased both regionally (within the EU) and internationally (within the UN) so too did the scope of issues for consideration by Irish foreign policy-makers and the world view of Irish citizenry. The extending vista is reflected strongly in the 1980s when there was a flourishing of groups campaigning for human rights issues in Central and South America, Asia, and in Africa. The Irish Nicaragua support group was particularly vocal during the 1980s, leading one politician to remark that no Irish diplomat would feel free to take anything other than a progressive line on Nicaragua (Kirby 1992: 162).

Such activism was not unique to Ireland but reflected a global demand for a pluralisation of global governance and the introduction of normative concerns into international relations (Gordenker and Weiss 1996). Furthermore, the rise of civil society activism in foreign policy issues in Ireland echoed the rise of Irish social movement politics, namely the women's movement and the birth of environmental politics.

The debate on human rights in South Africa prefigured that which was to come on East Timor in the 1990s. A significant difference between the two, however, was the nature of the state institutions. Much of the debate on South Africa was characterised by open confrontation (symbolised by the strike and picket lines which became a magnet for protest nationwide). By the mid-1990s, when East Timor was inserted onto the Irish foreign policy agenda, the state had formalised linkages between its foreign policy elite and the informed public. This reorientation arose out of specific initiatives, referred to earlier, but also from a statewide policy of social organisation based on partnership rather than adversarial politics.

Undoubtedly, the most significant change in Ireland's foreign policy landscape was the establishment of the parliamentary Joint Committee on Foreign Affairs in 1993. The committee's brief was to scrutinise legislation and to provide a forum for debate. In addition, foreign policy decision-makers – DFA officials and the government members – were accountable to the committee. This meant that officials were obliged to defend and explain policies and engage in discussions with committee members. An important function of the committee, furthermore, was its role as a conduit for public concerns on foreign policy into the government institutions. Committee procedures allowed the soliciting of submissions and any organisation or individual could seek to make a presentation, thus placing any item on the agenda. The committee's meetings became a key animating site for parliamentary debate on Irish foreign policy.

An unintentional impact of the committee's establishment was the reorganisation of the NGO sector under Dóchas, an umbrella group of NGOs involved in human rights, advocacy and developmental work, in 1993. Dóchas arose from a merger between two organisations seeking to coordinate NGOs when dealing with the committee and in the face of the growing influence of the EU on Irish foreign policy and development policies (CONGOOD 1993).

The 1994 elections, which saw a coalition of Fine Gael, the Labour Party and Democratic Left returned to power, were to usher in the initiatives, referred to above, that have further significantly changed the foreign policy landscape. One of the first initiatives of the new Minister for Foreign Affairs, Dick Spring (the Labour Party), was to launch the White Paper process including public consultations on a range of related themes. Seven such consultations took place early in 1995. One of their functions was to feed public opinion into the bureaucratic White Paper process. The document was eventually published (in 1996) just in time for Ireland's term at the helm of the EU beginning in July 1996.

The White Paper was indeed a radical departure in the history of Irish foreign policy, not least of all because it presented a comprehensive and coherent view of the totality of policy issues and how best to operationalise policy goals. Referring to the three relevant intergovernmental institutions through which Ireland works (the UN, the EU and the OSCE) the chapter on human rights set out the broad policy framework. Ireland was committed, *inter alia*, to the universality and indivisibility of human rights, strongly identified with the 1993 Vienna declaration, accepted that there was a society beyond the society of states from whence norms informing international relations could emanate, would seek to strengthen human rights instruments at intergovernmental level and recognised the importance of NGOs in promoting human rights. Separate subsections dealt with the relationship between human rights and development, human rights education, resources for human rights and issues of monitoring. Concrete proposals were included within the chapter, several of which arose from existing or pending commitments based on reporting requirements under international covenants or conventions.

Unlike many of the commitments, which required long-term policy evolution, the international changes proposed were put in place quite swiftly. The Human Rights Unit (HRU) was established in 1996 and the DFA/NGO Standing Committee on Human Rights the following year. Because of the commitments to the EU Presidency, however, the HRU did not function until 1997 – a delay which speaks of pressure on staffing within the department and the drain caused by the Presidency, but also underlines one of the difficulties facing the unit: resource allocation. A staff of four DFA officials was appointed to the unit.

The unit's work can be roughly divided into five categories. First, there is outreach work, including hosting the DFA/NGO standing committee but also acting as the public's port of call for any human rights queries to the department. The state/civil society dialogue was extended with the establishment in 1988 of an annual public forum on human rights. Secondly, the unit functions as the human rights expert within both the DFA and across other governmental departments. In this context the inter-departmental committee, chaired by the head of the HRU, provides a platform to discuss, for instance, the impact of conventions on social and public policy. Within the DFA itself, while the desk structure remains, the HRU fits somewhere between the desks to act as adviser, or informant, for any human rights issues that arise within any of the desk areas. Thirdly, the HRU is charged with responsibility for all reporting requirements such as compiling Ireland's national reports on the Rights of the Child. Fourthly, the HRU is charged with responding to parliamentary questions on human rights issues and, as with DFA officials generally, can be called upon by the Joint Committee on Foreign Affairs. The fifth responsibility involves representing Ireland at relevant intergovernmental meetings such as the CFSP Working Group on Human Rights (COHOM) which meets in Brussels.

A sixth, albeit less demanding, responsibility has been added to the HRU's brief with the establishment of Human Rights Commissions in Northern Ireland and in the south arising from the Good Friday Agreement. Primary responsibility for both commissions rests with the Department of Justice and, at the time of writing, the HRU's involvement was limited to information provision and maintaining a watching brief.

The DFA/NGO Standing Committee on Human Rights marked an unprecedented step in that it gave direct access by non-state actors to the foreign policy process. The White Paper charged the committee to provide a 'framework for a regular exchange of views between the department and representatives of the NGO community' (Department of Foreign Affairs 1996). Members of the committee are appointed by the DFA and tend to come from the NGOs with whom the DFA has an existing relationship or are individual experts. Two places are reserved for nominees of the NGO sector itself. The term of office for each member runs for two years. The committee meets several times a year, facing an extensive and varied agenda of items, and is chaired by the head of the HRU. It proceeds on the basis of presentations and discussions – the content of which is brought to the attention of the Minister of Foreign Affairs.

Human rights, East Timor and Ireland

When the Minister of Foreign Affairs, Dick Spring, walked out of a high-level EU meeting with his Indonesian counterpart, Ali Alatas, in New York in September 1995, the action may not have caused much of a stir beyond his surprised department officials. But for East Timor supporters back home in Ireland, the action was a valuable expression of the position that Mr Spring and his government had taken on East Timor over the previous period. In a press interview later, Mr Spring explained his decision to leave the meeting by the 'berating' he had received from Mr Alatas because of his (Spring's) public condemnation of the Indonesian government on East Timor (*Irish Times*, 13 July 1995). Mr Alatas, it appeared, would have preferred the more traditional diplomatic approach of 'quiet diplomacy'.

But how did this remarkable event come about? Why did the Irish Foreign Minister take such an interest in East Timor that he risked raising it at a meeting of EU officials and the Indonesian government on talks relating to EU/ASEAN trade? To understand this question I have below presented, first, a brief summary of the international dimensions of the East Timor case and, secondly, the evolution of East Timor within the Irish body politic.

East Timor – a brief background

With the collapse of the colonial system in 1975, Portugal's former colonies found themselves freed to assert the right of self-determination. East Timor, as a small Portuguese colony contiguous to Indonesian territory (Indonesia had been a Dutch colony until the end of World War II), declared itself an independent republic. However, within months the Jakarta government had invaded and annexed the former Portuguese territory. An estimated one third of the population of 680,000 people died in the months after the invasion from violence or from famine and disease.

In December 1975, after the invasion, the UN adopted a resolution that deplored the military action and asked Indonesia to withdraw (UN General Assembly 1975). Sub-sequently, the Security Council adopted Resolution 384 that called on all states to recognise the territory of Timor and the inalienable right of its people to self-determination (UN Security Council 1975). As far as the UN was concerned the Indonesian action was illegal and unacceptable. However, no mechanisms to enforce the resolutions were adopted and, while both the Security Council and the General Assembly regularly debated East Timor, neither punitive nor restorative action was taken.

Over time, support for East Timor within the UN began to weaken. East Timor had become a Cold War issue. Its supporters were primarily Portugal, the former Soviet bloc countries and China. Most European members of the UN, including Ireland, abstained on the eight resolutions debated between 1975 and 1982. That year, Ireland for the first time voted in favour of East Timor (UN General Assembly 1982). However, the voting pattern on that debate was dispiriting for Portugal which switched its diplomatic strategy. Portugal received sanction for trilateral negotiations (the UN, Portugal and Indonesia) and stopped raising East Timor at the General Assembly but brought it into the chambers of the Commission on Human Rights (CHR).

There were two significant events that changed the disinterested approach of the world community to East Timor. First was the 1986 ascension to power in Portugal of a left-wing government which prioritised a fresh diplomatic initiative on East Timor. The second event was the Santa Cruz massacre, the 1992 killing by Indonesian troops of 200 civilians at a peaceful gathering in a cemetery outside of Dili, the East Timor capital. The Santa Cruz massacre was captured on television and broadcast widely.

The event served to waken consciousness globally to life under Indonesian rule. In the aftermath, both the UN and the EU issued condemnations of Indonesia. It also acted as the catalyst for the rise of popular movements of solidarity with the people of East Timor. Amongst those who came together in response was a group of Dublin neighbours.

East Timor and Ireland

The unusual circumstances of the foundation of the Irish East Timor solidarity group have been often told. One evening in Dublin in December 1992 a group came together for a social gathering interrupted by agreement to watch a much-publicised documentary on the massacre. It had a lasting effect on some of the viewers.

Within months the East Timor Ireland Solidarity Campaign (ETISC) was launched. The campaign swiftly moved from a somewhat optimistic goal (hoping to change Indonesian policy in East Timor) to a more focused, politically sharpened objective to bring Irish political leaders to a position where it would be unacceptable for them to do nothing about East Timor.

Meeting the goal was translated to three levels of activity. First, the ETISC formed and solidified links with East Timorese leaders in exile and in the territory itself and made contact with solidarity groups worldwide. This was critical not only to establish the authenticity of the group *vis-à-vis* its public and the Irish political elite, but to ensure that the campaign was working as one voice with the East Timor opposition. The telecommunications revolution facilitated such linkages and ETISC members established hot lines for surveillance and monitoring of events within the territory. Secondly, the campaign set about bringing East Timor into the homes of Ireland. Careful cultivation of media relations as well as linking with other community groups (not just those involved with foreign policy issues but also local community organisations, youth groups and so on) occurred and the campaign successfully nurtured relations with the school system to speak to a huge audience of young people. Thirdly, the campaign set out to develop cross-party support for the issue of East Timor and directly lobbied government members and officials at the DFA. In this regard the ETISC took a pragmatic position that it would work with political leaders of all persuasions and would not identify with any particular ideology. By focusing on the human rights dimensions of East Timor and by linking East Timor's history with that of Ireland (both small nations suffering under the Goliath of big neighbours, both struggling in the post-colonial yoke), East Timor was presented as a situation which was highly politicised but at the heart of which lay a very human demand to basic human rights.

A brief summary of parliamentary activity underlines the impact of the ETISC over time. The first reference to East Timor in the Irish Parliament is found in a question from Opposition Deputy John Bruton in June 1987 (Ward 1999). In response, the Minister of Foreign Affairs, Brian Lenihan, remarked that Ireland had 'friendly relations' with Indonesia and that the dispute was best solved by UN negotiations. For Ireland, East Timor was clearly not of direct concern and was best managed elsewhere. No more questions were tabled or raised until 1992 and the Irish polity was silent on East Timor until that point.

In the period from 1992 to 1997, in sharp contrast, a total of 65 questions were asked about East Timor and between 1994 and 1996 eight protracted debates on East Timor took place in the second house, the Seanad. In particular, the Joint Committee on Foreign Affairs provided a significant venue for debates on East Timor. The ETISC had specifically targeted its members for lobbying. It was within this committee that the first full debate on East Timor occurred within the Irish Parliament when the ETISC and the Portuguese Ambassador to Ireland both made presentations in 1993. A seven-point resolution was adopted by the committee which, *inter alia*, called on the Irish government to do all it could to raise concern about East Timor at the EU and at the UN. The efficacy of ETISC lobbying was felt further afield and the campaign did not exclude members of the European Parliament in its activities. Within the European Parliament, several Irish parliamentarians became identified with the East Timor cause and sponsored and participated in debates within that forum.

A successful ETISC tactic was to bring visitors to Ireland both to meet with press and civil society groups and to directly lobby or brief DFA officials and parliamentarians. One such visitor (who was to return to Ireland several times over the coming years) was Nobel Peace Prize winner, José Ramos Horta, a leading East Timorese exile. During a trip in 1992, Mr Horta proposed that then Foreign Minister, David Andrews (Fianna Fáil) should become a negotiator in ongoing UN talks. In the event, Mr Andrews did not pursue the proposal but he did develop a relationship with East Timor that became a feature of his second tenure as Minister of Foreign Affairs in the coalition government formed in 1997.

The openness of the Irish polity to lobbying, derivative of the small size of the bureaucracy but also arising from the Irish tradition of clientelism, was carefully nurtured by the ETISC. In addition, the ETISC's hand was strengthened by the comparative advantage it had over the small number of hard-pressed officials it dealt with at the DFA: up-to-date information and analysis. In many circumstances, the ETISC was alerted of events within the territory before they became international news. As a result of its contacts the ETISC could produce expert analysis of any given situation that went into the pool of knowledge drawn upon by officials in developing their own policy position.

Should the ETISC's skills and capacity for generating support have been unclear in the first few years, the visit to Ireland by Australian Prime Minister Brian Keating in 1993 left no doubt. In a carefully planned campaign that required working with the media, members of parliament and with other NGOs, Mr Keating was confronted wherever he went by protestors linking his government's continued support for Indonesian rule in East Timor and human rights abuses going on there. When Mr Keating spoke in Dáil, he was surrounded by many parliamentarians wearing white carnations on their lapels as expressions of sympathy for East Timor (*Irish Times*, 21 September 1995).

Unusual for a foreign policy issue, but indicating just the extent of its penetration into Irish political discourse, East Timor was subject to party competition following the appointment of the new government in 1994. A public spat, run in the columns of the *Irish Times* in the summer of 1995, revealed the extent to which the former regime sought to best the incoming Minister on his East Timor policy. Previous Foreign Minister, Michael Kitt, who had been vocal on East Timor, accused his successor, Minister Spring, of failing to act on East Timor despite verbal commitments. Mr Spring's reply appeared six days later despite the fact that he was, at that time, involved in a critical stage of negotiations on the Northern Ireland peace process. The reply was unusual because of this circumstance but also because it revealed a great sensitivity to public criticism on the issue and, not least of all, because it was penned by Mr Spring himself. In his defence, Mr Spring stated that Ireland had gone beyond the ritualised condemnations to actually engage internationally with the issue of East Timor. The details of his response also indicated that his government was now pushing a more radical line than that pursued by the EU which had formed the Irish position some months previously, as revealed in a Senate debate.

But did all this domestic activity filter into how Ireland expressed itself on East Timor outside national territory? The answer is a clear yes. Again we can trace a progressive inclusion on the issue over time from 1992 onwards, notwithstanding changes of government in that period.

A commitment given by Minister David Andrews to José Ramos Horta in 1992 that Ireland would raise East Timor in both the EU and the UN at 'every level' may be difficult to test systematically (many multilateral levels of debate are not subject to public scrutiny) but we do see Ireland increasingly identifying itself within the EU as a vocal ally of East Timor and, conversely, a vocal critic of Indonesia. Continuing after the change of government in 1994, Ireland had raised the issue of human rights abuses in East Timor in the EU (at the level of the Council), at the UN, in direct talks between Ireland and the Indonesian Embassy, and in Ireland's capacity as a participant in the ongoing EU/ASEAN talks.

As we saw, in September 1995, Minister Spring walked out of the meeting with Indonesian Foreign Minister, Ali Alatas, in New York during EU/ASEAN negotiations. Commentators subsequently remarked that Irish–Indonesian relations were, at this stage, in tatters.

Just before Ireland took over the EU Presidency (July to December 1996), the efforts of many months of negotiations within the EU on East Timor bore fruit in the Common Position (CP) on East Timor (Common Position 1996). Irish officials participated in the process of agreeing on that CP. Prior to Ireland's Presidency of the EU the ETISC and other international solidarity organisations were confident that the Irish would produce a significant initiative on East Timor. Certainly, the signs augured well. Ireland had been identified within the EU as an ally of the East Timorese – a role perhaps shared with Portugal. Public support for the cause of East Timor was high. On the shopping list that the Irish Presidency brought to Europe was a prioritisation of the issue of East Timor. Prior to the presidency, Mr Ramos Horta visited the capital again and stressed the potential that the Irish Presidency had to include human rights in the EU's dialogue with Indonesia.

Not surprisingly, however, given the caution with which the EU normally moves on sensitive foreign policy issues, the CP itself did not contain a recipe for action on the part of the EU. Its overall emphasis was to defer to the ongoing UN talks. It failed to set out any specific goals or actions for the member states aside from proposing an EU humanitarian aid package. It did not, for instance, refer to self-determination but to the more legally and politically ambiguous notion of the 'legitimate aspirations of the Timorese people in accordance with international law' (Common Position 1996).

However, the CP could be seen as a maximalist document (nothing more than it set out would be done) or a minimalist document (it was broadly enabling of any unspecified action so long as the general framework was not violated). In CFSP mechanisms, a common position sets out the broad policy to which EU members are obliged to adhere. In an ideal world, a common position will be followed by a common action – a set of agreed actions which member states can collectively or individually implement. It was hoped that Ireland would guide the EU in a maximalist interpretation of the CP.

In his address to the European Parliament, when incoming Presidents set out their wares, Mr Spring did not make a single reference to East Timor despite the claim to its prioritisation during his period of office. Around that time, negotiations began in Brussels on the implementation of an aid package but went nowhere fast.

In July, Minister Spring raised the CP during an EU/ASEAN dialogue. In August of that year, during high-level EU/ASEAN talks, an initiative by the Irish Presidency to send a vote of congratulations to the newly named Nobel Peace Prize winners, José Ramos Horta and Archbishop Belo, was blocked by Germany. Within months, it was clear that Ireland was effectively hidebound by its position as representative spokesperson for the 12 states. It was no longer possible for an Irish policy to be implemented. Agreement on the CP appeared to represent the sum total of EU initiatives or capacity on East Timor.

By the time the Irish Presidency concluded, a more sober analysis was being offered by the ETISC. At least, commented Tom Hyland, the situation for East Timor *vis à vis* the EU had not got any worse. Expectation, fuelled by Deputy Spring's strong personal commitment to East Timor, had been high. What might not have been realised by the ETISC supporters was that, ironically, the position of Presidency of the EU carries a multilateral responsibility to be representative of all member states. The common position encapsulated the extent of agreement possible within the Union on East Timor. It would have been difficult for Deputy Spring to step beyond that.

In any event, Indonesian internal politics ultimately brought down the Suharto regime and with it, as reformers came to power, the grip over the disputed territory of East Timor. The collapse of the economy and the continuing running sore of East Timor, rendered it politically unattractive and costly to the new regime. As we know, as events swiftly unfolded in the spring of 1999, the Indonesian government agreed to relinquish control of East Timor if such was the outcome of a popular consultation. That vote went ahead in August of 1999 and resulted in over 90 per cent of the people of East Timor voting against autonomous status within Indonesia and in favour of independence.

Concluding remarks

Analysing foreign policy issues from a cause–effect perspective is a somewhat unattractive proposal. The environment within which decisions are taken and implemented is complex and multidimensional. And yet, some conclusions must be drawn that measure, say, Irish input to the outcome of the debate or, say, the impact of an NGO on the manner in which a human rights issue evolved within Ireland.

At the heart of this chapter was the relationship between Irish civil society actors and the state in the formulation and implementation of policy on East Timor with reference to human rights. Evaluating this relationship is not just a challenge to students of international relations but is critical for NGOs who must build strategies on what 'works' best.

What we can say is that had the ETISC not existed, it is highly improbable that Ireland would have paid any attention to East Timor other than what might have been required of it within the CFSP process. The pattern of emergence of the issue into public, parliamentary and diplomatic discourse shows this.

It is more difficult to make statements about Ireland's subsequent role in the international community's response to human rights abuses by Indonesia. Would the CP have evolved, limited though it was in use, had Ireland not stood as an ally of Portugal within EU discourse on East Timor? Even if we were to give an unambiguous 'no' to that statement, what role, if any, did the CP or the EU play in the eventual acceptance by Indonesia of the right to self-determination of the East Timorese peoples?

One difficulty here, of course, is that Ireland is a small state, with limited political, economic or diplomatic clout. Small states, even where they are equal participants in a regional organisation such as the EU, do not carry much weight on the world stage. It may be the case that human rights globally would not be improved one whit if Ireland were to actively, vigorously and consistently pursue a foreign policy in which human rights concerns took precedence over other concerns. Consequently, it could be argued that there is little point in Ireland pursuing such a policy orientation. The difficulties of the Irish EU Presidency to deliver on its prioritisation of East Timor in 1996 seem to provide evidence for such a conclusion.

Such a conclusion, however, is based on ethically questionable principles. It implies that a concern for human rights is contingent on the likelihood of their enforcement. This is diametrically opposed to the very conception of human rights as set out in the UN charter, and elsewhere, that the claim that human rights make on each of us arises from the very fact that we share a common humanity. An apparent or real impracticality in responding to that claim does not diminish the responsibility. But at the same time each state must match its capacity for influence with the demands of those grander ethical claims.

However, a further difficulty that students of international politics face is the epistemological resistance, to begin with, to the inclusion of normative dimensions in policy analysis. This, in turn, is related to the diplomatic traditions, dominated by a realist world view whereby human rights are, in fact, expendable.

This case study showed, however, that domestic ethical concerns for others outside of the national community can find a significant place in how a state behaves internationally. Something approximating an Irish national consensus on East Timor was generated by the activity of a small group of people. In forming this consensus, the institutions of the state were sensitised to the need to go beyond the rhetoric of human rights condemnations.

It may be the case that, while some human rights concerns are successfully operationalised and perhaps even proved to be efficacious, the measure of a successful human rights policy is how, in doing this, the state's own norms are altered and how it, in turn, participates in the norm-changing dynamics at the international level. This is, of course, a long-term and somewhat progressivist view of the evolution of human rights in international affairs.

It does not, in the meantime, imply that states, even small ones like Ireland, do not need to continue to expand the inclusion of human rights into the mix of concerns that arise when foreign policy orientations are being decided. There is considerable room for Ireland to develop a stronger voice within the CFSP where the principle of absolute sovereignty, one of the greatest barriers to human rights policy, has been weakened. Given the overarching influence of the EU, it is difficult to maintain that the development of new machinery and mechanisms, outlined in the early part of this chapter, would have made any difference to the case of East Timor. However, the establishment of the HRU, in particular, is a welcome and necessary step towards rendering human rights as 'defining' Irish foreign policy. It will be important that the unit is resourced to the maximum (including personnel) and that its deliberations are integrated across all dimensions of Irish foreign policy including trade, agricultural and defence policies.

References

Common Position (CP) (1996) 25 June.

CONGOOD (1993) 'Recommendations on the merger of CONGOOD and the national assembly' (Dublin).

Department of Foreign Affairs (1996) *Challenges and Opportunities Abroad: White Paper on Foreign Policy* (Dublin: Government Publications).

Donnelly, Jack (1993) *International Human Rights* (Boulder, CO: Westview Press).

Glasius, Marlies (1999) *Foreign Policy on Human Rights: Its Influence on Indonesia under Soeharta* (Antwerp, Groningen and Oxford: School of Human Rights Research, Intersentia-Hart).

Gordenker, Leon and Weiss, Thomas G. (1996) *NGOs, the UN and Global Governance* (Boulder, CO: Reimer).

Hayes, Mahon (1999) 'Human rights in the 21st century', Royal Irish Academy Conference Address, 12 February (Dublin).

Holmes, Michael, Nicholas Rees and Bernadette Whelan (1993) *The Poor Relation: Irish Foreign Policy and the Third World* (Dublin: Gill and Macmillan/Trocaire).

Irish Times (1992) 4 September.

Irish Times (1993) 21 September.

Irish Times (1994) 23 September.

Irish Times (1995) 7 July.

Irish Times (1995) 13 July.

Irish Times (1995) 21 September.

Irish Times (1995) 27 September.

Keatinge, Patrick (1973) *The Formation of Irish Policy* (Dublin: IPA).

Kennedy, Michael (1996) *Ireland and the League of Nations* (Dublin: Irish Academic Press).

Kirby, Peadar (1992) *Ireland and Latin America: Links and Lessons* (Dublin: Trócaire Gill and Macmillan).

Laffan, Brigid (1988) *Ireland and South Africa: Irish Government Policy in the 1980's* (Dublin: Trocaire).

Luard, Evan (1981) *Human Rights and Foreign Policy* (Oxford: Pergamon Press).

Maubere, Newsletter of the East Timor Ireland Solidarity Campaign, August (1996).

O'Donnell, Liz (1998) 'Human rights and foreign policy', Address at Conference on Human Rights and Democracy, 26 February (Dublin: Royal Hospital Kilmainham).

Skelly, Joseph (1997) *Irish Diplomacy at the UN, 1945–1965* (Dublin: Irish Academic Press).

Swift, John (1995) Irish Permanent Representative to the UN (Geneva), at DFA Seminar on Human Rights, January (Galway: UCG).

UN General Assembly Resolution 3485 (xxx) (1975) 'Question of East Timor', 12 December.

UN General Assembly Resolution 37/30 (1982) 'Question of East Timor', 23 November.
UN Security Council Resolution 384 (22 December 1975).
Ward, Eilís (1999) 'Cosmopolitanism and Irish Foreign Policy', Unpublished PhD, Trinity College, Dublin.

Chapter 11

The political economy of growth

Niamh Hardiman

Introduction

Between the mid-1980s and the late 1990s, social scientists' view of the principal issues involved in Ireland's social and economic development underwent profound change. Whereas Lee (1989), for example, sought to explain the under-performance of the Irish economy relative to the rest of the developed world, the issue for analysts such as Ó Gráda (1997), Barry (1999) and Nolan *et al.* (2000) was that of accounting for Ireland's remarkable successes. The economic climate has been transformed, from the dark days of fiscal crisis and a towering national debt, high inflation, perennially high unemployment and a massive haemorrhage of emigration, to the heady experience of economic boom, steady growth in population and employment levels, and a new confidence in the country's performance and prospects. Much as the policy combination adopted by the 'Dutch model' during the 1990s has attracted the attention of a wider public (see Visser and Hemerijck 1997), so also the policy configuration of the so-called 'Celtic Tiger' has fascinated many observers because of what it might contribute to our general understanding of models of economic development.

There is broad agreement about the role of the various elements of policy that have contributed to Ireland's recent and much-welcomed success story (see Barry 1999; MacSharry and White 2000). The long-standing commitment to promoting inward investment through a combination of preferential corporate tax rates and direct grant-aid has been vital. Since the 1980s these efforts have been targeted on particular sectors and world-class firms with a view to upgrading the quality of employment in industry and services. Ireland was well positioned to avail of the greatly increased flow of Foreign Direct Market (FDI) – especially American – attracted to Europe by the prospect of the completion of the Single European Market (SEM) in 1992. A large reservoir of skills and talents was available, in the form of a stream of well-educated new entrants to the labour market, the growth from a low base of female labour force participation, the return of skilled emigrants of the earlier phase and the inward migration of non-nationals.

All these and other factors combined to enable the economic boom to take off from the mid-1990s on. But what is often missing from analyses is an account of the institutional and political conditions underlying the economic successes. These ensured that the benefits of rapid growth were not dissipated in wage inflation but were translated into a rapid expansion in employment alongside a steady rise in overall living standards. Together, the elements of this policy configuration amount to what is termed 'social partnership'. The next section outlines the origins and course of the social partnership process. The following section surveys some of the respects in which the social partnership model has contributed to managing economic development more stably than would have been possible in its absence. The final section explores some possible sources of weakness in Ireland's capacity to adjust to changing external and internal economic circumstances.

From managing crisis to managing growth

Internal crisis, external constraints: the origins of social partnership

At the heart of recent Irish governments' approaches to economic management has been a reliance on 'social partnership'. This refers to a process of consultation between government and the principal organisations representing employers, trade unions and farmers. Increasingly, organisations from the 'community and voluntary sector' have also been drawn into this network. Consultations principally take place through the National Economic and Social Council (NESC). A series of five national framework pay agreements, each of roughly three years' duration, has been negotiated in Ireland since 1987, most recently in March 2000, on the basis of the periodic strategy reports worked out through NESC.

Centrally negotiated pay agreements have a precedent in Ireland's 'policy repertoire'. Collective bargaining over the post-war decades had taken the form of a loose sequence of pay 'rounds'. During the 1970s, in an attempt to dampen wage inflation and contain industrial conflict, governments had sponsored the negotiation of a series of national wage agreements, through which pay and tax had come to be explicitly linked. But these never really approximated to the continental European model of 'societal corporatism' or 'social concertation' (Hardiman 1988). In view of the upward trend in nominal pay increases, rising inflation and mounting strike rates, private sector employers withdrew their support in 1981. They were determined to make pay settlements more responsive to firm-level conditions and to ensure that real concessions were secured in exchange for productivity-based pay increases. A period of decentralised bargaining ensued between 1981 and 1987, during which high and rising unemployment dampened wage pressures.

The construction of the new institutions and practices of social partnership may be attributed primarily to the gravity of the economic crisis faced by the country in the mid-1980s (Hardiman 1988: 231–4; Hardiman 1992; MacSharry and White 2000: 122–3). A series of fiscal mistakes had resulted in a debt–GDP ratio of over 120 per cent by 1987. Unemployment stood at over 17 per cent, and almost two-thirds of these were long-term unemployed (Sexton *et al.* 1999: 42–8). Emigration once again approached the catastrophic levels of the mid-1950s. Government policy managed to stabilise the fiscal crisis through a very difficult tax-based adjustment (Honohan 1999). But it seemed to be impossible to reverse the downward spiral of recession and unemployment. A spirit of fatalistic pessimism prevailed.

Against this backdrop, NESC prepared a document, *A Strategy for Recovery* (1986), setting out an analysis of the economic crisis agreed on by all participants. This NESC report committed the participant organisations to the attainment of specific targets on the public finances, recognising that this would necessarily entail painful cuts in public expenditure. As one participant noted, 'NESC developed the debt/GDP ratio as a performance measure long before Maastricht'.[1]

This proved to be the genesis of an 'expectations consensus' which made it possible to alter macroeconomic priorities (Dore 1994: 29). While employers and unions had worked out common priorities regarding the medium-term requirements of the Irish economy, it required political impetus to convert this into a coherent economic strategy. The minority Fianna Fáil government that took office in 1987 convened tripartite talks that led to the negotiation of the Programme for National Recovery (PNR): the central element of this deal was that a modest pay settlement would be offset by cuts in personal income taxation (see Table 11.1). The intervention of government was crucial to achieving co-ordination between unions and employers, the need for which had already been recognised in principle.

The role of acute economic crisis in recasting the conventional style of industrial relations has its counterpart in other countries. The sense of domestic economic crisis concentrated the minds of all participants on identifying the Irish economy's medium-term prospects and on developing a strategy for escaping the current policy stalemate.

It is interesting to note that a consensus-oriented style of pay bargaining linked to macroeconomic management emerged elsewhere on the European political landscape around this time – most strikingly perhaps in the Netherlands, but also in Finland, Spain, Italy (see Visser and Hemerijck 1997; Regini 1998; Rhodes 1998; Pérez 1999). Employer and union bodies that were well organised, but not highly centralised, perceived a variety of advantages in adopting a co-ordinated approach to pay determination, rather than relying on decentralised and market-led procedures (see also Soskice 1990, 1999). Ireland's closest neighbour, Britain, has often initiated policy models that were subsequently adopted in Ireland. Yet while Britain in the 1980s was proceeding with one of the most advanced experiments in neo-liberal economic management, Ireland moved in the direction of increasing co-ordination in the labour market. Their respective labour market institutions had common origins, but different political choices pressed each towards contrasting strategies of domestic adaptation to new economic conditions.

The contingency of the first agreement is easy to forget in hindsight. What secured the success of the package was an upturn in the international economy and a drop in the inflation rate which turned a modest pay-and-tax-cuts deal into an increase in real disposable income (see Barry 1991; Honohan 1999). This contrasted with the period 1981–87, when the nominal earnings of manual workers rose by 101 per cent but real take-home pay dropped by 7 per cent (NESC 1999: 237). Fortuitous external circumstances helped the PNR to initiate a 'virtuous circle' of

Table 11.1 Pay terms of partnership agreements

Programme for National Recovery, 1987–1990 (PNR)
Pay – private and public sector Duration 36 months. 3% on first £120 of weekly basic, 2% on balance.
Low-paid Floor £4 per week.
Other terms Weekly working hours reduced from 40 to 39 hours. Inability to pay clause. Ongoing cooperation with change.
Tax cuts £225m promised over three years.

Programme for Economic and Social Progress, 1991–1993 (PESP)
Pay – private and public sector 10.75% over three years: 4.0% in first year, 3.0% in second, 3.75% in third.
Low-paid Floor of £5.00 per week in 1991, £4.25 in 1992, £5.75 in 1993.
Other terms Local bargaining permitted for 'exceptional' increases of up to 3%, not earlier than 1992. In public service, negotiable with reference either to 'grade restructuring', or to 'special' claim, not before third year. Private sector inability to pay clause. Industrial peace clause. Ongoing cooperation with change.
Tax cuts £400m promised over three years.

Programme for Competitiveness and Work, 1994–1997 (PCW)
Pay – private sector (excluding construction – separate) 8% in total, over 39 months. 2.0% in first year, 2.5% in second year, 2.5% for 6 months, 1% for 6 months.
Public service 8% in total, over 42 months. Five-month pay pause, then 2% in first year, 2% in second year, 1.5% for 4 months, 1.5% for 3 months, 1% for 6 months.
Low-paid Private sector floor of £3.50; public sector: £2.80 in first two years, £2.20 in later phases.
Other terms Public sector implementation of 3% PCW local bargaining clause: 1% payable, balance subject to local negotiation. Private sector inability to pay clause. Industrial peace clause. Ongoing cooperation with change.
Tax cuts No specific amount; to be targeted on low and middle earners.

Partnership 2000 for Inclusion, Employment and Competitiveness, 1997–2000 (Partnership 2000)
Pay – private sector 7.25% over 3 years: 2.5% in first year, 2.25% in second year, 1.5% for 9 months, 1.0% for 6 months.
Public service In first year, 2.5% of first £220 of weekly basic pay for 9 months, then 2.5% of the balance for 3 months. Second and third years as private sector.
Low-paid From second year, floor of £3.50 per week, then £2.40 next 9 months, then £1.60 next 6 months.
Other terms Local negotiation of up to 2%, not before mid-1998 (private sector) or mid-1999 (public sector). Private sector inability to pay clause. Industrial peace clause. Ongoing cooperation with change.
Tax cuts £1bn in total, 90% to go on employee income taxes.

Programme for Prosperity and Fairness, 2000–2003 (PPF)
Pay – private and public sector Duration 33 months. Cumulative 15%. 5.5% for 12 months, 5.5% for next 12 months, 4% for next 9 months.
Low-paid Floor of £12, £11, £9 per week respectively in each phase. Statutory minimum wage of £4.40 per hour from April 2000, £4.70 from July 2001, £5 from October 2002.
Other terms Private sector inability to pay clause. Industrial peace clause. Ongoing cooperation with change.
Tax cuts No specific sum, but commitment that net take-home pay will increase by up to 25% or more by Budget 2003. Commitment to reform of tax administration and personal taxation.

Sources: PNR (1987), Programme for Economic and Social Progress (1990), Programme for Competitiveness and Work (PCW) (1993), Partnership 2000 for Inclusion, Employment and Competitiveness (1996), PPF (2000).

Table 11.2 Governments in power, 1987–2000

Date	Government	Taoiseach	Minister for Finance
1987–89	FF minority	C.J. Haughey	Ray MacSharry
1989–92	FF–PD	1989–90 C.J. Haughey	Albert Reynolds
		1990–92 Albert Reynolds	Bertie Ahern
1992–94	FF–Labour	Albert Reynolds	Bertie Ahern
1994–97	FG–Lab–DL	John Bruton	Ruairí Quinn
1997–	FF–PD minority	Bertie Ahern	Charlie McCreevy

Note:
Abbreviations:
DL Democratic Left
FF Fianna Fáil
FG Fine Gael
PD Progressive Democratic Party
Lab Labour Party

improved domestic economic performance, which paved the way for successor agreements (see also Prondzynski 1997; Durkan 1999: 47).

Undoubtedly the shared sense of economic crisis helped to bring trade union and employer leaders together; in this sense, patriotism and a sense of responsibility to the wider community played an important part in shaping participants' views (see also Dore 1994: 29). But the institutional and political bases for maintaining the 'virtuous circle' were now in place. While the negotiation of a new agreement could never be taken for granted, there was a bias in favour of renewal of the process with the expiry of each old agreement. Furthermore, as Table 11.2 shows, all the major political parties participated in government over the period since 1987, which tended to further stabilise the social partnership approach to pay determination. All parties in government also agreed that Ireland should aim to qualify for membership of the European Monetary Union (EMU) by 1999 – a priority also shared by the social partners within NESC. The 'Maastricht convergence criteria' provided an additional, externally based pressure towards negotiation of moderate pay agreements. And despite criticism from individual commentators (see for example Teague 1995), there was no organised bloc of political opposition either to the process of social partnership or to its outcomes.

The negotiation of the next two three-year programmes, the Programme for Economic and Social Progress (PESP 1990–93) and the Programme for Competitiveness and Work (PCW 1993–96) broadened the range of bargaining issues surrounding the central framework pay agreement. The process of social partnership, it may be argued, gained in problem-solving capacity.

Turning the corner: managing prosperity

By 1996, when the PCW was nearing expiry and NESC was preparing its background strategy document for a new agreement (NESC 1996), the sense of economic crisis, of an economy near collapse, of a polity running out of ideas, had receded into the past.

The growth that was to continue for the rest of the decade was already well under way. As Barry *et al.* note, 'foreign direct investment inflows into Ireland increased substantially in the 1990s; this reflected not just increased inflows into the EU, but also a substantial increase in Ireland's share of these inflows' (1999: 68). Linkages between the foreign sector and the rest of the domestic economy also increased, generating more jobs. The Irish economy grew at an average annual rate of 8.5 per cent per annum between 1994 and 1999, almost four times as fast as the EU15. Inflation averaged just above 2 per cent, below the EU15 average of 2.7 per cent (NESC 1999: 10). The debt–GDP ratio scarcely featured in economic commentary – the economy grew so rapidly that the debt declined to 52 per cent of GDP by 1998, or 68 per cent of GNP (NESC 1999: 12). Far from having to deal with fiscal deficits, steady growth and greatly increased labour force participation levels resulted in recurrent revenue overshoots, enabling governments to run a fiscal surplus from the mid-1990s on (see Duffy 1999: 12).

Concerns about 'jobless growth' were now all but forgotten as employment levels began to grow rapidly from 1994 on (Barry *et al.* 1999: 69). Inward migration began to pick up, and unemployment also fell from almost 15 per cent in 1994 to under 12 per cent in 1996. The trend continued in subsequent years, with unemployment falling continuously to 10 per cent in 1997, below 8 per cent in 1998, to an average of 4.1 per cent in 2000, falling even further in 2001.[2] Amazingly for Ireland, the talk was of the growing problem of skill shortages and even of labour shortages in general. Cumulative employment expansion in Ireland between 1994 and 1999 was estimated at 28 per cent, compared with 13 per cent in the Netherlands, 5 per cent in Britain and 3 per cent in the EU (NESC 1999: Tables 9.8, 9.9).

Against this backdrop, commitment to the 'virtuous circle' was maintained: a new pay agreement was negotiated, termed Partnership 2000 (1996–99). Despite the fairly modest nominal pay terms, total average increase in take-home pay was estimated to average 14 per cent for single people and 16.2 per cent for married people. In fact, cumulative increases in real take-home pay over the whole period 1987–99 for an employee on average manufacturing earnings were estimated to amount to over 35 per cent (NESC 1999: 237).

Pay determination in a new era

Ireland became a member of the EMU in January 1999. With no further domestic control over monetary or exchange rate policy, adjustment to external shocks could only be mediated through fiscal policy or pay adjustments. This gave pay agreements an even more important role in economic management than hitherto. A new pay agreement was negotiated, under the title of Programme for Prosperity and Fairness (PPF) (2000–03). The pay terms, at about 15 per cent over 33 months, were a good deal higher than in any previous agreement. Tax cuts were due to give a further substantial boost of about 10 per cent to disposable income. The rather high nominal pay terms reflect the tightness of the labour market – pay trends have always, of course, been subject to market forces as well as to pay agreements (see Fitzgerald 1999). The economic projections continued to forecast high and steady growth into the future.

Growth with equity

The pay agreements negotiated through the evolution of social partnership since 1987 undoubtedly contributed to the remarkable turnaround in the economy. Real increases in disposable income were delivered while keeping industrial conflict at low levels; inflation was curbed effectively, at least until early 2000; the national finances were transformed. The national framework of pay bargaining made it possible for the far-reaching trade-offs between wage moderation and tax reform to take effect. Once growth began in earnest, the pay agreements helped to ensure that the gains were not dissipated by wage inflation and industrial conflict.

In common with the adjustment strategies of other European countries since the 1980s and 1990s, social partnership in Ireland combined with a new emphasis on promoting competitiveness with some concern for the distributive outcomes of the growth that ensued. A centralised pay strategy combining these twin objectives has been termed 'competitive corporatism' (Rhodes 1998; see also Aust 1999). Ireland displays both features of this model of economic adaptation but with varying degrees of success.

Managing structural change: competitiveness in diverse sectors

Since 1987, Irish business has been improving its profitability; the OECD comments that this has undoubtedly been helped by the wage restraint entailed by the social partnership pay agreements. The share of capital income as a proportion of GDP rose from 25 per cent in 1987 to about 38 per cent in 1998, close to the European average (OECD 1998; NESC 1999: 240). The wage share has been correspondingly declining, especially in manufacturing. The unions have had to accept this as the necessary cost of continued growth. Over the same time-period, cost competitiveness has also been improving across the economy taken as a whole. Even though earnings in national currency rose faster than competitor countries in 1998 and 1999, exchange rate movements offset the negative consequences.

Yet any pay agreement purporting to span the whole economy is likely to encounter problems accommodating the diverse needs of different sectors. The Irish economy has been experiencing profound structural change since 1987. Some sectors have been very successful indeed, generating large productivity gains and profits. The foreign-owned sector overall has been far more successful than the indigenous sector (NESC 1999: 241, 325). This is partly a function of enterprise scale, but is also a feature of the industrial sectors in which they are concentrated, among them pharmaceuticals and chemicals, and microelectronics and engineering. On the other hand, some parts of the traditional manufacturing sector were hard-pressed to accommodate the terms of the pay agreements.

One of the dangers of a situation like this is the risk of developing 'Dutch disease' – where a successful, export-oriented, high-tech sector pulls wages unsustainably upward in other sectors. However, the OECD found little evidence of such a development in Ireland (OECD 1999: 6, 102). It would appear that the pay agreements themselves contributed to avoiding a pay squeeze on the traditional, low-pay, labour-intensive manufacturing sector. They helped restrain the upward movement of basic pay rates in the modern sector to some degree, and prevented any serious spill-over of wage-cost increases into the lower-skilled sectors. There was, besides, a surplus supply of labour in the lower-skilled end of the labour market until the late 1990s (OECD 1999: 61). The decline in the traditional sector is irreversible but can be managed more or less well (OECD 1999: 102), and social partnership has a vital role to play in this.

That is not to deny that wage drift has been a problem in some sectors. In much of the software industry, for example, the supply of skilled labour was at a premium from the mid-1990s on. Most of this sector is not unionised, and wage increases in excess of the pay agreement norms were common. It was estimated that wage-cost increases were running at between 10 per cent and 15 per cent per annum in the latter part of the 1990s (Ó Riain 1999: 37–42).[3] Nor can it be denied that cost competition in the more labour-intensive, lower-productivity and low-paid traditional manufacturing sector (both indigenous and foreign-owned) was keenly felt. Even the modest basic pay increases of the framework agreements constituted a threat to the viability of some enterprises.

These employees also found themselves at the critical edge of the conflicting exchange-rate priorities which Irish governments were trying to balance during the 1990s. The Irish pound approached parity with sterling for a time during the mid-1990s. The value of non-sterling exports was growing in significance compared with the value of exports to Britain. But a disproportionate number of jobs in marginally profitable and labour-intensive firms in traditional industries such as clothing, textiles and food production depended on sales in Britain. The problem was not unique to Ireland: conflicts of interest over exchange-rate priorities between different groups of employees were felt in other European countries during the 1990s too (see, for example, Frieden 1995).[4]

The main participants in the partnership process accepted that low-cost-based competition was not sustainable in the long run, and that these sectors were in irreversible decline. On balance, the risk of job losses was outweighed by the benefits of securing sustainable agreements throughout the rest of the economy. The emphasis was placed instead on pressing for skills upgrading and improved productivity in the small-enterprise and low-skill sector, complemented by politically initiated task forces to seek to find replacement industry for regional job losses. Social partnership had thus facilitated the unpalatable but inevitable process of structural adjustment in the country's industrial composition.

Interest representation and the commitment to 'social justice'

The first three social partnership agreements were negotiated by the 'traditional' social partners, unions, employers and government. Representation at Partnership 2000 was extended to a range of groups representing a 'third strand', or the 'community and voluntary sector' (see Table 11.3). This reflected a shift in the emphasis of government policy, associated with the development of the National Anti-Poverty Strategy (NAPS) in the mid-1990s, from 'social equity' to 'social inclusion', 'a strategic objective in its own right' (see NESC 1999: 12). According to one key participant, it arose from 'the concern to ensure the fairness necessary for social cohesion, an essential underpinning to successful policy implementation' (McCarthy 1999: 9).

The inclusion of the community sector as 'new' social partners reflects the growing importance of the consultative process in shaping a range of policy choices. Partnership 2000 gave rise to many new partnership-based working groups on issues such as childcare, women's health, domestic violence, the needs of the travelling community, people with disabilities, and racism (see NESC 1999: Appendix Box A2.1). The Programme for Prosperity and Fairness involves about 35 partnership-based working groups at national level, some set up under Partnership 2000, some new.

It might be expected that the participation of the community and voluntary sector would also result in measurable progress on issues of poverty and inequality. The evidence of developments on these issues is rather mixed. There has in fact been an increase in income inequalities. In a rapidly growing economy which was experiencing big shifts in the composition of employment, returns to the top section of the income distribution grew rapidly (see Barrett *et al.* 1999). Thus more people were poor in relative terms. The profile of those at risk of poverty changed very little. There continued to be a strong association between labour market status and the risk of poverty (NESC 1999: Table 9.2).

The community and voluntary sector found that the issue of the scale of inequality was difficult to mobilise onto the political agenda and that they lacked 'clout' to secure their objectives in the negotiations (Hardiman 1998). Their involvement gives a voice to the interests of marginalised groups, but it cannot be seen as a functional substitute for redistributive government policy commitments.

The reason may be traced back to the nature of the central political bargain in the social partnership process. Neo-corporatist 'political exchange' agreements in other European countries in the earlier post-war decades had been based, in large part, on an understanding that wage moderation would be compensated by improvements in welfare provisions; this facilitated the construction of the continental European and Scandinavian welfare states (see, for example, Lehmbruch 1984). In the Irish case, however, even though a key section of the trade union leadership advocated development of the 'social wage', the heart of the pay agreements lay in the provision of tax cuts in exchange for wage moderation. In other words, the emphasis was on boosting private consumption through increased real disposable income, rather than on investment in collective or public consumption.

Table 11.3 Participation in agreements

Partnership 2000 for Inclusion, Employment and Competitiveness

Submissions were formally presented in the Opening Discussions for a new agreement by 19 organisations. These were:

Irish Business and Employers' Confederation (IBEC)
Irish Congress of Trade Unions (ICTU)
Construction Industry Federation (CIF)
Irish Farmers' Association (IFA)
Irish Creamery Milk Suppliers' Association (ICMSA)
Irish Co-operative Organisation Society Ltd (ICOS)
Macra na Feirme
Irish National Organisation of the Unemployed (INOU)
Congress Centres for the Unemployed
The Community Platform (Community Workers Co-operative, the Irish National Organisation of the Unemployed, the National Women's Council of Ireland, Irish Rural Link, Irish Traveller Movement, Focus on Children, Gay and Lesbian Equality Network, One Parent Exchange Network, Conference of Religious of Ireland, Forum of People with Disabilities, Pavee Point, Community Action Network, European Anti-Poverty Network and Irish Commission for Prisoners Overseas)
Conference of Religious of Ireland (CORI)
National Women's Council of Ireland (NWCI)
National Youth Council of Ireland (NYCI)
Society of Saint Vincent de Paul
Protestant Aid
Small Firms Association (SFA)
Irish Exporters Association (IEA)
Irish Tourist Industry Confederation (ITIC)
Chamber of Commerce of Ireland (CCI)

Programme for Participation and Fairness

Note: The parties to the negotiations of the PPF included the Government, employers, trade unions, farmers and the community and voluntary sector. The list of participants was substantially the same as that given above, with some variations in the range of groups represented by the umbrella group, the Community Platform.
Fourteen organisations were named as members of Community Platform in Partnership 2000, 21 in the PPF. In the latter programme, the National Women's Council of Ireland is not listed as part of the Community Platform (though it had its own direct representation), while additional groups are. These are: Irish Association of Older People, National Adult Literacy Agency, National Traveller Women's Council of Ireland, Threshold, Vincentian Partnership for Justice, St Vincent de Paul, Women's Aid, Voluntary Drug Treatment Network.

Sources: Partnership 2000 for Inclusion, Employment and Competitiveness (December 1996), p. 5; PPF (March 2000), p. 3.

Nevertheless, the incidence of poverty and deprivation fell from 15–16 per cent in the late 1980s and early 1990s to under 10 per cent, a welcome development (Callan *et al.* 1999; Layte *et al.* 2000). Fewer people were in deep poverty. The living standards of the poorest may have increased, on average, less quickly than other groups, but they did not fall in real terms. To that extent, the process of social partnership may be seen to provide a point of access to voices that would otherwise, in a typical liberal polity, fall to the margins. Social partnership does not spring from redistributive or Social Democratic politics. But it does appear to have helped to prevent the decline in real living standards of the poorest which has been associated with the Anglo-American neo-liberal model (Atkinson 1997; Sexton *et al.* 1999: 64).

Maintaining the domestic coalition

The model of social partnership has stood the Irish economy and Irish society in good stead. It has played a vital role in facilitating the maintenance of competitiveness and the conversion of growth into rising employment. It represents a successful example of the institutionalisation of bargained co-operation between the 'social partners'. It has provided a political space in which wider issues of social development can be aired.

But no model of consensus-oriented bargaining can be expected to be without stresses (see also Hardiman 2000a). Several issues may be identified which make it difficult to maintain the political coalition intact. We may identify these according to the actors primarily affected, looking in turn at stresses within the trade union movement, among employers and within government.

Trade union organisation and strategy

The organisational capacity to hold diverse interests together on the part of the trade union federation, the Irish Congress of Trade Unions (ICTU), has been greater during the current period of social partnership than it had been during the 1970s (see Hardiman 1988: ch. 5). This was partly due to rationalisation within the trade union movement, and partly due to the enhanced prestige of ICTU arising from the process of social partnership itself. Unions affiliated to ICTU numbered 77 in 1970 and 65 in 1983. In 1999 there were 63 unions, 46 of which, with some 523,700 members, organised in the Republic.[5] The most significant merger resulted in the creation of the Services Industrial, Professional and Technical Union (SIPTU) in 1990, whose 200,000 members in the Republic now constitute almost 40 per cent of total trade union membership. The organisational basis on which 'encompassing' analyses of the economy can be undertaken has been strengthened.

However, the trade union movement sought to represent the interests of a membership the conditions of whose employment were growing more not less diverse. This is most evident when considering the tensions between employees in the public sector and those in the private sector, and tensions between high- and low-paid employees.

Public versus private sectors

The size of the public sector pay bill makes it a priority issue for government: it amounts to some 60 per cent of current supply services expenditure (NESC 1999: para. 6.4.3), and about 40 per cent of total current government spending (Gunnigle and Roche 1995: 11). The framework pay agreements since 1987 were supposed to facilitate improvement in the competitiveness of the national economy. This implies giving priority to the needs of the market-oriented sector.

But control over public sector pay proved a recurrent problem. Public sector pay determination had neither market disciplines to respond to, nor any tradition of productivity-based assessment. Pay bargaining was mainly driven by well-established relativities, which had an in-built tendency to foster leap-frogging pay claims. It was further complicated by 'special' pay increases, which tended to spread through the relativities networks.

Compared with pay trends in the economy as a whole, the public sector between 1988 and 1999 displayed 'real increases noticeably greater than the general body of employees in manufacturing industry and in financial and insurance industries' (Sexton *et al.* 1999). This need not reflect preferential pay increases – issues of public sector workforce composition are involved as well. Nevertheless, pay movements in the public sector proved, and continue to prove, a recurring problem for the social partnership process.

It is by now widely agreed that the industrial relations procedures underlying the deeply entrenched attachment to relativities in the public sector need to be reformed.[6] Yet the opinion of one commentator was equally widely shared, that 'the last attempt at public sector restructuring (under the PCW) was a disaster',[7] which gave rise to successive waves of discontent and industrial conflict over the following years. One senior civil servant described how the issue of public sector pay reform was continually postponed in the course of three-year-long agreements. Initially a lot of time is focused on the negotiations, and no time is available to think about reform; then once an agreement is in place, everyone gets complacent and there is no impetus to get on with thinking about reform; then the pressure builds up again to negotiate a new agreement, and change is too sensitive an issue to broach.[8] Government had relatively little appetite to confront public sector pay claims during the 1990s. Strikes by gárdaí or nurses or transport workers or teachers are inevitably unpopular and politically difficult to withstand.

By the end of the 1990s, the principal cleavage in the trade union movement could be identified as running between the public sector and the rest (Roche 1997: 218). Organisationally, public sector employees accounted for some 50 per cent of total trade union membership (Roche 1997: 200). They continued to be highly unionised, whereas some of the newer sectors, especially in high-tech manufacturing and in private-sector services industries, proved difficult or impossible to unionise, and total private sector unionisation was estimated in 1999 to be about 30 per cent.[9] Public-sector-only unions constitute a powerful bloc within ICTU. SIPTU itself, the single largest union, is estimated to have 80,000 members in the public sector and 120,000 in the private sector. On the trade union side, therefore, the leadership of ICTU has been hard-pressed to balance the interests of its public sector membership against the rest.

The PPF (2000–03) finally committed the social partners to work on reforming of public sector pay, tying it more closely to private sector pay trends. Work on a report on 'benchmarking', due in 2002, was brought forward by a difficult dispute involving second-level teachers.[10] So while the issue is being addressed at the time of writing, it cannot be said to have been satisfactorily resolved.

Wage dispersion in exposed and sheltered sectors

The pay agreements were not primarily designed to manage income distribution, but to prevent wage inflation through negotiation of moderate pay increases. The combination of special provision for the low-paid and moderate settlements for everyone else might have been expected to result in some degree of wage compression in the economy.

The evidence suggests that inequality in the overall income distribution increased over the period since 1987 (Sexton *et al.* 1999). The main factors accounting for wage dispersion appear to be the compositional changes in the Irish economy, including the large increases in employment in high-tech industries, the continuing decline of the traditional sector, and the availability of a relatively highly educated workforce. The highest range of incomes pulled furthest away from the median (a trend familiar in other OECD economies too – see, for example, Dore 1994). Much of this is attributable to increased rates of return to education (Barrett *et al.* 1999).

The exposed, competitive sector saw some of the most rapid increases in pay rates, reflecting not only improved productivity but also skill shortages. There was little evidence of serious wage drift within most of the unionised sectors of the economy for much of the 1990s (Sheehan 1996; Roche 1997). But by the end of that decade, many profitable sectors were conceding often significant additional benefits, mainly in the form of productivity-related increases or non-wage fringe benefits. The strain on the terms of the pay agreements was becoming quite acute among higher earners.

On the other hand, the very successes of social partnership in averting pervasive wage inflation also increased discontent among those confined to the basic terms of the agreements who had little or no option of engaging in productivity-related bargaining. Representatives of employees in sheltered sectors expressed some of the most vociferous complaints about the paucity of the gains made by their members relative to other groups. For example, the general secretary of Mandate, a union representing some 31,000 employees in retail and distributive trades, claimed that members in the retail trade had secured only a 32 per cent increase since national agreements began in 1987, while the average industrial wage rose by 56 per cent.[11]

Nor was dissatisfaction confined to the private sector. One of the largest public sector unions, the Civil and Public Sector Union (CPSU), organising some 14,000 employees, argued that while restructuring at the top of the civil service had seen the pay of a Secretary-General increase by 120 per cent during the 1990s, clerical workers gained about 60 per cent. Indeed, in the civil service, while the average pay rate was a good deal higher than the average industrial wage (see Tansey 1998: 6), 35 per cent of employees, mainly clerical workers, earned less than the relevant amount (about £15,000 in July 1998; see NESC 1999: 244).

The trade union movement possessed limited powers to deal with such inequalities. On the advice of a partnership-based working group, government introduced a Statutory Minimum Wage in April 2000, to be increased over the term of the pay agreement. But in a climate of ongoing rapid economic growth, the tensions between high- and low-paid, exposed and sheltered sectors, as well as the ongoing tensions between public and private sectors, proved increasingly difficult to contain.

Employers and workplace social partnership

In an economy experiencing profound structural shifts in composition, employer preferences may be quite diverse. The most difficult issues for employers were those of trade union recognition and workplace social partnership. Ireland is heavily reliant on direct foreign investment, especially American. The Irish Business and Employers' Confederation (IBEC), the principal employers' federation, is cautious about proposals that might prove unacceptable to a section of its membership.

Some of the most highly profitable sectors of industry and services, especially American microelectronics and software companies, do not recognise trade unions and are opposed to union organisation in their enterprises (see Geary 1999). Trade union recognition became a particularly difficult issue in the run-up to Partnership 2000 in the wake of a bitter dispute at Ryanair. A high-level working group, set up under the terms of Partnership 2000, set out a protocol for dealing with issues of recognition on a voluntary basis.

The issue of deepening social partnership at the level of the enterprise, which the unions would also like to advance through the national framework agreements, proved more difficult. The tripartite National Centre for Partnership plays a facilitating and advisory role. But employee workplace participation, whether in consultative procedures or financial participation, is not well developed.

Chapter 9 of Partnership 2000 was devoted to the need to deepen partnership at workplace level. ICTU encouraged its affiliates to move away from adversarial industrial relations toward a new role as 'business partners' committed to quality improvement.[12] A number of workplace participation schemes were developed on a pilot basis (NESC 1999: 308). But these are still quite weakly developed, relative to European systems (NESC 1999: 268). One authoritative investigation concluded that '"exclusionary" forms of decision-making are shown to dominate the postures of establishments towards the handling of change'. Where changes in workplace practices have taken place, they tend to be in line with those of the Anglo-American industrial systems, 'which are not readily permeable to collaborative production', nor very favourable towards consultative or inclusive forms of decision-making (Roche and Geary 1998).

Firm-level social partnership of a purely financial kind, in the form of profit- and gain-sharing schemes, would appear to be an imaginative way of managing pay pressures in profitable sectors, as well as increasing employee commitment at enterprise level. But as yet these are not widely in evidence. Research evidence produces very different estimates of the extent of all kinds of financial participation, ranging from 22 per cent to 58 per cent of enterprises (NESC 1999: 251–2). They are most common in larger than in smaller enterprises, but are more likely to apply to management than to all employees. SIPTU criticised the fact that more was not achieved in this area during Partnership 2000. But given the diversity among Irish employers, this outcome is hardly surprising.

Government and social partnership

A plausible case may be argued that social partnership in Ireland has evolved from a mechanism to deal with emergency to a more embedded set of institutionalised relationships within the political system (O'Donnell 1998: 19–20; O'Donnell and Thomas 1998).

However, social partnership is less securely anchored in the political process than might be assumed, and is heavily dependent on maintaining performance in the core areas of wage moderation, competitiveness and productivity. The influence of the consensus-building networks on government decision-making remains both limited and contingent. Government decisions may at times run counter to the priorities set within the context of social partnership. Examples may be seen in two areas, general macroeconomic management and tax reform priorities.

Government's role in co-ordinating pay bargaining with broader macroeconomic priorities has become, if anything, even more important in the context of EMU. Between 1999 and mid-2001 various commentators, including the European Central Bank and the European Commission, had expressed concerns that the economy was at risk of over-heating. Rising inflation – 7 per cent on an annualised basis by the end of 2000 – was eroding the real purchasing power of employee incomes, and trade union discontent with the terms of the pay agreement grew more acute. Capacity constraints, particularly in the areas of labour supply, housing and transportation, were becoming severe. A domestic central bank would certainly have raised interest rates; that option no longer existed. In December 1999, a one-off upward revision of the pay terms of the current agreement was negotiated, saving the partnership process for the time being. But the episode demonstrated that the difficulties involved in balancing the various objectives of economic management could undercut support for the pay agreements.

The priorities reflected in tax strategy have also, at times, run counter to the requirements of the social partnership process, whether in the area of enforcing tax compliance, or in the design of the personal income tax cuts which underpin the pay agreements.

The stream of scandals and revelations during the 1990s about the financial misdeeds of prominent business and political figures, including their poor tax compliance, created a mood of public disgust and disillusionment. Des Geraghty of SIPTU, following revelations about off-shore bank accounts, wrote that:

> The whole of Ireland is angry . . . Clearly, the 'little people' were the only ones who paid their taxes, accepted pay moderation and worked for the common good. They were also the ones to pay the price for economic failure . . . Here was a classic case of one section of society writing the rules and ethics for the others, but not for themselves.

The trade union movement has been committed to promoting reform on issues such as these through the social partnership mechanisms. The General Secretary of ICTU, Peter Cassells, commending trade union delegates' vote to enter new talks in late 1999, said that 'the decision was about more than pay. It was about trying to develop a fairer society purged of institutional corruption, the gold-collar fraud, the money politics, the abuse of power, the political cronyism and the massive tax fraud.'[13] But the point was clear: government must be seen to act convincingly on these issues if the legitimacy of social partnership is to be maintained.

Tax concessions have been vitally important in securing union support for the moderate pay deals.[14] But the priorities established through the partnership process were not consistently reflected in government actions. NESC reports repeatedly drew attention to the need to concentrate tax reform on two areas: the lowest-paid, and the low-to-middle-income threshold at which the higher rate of tax begins to apply. Yet tax-cutting priorities paid relatively little attention to these arguments. Greatest emphasis was placed on cutting rates rather than increasing allowances or widening bands, which resulted in most benefits being channelled to those on higher incomes (Ruane and O'Toole 1995; Cahill and O'Toole 1998; Hardiman, 2000b). What is striking is the ease with which governments can take decisions on these matters outside the parameters agreed by the process of consensus-oriented consultation – evidently responding more to specific electoral priorities than to the consensus-oriented partnership process, yet without any overall guiding principles in evidence (O'Toole 1993/94; Sandford 1993). This is quite unlike the process of achieving tax reform in Sweden, for example, through negotiation with the social partners (see Steinmo 1993), or in the Netherlands (Visser and Hemerijck 1997). Government retains the absolute right to adopt any priorities it wishes, of course; it is not merely one social partner among others. But episodes such as these reveal the limits of the embeddedness of social partnership in the political arena, and tend to erode the foundations of the social partnership process itself.

Conclusion

Social partnership has been central to the enormous successes of the Irish economy since the late 1980s. Having emerged as a medium-term response to fiscal crisis, it evolved into a strategy for facilitating steady growth and the continuing inward investment that fuelled it, over a longer time-span than anyone might have predicted at the outset. As in other cases of 'competitive corporatism', it has been premised primarily on the advancement of economic competitiveness while also attending to issues of social equity.

The organisational and political conditions underlying a strategy of 'competitive corporatism' will, of course, vary from one country to another, giving rise to distinctive sources of tension or difficulty. In the Irish case, social partnership was worked out in the context of a far-reaching process of structural adjustment of the economy. While social partnership proved highly successful in both promoting growth and enabling rapid expansion in employment, the underlying conditions also help to account for many of the sources of tension within the social partnership system itself. Moreover, the commitment to social equity was not primarily based on a strategy of welfare state expansion, but was linked to a process of personal income tax reform focused on individual disposable income. This raised the interesting question of the limits to the strategy of tax cuts in exchange for wage moderation, at a time when demand was increasing for improvements in public services. Despite record gross tax revenues, in relation to the size of its economy, Ireland in the early twenty-first century was fast becoming a low-tax, low social spending society (NESC 1999; Ó Riain and O'Connell 2000: 330–2). Yet despite the centrality of social partnership to macroeconomic management, its embeddedness in the political process, and the extent of its influence over key taxing and spending decisions, were less pervasive than some of its advocates – particularly in the trade union movement – might have wished.

Some form of co-ordinated pay policy has been a recurring theme in Ireland's policy repertoire. Despite the voluntarist character of the industrial relations system and the British institutional inheritance of the trade union movement, Irish politics has consistently been drawn to a more continental European style of labour market management, rather than to the neo-liberal strategy of its close neighbour, Britain. The weak left–right differentiation of the party political system and the cross-class support base of the largest parties (particularly the single largest party, Fianna Fáil) contribute to making decision makers strongly averse to overt manifestations of distributional conflict. The strong reliance on direct foreign investment as the primary motor of growth gives a distinctively liberal flavour to the outcomes of government policy deliberations, and constrains the nature of the issues that can be dealt with through the institutions of social partnership. Overt and emergent tensions within the current model of pay-tax agreements need to be attended to. But some form of politically mediated wage formation process seems likely to exert a recurring strong attraction for government and organised interests alike.

Endnotes

1. Interview with Dermot McCarthy (Secretary-General to Government, vice-chair of NESC).
2. *Quarterly National Household Survey*, Central Statistics Office, March 2000, Table 9; *Labour Force Statistics*, Central Statistics Office.
3. Labour shortages in a range of other skill areas also began to emerge as a serious problem in the late 1990s, earlier in

some sectors. For example, earnings in the building industry show 'spectacular gains' from about 1994 on, especially for skilled manual trades (Sexton *et al.* 1999: 67).

4. In fact the anticipated difficulties of living within the Euro-zone from 1999 on were postponed when the Euro unexpectedly drifted downward relative to sterling. This helped to maintain Ireland's competitiveness on the British as well as the broader European market. But it was likely to be a temporary benefit – and to mask growing disparities in cost-based competitiveness between Irish and British manufacture.
5. These figures conceal a great many organisational changes. There were 30 amalgamations between 1989 and 2000; in addition, 10 new organisations affiliated to Congress (Department of Trade, Enterprise and Employment).
6. The public sector Strategic Management Initiative (SMI) was intended to improve service and increase productivity. But while it was welcomed and supported by government, it had originated among senior civil servants and had no political 'sponsor' to drive through difficult institutional changes (Roche 1998). It did not engage with the extremely difficult issues of relating pay to measurable productivity. See, for example, the emphasis on service delivery in Teahon 1997; *Administration*, 1995.
7. Pádraig Yeates, *Irish Times*, 8 February 2000.
8. Interview with Paddy Teahon, former Secretary-General, Department of the Taoiseach and chair of NESC.
9. ICTU estimate, cited in *Irish Times*, 22 October 1999.
10. The Association of Secondary Teachers of Ireland (ASTI) withdrew from ICTU before negotiation of the PPF, and submitted a claim for a 30 per cent pay increase, well outside the parameters of the social partnership pay terms. However government stood firm concerning the need to negotiate within recognised procedures.
11. See *Irish Times*, 5 November 1999.
12. See, for example, ICTU policy documents *New Forms of Work Organization* (1997), *Profit Sharing Guidelines for Employee Share Ownership* (April 1999), *Challenges Facing Unions and Irish Society in the New Millennium* (June 1999).
13. See *Irish Times*, 5 November 1999.
14. In fact, budgetary tax cuts have been far more extensive and have significantly exceeded the levels promised in the agreements. For example, cumulative cuts in personal and corporation income tax between 1997 and 1999 amounted to £1,730, or 73 per cent more than the amount pledged under the terms of Partnership 2000 (OECD 1999: 95). By the termination of that agreement, total tax cuts were estimated to have come to some £3 billion (Pádraig Yeates, *Irish Times*, 4 October 1999).

References

Administration (1995) Special issue on 'Strategic management in the Irish civil service', 43(2), Summer.

Atkinson, A.B. (1997) 'Poverty in Ireland and anti-poverty strategy: a European perspective', in Alan Gray (ed.), *International Perspectives on the Irish Economy* (Dublin: Indecon).

Aust, Anders (1999) 'The "Celtic Tiger" and its beneficiaries: "competitive corporatism" in Ireland', ECPR Joint Sessions, Mannheim, March.

Barrett, A., Callan, Tim and Nolan, Brian (1997) *The Earnings Distribution and Returns to Education in Ireland 1987–1994*, working paper no. 85 (Dublin: ESRI).

Barrett, Anthony, Callan, Tim and Nolan, Brian (1999) 'Rising wage inequality, returns to education and labour market institutions: evidence from Ireland', *British Journal of Industrial Relations*, 37(1): 77–100.

Barry, Frank (1991) 'The Irish recovery 1987–90: an economic miracle?', *Irish Banking Review*, pp. 23–40.
Barry, Frank (ed.) (1999) *Understanding Ireland's Economic Growth* (Basingstoke: Macmillan).
Barry, Frank, Hannan, Aoife and Strobl, Eric A. (1999) 'The real convergence of the Irish economy and the sectoral distribution of employment growth', in Barry (1999).
Cahill, Noel and O'Toole, Francis (1998) 'Taxation policy', in Healy, Seán and Reynolds, Brigid (eds), *Social Policy in Ireland* (Dublin: Oak Tree Press).
Callan, Tim, Nolan, Brian, Walsh, John and Nestor, Richard (1999) 'Income tax and social welfare policies', in *Budget Perspectives*, ESRI Conference, 27 September.
Dore, Ronald (1994) 'Introduction: incomes policy: why now?', in Dore, Ronald, Boyer, Robert and Mars, Zoe (eds), *The Return to Incomes Policy* (London: Pinter).
Duffy, David (1999) 'Budget 2000: a macroeconomic perspective', in *Budget Perspectives*, ESRI Conference, 27 September.
Durkan, Joe (1999) 'The role of budgetary policy in social consensus', in *Budget Perspectives*, ESRI Conference, 27 September.
Fitzgerald, John (1999) 'Wage formation and the labour market', in Barry (1999).
Frieden, Jeffry (1995) 'Labor and the politics of exchange rates: the case of the European Monetary Union', in Sanford Jacoby (ed.), *The Workers of Nations: Industrial Relations in a Global Economy* (New York: Oxford University Press).
Geary, John (1999) *Multinationals and Human Resource Practices in Ireland* (Dublin: University College Dublin, Centre for Employment Relations and Organizational Performance).
Gunnigle, Patrick and Roche, William K. (1995) 'Competition and the new industrial relations agenda', in Patrick Gunnigle and W.K. Roche (eds), *New Challenges to Industrial Relations* (Dublin: Oak Tree Press).
Hardiman, Niamh (1988) *Pay, Politics and Economic Policy in Ireland* (Oxford: Clarendon Press).
Hardiman, Niamh (1992) 'The state and economic interests', in J.H. Goldthorpe and C.T. Whelan (eds), *The Development of Industrial Society in Ireland* (Oxford: Clarendon Press).
Hardiman, Niamh (1998) 'Inequality and the representation of interests', in W. Crotty and D. Schmitt (eds), *Ireland and the Politics of Change* (Harlow: Addison, Wesley, Longman).
Hardiman, Niamh (2000) 'Social partnership, wage bargaining, and growth', in Nolan, B., O'Connell, P.J. and Whelan, C.T. (eds), *Bust to Boom? The Irish Experience of Growth and Inequality* (Dublin: IPA/ESRI).
Hardiman, Niamh (2000b) 'Taxing the poor', *Policy Studies Journal*, vol. 28, no. 4, 779–894.
Honohan, Patrick (1999) 'Fiscal adjustment and disinflation in Ireland: setting the macro basis of economic recovery and expansion', in Barry (1999).
Kitschelt, Herbert, Lange, Peter, Marks, Gary and Stephens, John D. (1999) *Continuity and Change in Contemporary Capitalism* (Cambridge: Cambridge University Press).
Layte, Richard, Nolan, Brian and Whelan, Christopher T. (2000) 'Trends in poverty', in Nolan, B., O'Connell, P.J. and Whelan, C.T. (eds), *Bust to Boom?: The Irish Experience of Growth and Inequality* (Dublin: IPA/ESRI).
Lee, J.J. (1989) *Ireland 1912–1985: Politics and Society* (Cambridge: Cambridge University Press).
Lehmbruch, Gerhard (1984) 'Concertation and the structure of corporatist networks', in Goldthorpe, J.H. (ed.), *Order and Conflict in Contemporary Capitalism* (Oxford: Oxford University Press).
MacSharry, Ray and White, Pádraic (2000) *The Making of the Celtic Tiger: the Inside Story of Ireland's Boom Economy* (Cork: Mercier Press).
McCarthy, Dermot (1999) 'Building a partnership', Dept of the Taoiseach.

NESC (1986) *A Strategy for Development 1986–1990*, Report No. 83, Dublin.
NESC (1990) *A Strategy for the Nineties: Economic Stability and Structural Change*, Report No. 89, Dublin.
NESC (1993) *A Strategy for Competitiveness, Growth, and Employment*, Report No. 96, Dublin.
NESC (1996) *Strategy Into the 21st Century*, Report No. 99, Dublin.
NESC (1999) *Opportunities, Challenges, and Capacities for Choice*, Report No. 105, Dublin.
Nolan, Brian, O'Connell, Philip J. and Whelan, Christopher T. (eds) (2000) *Bust to Boom?: the Irish Experience of Growth and Inequality* (Dublin: Institute of Public Administration).
O'Donnell, Rory (1998) *Ireland's Economic Transformation: Industrial Policy, European Integration and Social Partnership*, working paper no. 2 (Pittsburgh: Center for West European Studies, University of Pittsburgh).
O'Donnell, Rory and Thomas, Damian (1998) 'Partnership and policy-making', in Healy, Seán and Reynolds, Brigid (eds), *Social Policy in Ireland* (Dublin: Oak Tree Press).
Ó Gráda, Cormac (1997) *A Rocky Road: the Irish Economy Since the 1920s* (Manchester: Manchester University Press).
Ó Riain, Seán (1999) 'The flexible developmental state: globalization, information technology and the "Celtic Tiger"', unpublished MS, Dept of Sociology, University of California-Davis.
Ó Riain, Seán and O'Connell, Philip J. (2000) 'The role of the state in growth and welfare', in Nolan, B., O'Connell, P.J. and Whelan, C.T. (eds), *Bust to Boom?: The Irish Experience of Growth and Inequality* (Dublin: IPA/ESRI).
O'Toole, Francis (1993/94) 'Tax reform since the Commission on Taxation', *Journal of the Statistical and Social Inquiry Society of Ireland*, xxvii, Part 1, pp. 85–123.
OECD (1998) *Economic Outlook*, June, Paris.
OECD (1999) *Economic Survey: Ireland*, Paris.
Pérez, Sofia (1999) *The Resurgence of National Social Bargaining in Europe: Explaining the Italian and Spanish Experiences*, working paper 1999/130 (Madrid: Juan March Institute).
Prondzynski, Ferdinand von (1997) 'Ireland: corporatism revived', in Anthony Ferner and Richard Hyman (eds), *Changing Industrial Relations in Europe*, 2nd edn (Oxford: Blackwell).
Regini, Marino (1998) *Between De-Regulation and Social Pacts: the Responses of European Economies to Globalization*, working paper no. 1999/133 (Madrid: Juan March Institute).
Rhodes, Martin (1998) 'Globalization, labour markets and welfare states: a future of "competitive corporatism"?', in Rhodes, Martin and Mény, Yves (eds), *The Future of European Welfare: A New Social Contract?* (London: Sage).
Roche, William K. (1997) 'Pay determination and the politics of industrial relations', in Murphy, Tom and Roche, W.K. (eds), *Irish Industrial Relations in Practice*, 2nd edn (Dublin: Oak Tree Press).
Roche, William K. (1998) 'Public service reform and human resource management', *Administration*, 46(2), Summer, 3–24.
Roche, William K. and Geary, John (1998) *'Collaborative production' and the Irish Boom: Work Organization, Partnership and Direct Involvement in Irish Workplaces*, working paper no. 26 (Dublin: University College Dublin, Graduate School of Business).
Ruane, Frances and O'Toole, Francis (1995) 'Taxation measures and policy', in J.W. O'Hagan (ed.), *The Economy of Ireland* (Dublin: Gill and Macmillan).
Sandford, Cedric (1993) *Successful Tax Reform* (Bath: Fiscal Publications).
Sexton, J.J. and O'Connell, Philip J. (eds) (1996) *Labour Market Studies: Ireland* (Luxembourg: European Commission).

Sexton, J.J., Nolan, Brian and McCormick, B. (1999) 'A review of earnings trends in the Irish economy since 1987', *Quarterly Economic Commentary*, ESRI, December.
Sheehan, Brian (1996) *Crisis, Strategic Revaluation and the Re-emergence of Tripartism in Ireland*, unpublished thesis (Dublin: University College Dublin, Graduate Business School).
Soskice, David (1990) 'Wage determination: the changing role of institutions in advanced industrial countries', *Oxford Review of Economic Policy*, 6, pp. 36–61.
Soskice, David (1999) 'Divergent production regimes: coordinated and uncoordinated market economies in the 1980s and 1990s', in Kitschelt *et al.* (1999).
Steinmo, Sven (1993) *Taxation and Democracy* (New Haven, CT: Yale University Press).
Tansey, Paul (1998) *Ireland at Work: Economic Growth and the Labour Market, 1987–1997* (Dublin: Oak Tree Press).
Teague, Paul (1995) 'Pay determination in the Republic of Ireland: towards social corporatism?', *British Journal of Industrial Relations*, 33(2), pp. 253–73.
Teahon, Paddy (1997) 'The Irish political and policy-making system and the current programme of change', *Administration*, 45(4), pp. 49–58.
Visser, Jelle and Hemerijck, Anton (1997) *'A Dutch Miracle': Job Growth, Welfare Reform and Corporatism in the Netherlands* (Amsterdam: Amsterdam University Press).

Chapter 12

Ireland on the world stage: conclusions and challenges

David E. Schmitt

The processes of globalisation and internationalisation have produced profound change in Ireland since the 1950s. This transformation, however, was also created by the conscious decision of Irish political and other leaders to aggressively pursue an international strategy of modernisation and economic growth. Entering the then EEC (today the EU) as one of the less economically advanced states, Ireland today has the reputation as a Celtic Tiger because of the rapid growth of its economy in the 1990s. Reforms in education and the successful quest to attract foreign investment have increased job opportunities and dramatically improved the standard of living for Irish citizens. Participation in the EU has moved Ireland from economic dependence on Britain to a relationship of interdependency. Indeed, in one scholar's view, '. . . Europe symbolizes the end of empire and, therefore, the obsolescence of the ancient English-Irish quarrel' (Garvin 2000: 43). The impact of international media and participation in the EU has produced important cultural change. Although the Irish continue to participate in religion at much higher levels than other modern nations, there has been a significant degree of secularisation. Women have acquired a greater voice in Irish life and more access to jobs (Galligan 1998a). In brief, while retaining some aspects of its traditional culture, Ireland has become a modern nation.

The conflict in Northern Ireland has also been heavily affected by globalisation. Many of these changes have improved the prospects for peace. Of course, the final outcome of the ongoing, evolutionary peace process is uncertain, but the successes thus far are due in large measure to international cooperation and developments within the international system.

Referring mainly to the chapters in this book, this chapter will provide an overview of Ireland on the world stage and offer a few additional observations. Ongoing risks and challenges will be considered in the final section of the chapter.

The foreign policy establishment

The Irish government is the principal leader in Ireland's relations with the world community. Although its freedom of action has been progressively constrained by membership in the EU, the Irish government has implemented major reforms, overcome the errors of earlier fiscal policy decisions and ushered in the rapid economic growth of the 1990s. Even though its manoeuvring room has been reduced in such areas as tax benefits for direct foreign investment and certainly monetary policy, the government nevertheless has the crucial task of promoting and protecting Ireland's interests within the EU. It has substantial latitude in educational policy, the development of infrastructure and many other areas that help determine Ireland's economic success and social stability, although EU bodies monitor these areas for such purposes as determining the adequacy of Ireland's use of EU structural and social funds.

As Ben Tonra (Chapter 2) pointed out, several different government entities have an important role in the development of Ireland's foreign policy. The Taoiseach (Prime Minister) and Cabinet have ultimate responsibility for all decisions and policies, but several departments and government entities also play an important role. The Department of Finance has both a direct and indirect impact upon foreign policy, through, for instance, its input into the EU budget as well as its role in helping to determine such matters as the number of overseas missions. Indeed, either the Department of Finance or the Cabinet must authorise the funding of any foreign policy proposal.

Other departments also have an important role in the development of foreign policy. The Department of Justice, Equality and Law Reform, the Department of Enterprise, Trade and Employment and the Department of Agriculture and Food all deal with significant aspects of foreign policy in their respective areas. Among the Department of the Taoiseach's important roles is providing leadership on the Northern Ireland issue and dealing with Ireland's role in the European Council. As Tonra emphasised, a co-ordinating body such as the US National Security Council does not exist in Ireland, with foreign policy being developed on a more *ad hoc* basis. On the other hand, he notes that this may be the result of the relatively small size of the Irish administration and the personal connections that form a constructive basis for more informal avenues of co-ordination. Decisions can be made more expeditiously and negotiations more effectively co-ordinated (Cullen 2000: 47).

The Minister of Foreign Affairs is the most important cabinet member on external relations and has overall responsibility for the co-ordination of foreign affairs policy; issues relating to the EU are an especially important area requiring the Minister's attention. Many of the policies dealt with by the Minister of Foreign Affairs have direct implications for domestic policy; this is obviously the case, for example, regarding EU policy and regulations. The Department of Foreign Affairs has grown in both size and function as the result of Ireland's involvement in the EU and plays an important role in a broad range of foreign policy issues. The important Anglo-Irish division is concerned mostly with the Northern Ireland issue, and Political, Economic and other divisions also play important roles. The Human Rights Unit established in 1997 reflects the growing importance of NGOs in the development of policy in this area. It should be noted that Former Irish President Mary Robinson took a strong interest in human rights issues and became United Nations High Commissioner for Human Rights.

As Eunan O'Halpin's contribution (Chapter 9) demonstrated, the internationalisation of Ireland's military and police functions has brought important changes and challenges. The development of an EU CFSP has compelled Irish leaders to reconsider Ireland's traditional policy of neutrality. Traditionally the Republic has been a good world citizen in providing peacekeeping forces under UN auspices in a number of the world's hot spots, providing over 42,000 troops for these missions since 1958 (Brown 1999: 164). Under the CFSP the EU is developing an independent capacity for the use of military force. In addition to humanitarian, rescue and peacekeeping functions, the EU has committed itself to having an effective capability for the use of military force in crisis-management operations. Participation by member states in EU military operations will be voluntary, and the Irish government has emphasised that it will make sovereign, independent decisions about participation. Also, the Irish government is committed to maintaining a policy of neutrality, an orientation necessitated by public sentiment, active NGO lobbying and the attitudes of many politicians themselves. Yet the clear movement toward greater involvement by Irish military forces is indicated by the decision of the Irish government to join the Partnership for Peace in 1999, however reluctant and delayed this decision might have been. Also instructive is the decision to send a detachment of special-forces Rangers to East Timor to monitor and prevent infiltration by insurgents from West Timor.

The Irish economy in international perspective

The stellar performance of the Irish economy in the 1990s was the product of wise policy decisions begun in the 1960s. As John Bradley (Chapter 3) pointed out, the Irish government responded positively to the changes in the international economic order such as the liberalisation of world trade and less expensive transportation and telecommunications. A more interdependent international economy provided more opportunities for growth and modernisation. The effort to seek direct foreign investment, to join the EEC and to reform education were major factors contributing to Ireland's impressive successes. But there were considerable costs resulting from the quest for growth and modernisation. Ireland in the 1980s had one of the worst-performing economies in Europe. Adaptation to a single market proved to be a painful process for traditional Irish businesses with the collapse of some traditional firms leading to high unemployment. Government overspending and misjudgements contributed to inflation and other difficulties. Indeed, one scholar analysing Ireland's handling of European integration observes that '. . . the severe difficulties experienced in the first fifteen years of membership should be seen as, in large part, a failure to adjust to the demands of internationalization and European integration' (O'Donnell 2000: 209).

Yet over the long term growth-oriented policies had a powerful effect. Aggressive and imaginative plans to encourage DFI netted Ireland massive growth in the foreign-owned component of its economy. Much of this investment, especially from the United States, was in high technology areas and produced many residual benefits such as the introduction of modern and more efficient business and management practices. John Fitz Gerald (Chapter 4) noted that American investment was particularly important, accounting in 1997 for one quarter of Irish employment in manufacturing, with other foreign firms accounting for an additional quarter. The zero-level tax (later raised to a modest 10 per cent under EU pressure) on exported manufactured products gave a substantial incentive to multinational corporations deciding where to invest. As Bradley (Chapter 3) pointed out more than two-thirds of gross manufacturing output and approximately 50 per cent of employment in manufacturing is accounted for by the foreign sector of the Irish economy. Irish employees of these international firms often were promoted into positions abroad and returned as managers with top-level skills.

One of the most important strategies of government was the social partnership endeavour. Essentially this involved a government-sponsored effort for responsible wage agreements between business and labour. A series of national pay agreements helped produce employment growth and higher living standards rather than a wage-driven inflationary spiral. These agreements created a stable and attractive environment for international investors. Of course, a favourable international economic climate contributed to the rapid growth and the success of these strategies as well.

Fitz Gerald (Chapter 4) documented the importance of demographics in accounting for Ireland's successes. Most fundamental has been the reversal of Ireland's historically high levels of emigration. Although some of Ireland's best-trained people emigrate, the majority today are 'homing pigeons' who return with valuable skills learned abroad. Additionally, as Fitz Gerald pointed out, the decline in birth rate after 1980 combined with returning immigrants means a higher percentage of the population in the workforce; Ireland's formerly high economic dependency ratio has thus dropped to the EU average. Immigrants from abroad are an increasingly important component of the Irish economy. They are often highly qualified, and well-educated immigrants from continental EU countries typically have excellent command of the English language as well as skills well suited to Ireland's high-tech economy.

Membership in the EU has been central to Ireland's economic success. In addition to the benefits of belonging to a single market, development funding from the EU has had a dramatic impact on Ireland's growth rates. Structural Funds were intended in part to assist the peripheral, less advanced economies of Ireland, Greece, Spain and Portugal to adjust to a single market and assist in the development of greater competitiveness. The EU's CAP of price supports was also of great benefit to the economy and to the incomes of farmers. As Brigid Laffan (Chapter 5) noted this was an important improvement over the cheap food prices of the United Kingdom. Indeed, in this and other important ways the EU has dramatically reduced Irish dependency upon Britain. The impact of the EU as well as other forces contributing to Ireland's rapid economic growth and creation of jobs has filtered down to employees through increased real wages and an improved living standard. Bradley (Chapter 3) noted that compared to the European average in living standards of 100, Ireland began at 64 in 1986 and has today reached the level of 111, a performance far better than the other peripheral countries.

The EU and Europeanisation

As a small state economically dependent on Britain, Ireland had little flexibility. Its economic destiny was tied to a large neighbour who maintained relatively low prices on agricultural products. Like all of the small states of Europe Ireland was concerned that lack of self-restraint by the larger powers could lead to instability or war. It also feared that these bigger states could attempt to maximise their own economic advantage at the expense of the smaller states. Certainly much of the violent history of the 20th century in Europe has been the product of rampant nationalism and unrestrained self-seeking by large powers. Ireland does not typically vote in Council together with the other small states or take identical policy positions. Yet it does make common cause with these countries in the matter of institutional reform and methods of representation.

The advantages for small states of an integrated economic and political framework are clear. The cooperative, consensual nature of the decision process serves as a significant restraint on potential excesses by large powers. Furthermore, by having a structured input into the decision process, smaller countries such as Ireland can be sure they will have a voice even though, as in Ireland's case, they may have to choose their issues very carefully. Ireland has been especially effective for a small state partly due to the skill of Irish politicians and administrators in networking and building support, although this personal style may become less of an advantage as the EU becomes more institutionalised (Laffan and O'Donnell 1998: 177).

The European Parliament has provided a forum in which Irish politicians could interact and build support with members from other countries. Arguments by the Republic in favour of minority rights and reform in Northern Ireland have received a sympathetic hearing in this and other institutions of the EU, partly because all members have an interest in stemming ethnic violence. The European Court of Justice constitutes a real constitutional framework in its ability to limit and regulate the behaviour of national governments. Illustrating the point that EU institutions and regulations have significantly affected the institutions and processes of Irish government is the role of Irish courts in interpreting EU law and seeking advice from the European Court of Justice. In areas where EU law operates it is supreme over domestic legislation and constitutional provisions, and domestic courts are obligated to apply EU law. In effect national judges become Community judges (Barrington 1999: 36–8).

Public support in Ireland for the EU is very high. According to survey data cited by Laffan, over 80 per cent of respondents believe that Ireland has benefited from membership. Even with a declining percentage of the Irish electorate voting favourably on treaty issues, support for further integration has been quite solid. The overwhelming majority of Irish citizens believe that the European connection has been good for Ireland. For Irish political leaders the importance of European partnership goes beyond economic gain:

> Ireland's membership of the Union has always been about more than free trade and financial transfers, important as these may be. The period of our membership in the

> Union has coincided with an increase in national self-confidence, a strengthening of our identity and an increase in our international profile. (Government White Paper 1996: 3.11)

Northern Ireland in international perspective

The enormous progress toward resolving the Northern Ireland conflict represented by the Good Friday Agreement of 1998 is in large part the result of the changing nature of the international system. To be sure, prospects for the future are uncertain and, as Joseph Ruane and Jennifer Todd (Chapter 7) pointed out, the processes of globalisation have produced contradictory pressures. Changes in the international system have assisted the peace process in many ways but may also have increased the sense of communal identity and allowed political leaders to use widely accepted concepts such as democracy and pluralism to their own advantage.

Nevertheless, it can be argued that on balance international change has been a critical factor in producing the extraordinary compromises and concessions that led to the Good Friday Agreement and the establishment of the Northern Ireland Assembly and new international structures. Major world events have been a key part of this process. As Adrian Guelke (Chapter 8) pointed out, the end of the Cold War enabled the British government to credibly claim it no longer had a strategic interest in Northern Ireland and contributed to Sinn Féin and the IRA reconsidering their positions. The settlement of the South African conflict meant that the republican movement could no longer compare itself to the ANC as a means of gaining legitimacy for the armed struggle against the British government. Similarly, the 1993 agreement between Israel and the PLO removed another source of legitimacy for the armed struggle. Guelke also noted that plans for the devolution of power to Scotland provided a vehicle for the development of the British–Irish Council.

The European Court of Human Rights has heard cases by individuals brought against the British government. The European Convention on Human Rights was also important in shaping the Good Friday Agreement and has been an important moral force in shaping ideas. NGOs also played a role in pressuring the British government to make reforms. Amnesty International and Human Rights Watch, for example, publicised violations of human rights to an international audience.

The EU has been a central force that has encouraged the peace process in many ways. The British and Irish governments have worked as close and friendly collaborators on many different policy issues, and each government has given up significant aspects of its sovereignty as a member of the Union. This collegiality helped overcome differences between them and led to a successful cooperative effort to create a conducive environment for compromise by the contending parties. The Republic of Ireland was given an important voice in the affairs of Northern Ireland by the Anglo-Irish Agreement of 1985, and had a key role in bringing about the Good Friday Agreement.

The EU itself was a model for international cooperation crossing the traditional lines of national sovereignty. Two innovative institutions established by the Good

Friday Agreement were the North/South Ministerial Council, which constituted an important concession to nationalist sentiment, and the British–Irish Council, which included representatives of the British and Irish governments as well as representatives from the devolved political institutions of Scotland, Wales and Northern Ireland (Good Friday Agreement, Strand Three). This latter institution was, of course, an important concession for the unionist community.

Political support and generous funding from the EU aided economic and social development and were important also from the standpoint of psychological pressure and support for the contending parties. The border between the Republic and Northern Ireland has grown progressively less important politically, economically and socially as a result of British and Irish membership in the EU. Common policies, the single market and political partnership have diminished the significance of the divide between the two regions in many ways.

Globalisation has also had a significant impact upon the dispersal of ideas and principles that created a more supportive climate for the peace process. Although some concepts have been adopted by the contending parties for their own political agenda, other ideas such as civil, minority and human rights have gained wide international acceptance and have been part of the moral suasion that has contributed to compromise. As Guelke (Chapter 8) explained the principle of consent has also been important in eliciting the cooperation of the republican movement (which was committed to a campaign of violence to end British rule). The consent principle states that Ireland can be unified only by majority vote and cannot be unified without such support. As the percentage of Catholics in Northern Ireland continues to grow, there is a potential at some future date for a vote in favour of unification, and of course the British government is committed to honouring such an outcome. For many reasons such a vote appears rather unlikely in the foreseeable future, but the potential gives hope to nationalists and republicans seeking unification.

International mediation has become a much more accepted and common form of conflict resolution within the international community and has played a crucial role in the Northern Ireland peace process. Of particular importance has been the role of the United States. Richard Finnegan (Chapter 6) explained how many in the large Irish American community as well as Irish–American politicians initially supported the radical republican nationalists in Northern Ireland. Key legislators such as Senator Ted Kennedy and Speaker Thomas P. O'Neill, however, were persuaded by Irish politicians to adopt the position of moderate Irish nationalism, which supported human rights and reform within Northern Ireland. Many components of the American political and administrative systems have been involved in the conflict. The courts and the FBI have played an important enforcement role in dealing with such matters as arms smuggling. State and local governments passed various resolutions they viewed as supporting the Catholic minority of Northern Ireland. Congress has passed aid legislation, and American presidents have been involved on several occasions. Clearly it has been President Clinton who has been most active in the peace process, placing Northern Ireland high on his list of key foreign policy issues. Among his most important actions was the decision to allow the leader of Sinn Féin, Gerry Adams, into the United States over the strong protests of the British government. This helped legitimise the newly moderate approach of the Sinn Féin leadership and gave support to Adams in his struggle with party and IRA militants. President Clinton also travelled to Northern Ireland to lend support to the ratification of the peace accord and promised American aid to Northern Ireland. He also lobbied political leaders by telephone in order to encourage support for the GFA. US Senator George Mitchell also played an instrumental role as a mediator. It should be added that Canada, Finland and South Africa have also been contributors to the peace effort.

In sum, globalisation and international institutions and actors have played a vital role in bringing about the Good Friday Agreement and the progress thus far in resolving the Northern Ireland problem. As Ruane and Todd (Chapter 7) emphasised, however, globalisation has produced contradictory effects. Community identity may have grown more intense and political leaders have learned to use symbols such as pluralism and democracy for their own political ends. There is certainly no guarantee that the peace process will continue or that violent conflict might not re-emerge. Any successful outcome is likely to face obstacles and setbacks along the way. On balance, however, it seems clear that the forces of internationalisation have both directly and indirectly contributed substantially to the successes thus far.

Ireland and the Third World

Ireland has traditionally had a far greater impact upon the poorer regions of the world than its size would indicate. Historically, the religious orders played an important role in many ways such as providing health care and education. Today various NGOs give aid and assistance to the Third World. Although the religious community continues to play an important role in these endeavours, many secular organisations have become increasingly active and influential in recent years. Additionally, the Irish government's provision of aid to developing countries has been higher than most OECD countries as a percentage of gross national product (O'Neill 1998: 161).

Ireland has been a strong advocate of human rights. Liz O'Donnell, Minister of State for Foreign Affairs, is responsible for human rights issues and is an effective spokesperson. Within the Department of Foreign Affairs there is a Human Rights Unit and a joint DFA/NGO Standing Committee on Human Rights. Irish politicians and NGOs have been especially interested in human rights issues in Asia. Eilis Ward's analysis (Chapter 10) of the East Timor problem documented an important case of recent and strong activity in the cause of human rights. The East Timor Ireland Solidarity Campaign was a highly effective NGO that generated interest among politicians and brought key speakers from East Timor to Ireland. Already mentioned was the decision by the Irish government to send a Ranger unit to East Timor. Irish politicians were not successful in seeking a strong common East Timor policy by the EU, which tends to be cautious on sensitive international issues. Nevertheless, it is fair to say that Ireland has had a positive impact not only on this issue but also on other important areas of humanitarian concern in the Third World.

Yet civil liberties groups, Church leaders, trade unions, opposition parties and others have heavily criticised Irish government for its recent restrictive policies on refugees and those seeking asylum. The government's concern, like that of many of its EU partners, is that easy amnesty and excessively liberal policies concerning asylum and immigration will create serious social problems and financial pressures. In this area, Ireland is struggling to find a balance between the need all countries have for immigration controls and the historic international humanitarian outreach for which Ireland has been rightly praised.

The impact of internationalisation on culture and identity

Through the mass media, travel and other forms of international communication Ireland has had great exposure to the ideas and values of the modern world. This has had a powerful effect on Irish culture. Already noted was the decline in the authority of the Catholic Church. Modern ideas on women's rights, premarital sex, birth control and even abortion have penetrated Ireland and resulted in less restrictive policies. Many see the liberalisation of attitudes regarding sex, marriage and related subjects as an indication of greater freedom. Yet many other Irish citizens with more traditional values see these changes not as progress but rather as decline (Fahey 1998). From this perspective modern values have contributed to the breakdown of the family and an increase in non-marital births, among other things. The international media have thus contributed to some of Ireland's most contentious political conflicts such as the fight over constitutional amendments on divorce and abortion.

Television, film, music and other aspects of popular culture are mostly dominated by Anglo-American media; the cultural impact of the media from continental EU states has been much less pronounced (Ryan 2000: 61). Nevertheless, many aspects of EU membership contribute to a modification of Irish culture and identity. Tom Garvin cites, for example, the importance of large numbers of third-level students studying in countries of the EU (Garvin 2000: 41).

Although Irish citizens have strong national identity, as noted above survey data demonstrates that Irish men and women support European integration and overwhelmingly believe that membership in the EU has been good for Ireland. While one of the hopes of advocates of European integration was to reduce nationalism in its negative forms, the encouragement of support for a wider Europe has not resulted in efforts by the EU to weaken national cultures. EU policy, however, has had the effect of challenging some traditional values such as limited career options for women. But the institutions of the EU such as the Court of Justice appear to be especially sensitive to issues of national culture (O'Higgins 1999: 107).

Administrators, politicians and others who regularly participate in the affairs of the European Union inevitably internalise their experiences, adding a European dimension to their Irish national identity. The White Paper on Foreign Policy states that 'Irish people increasingly see the European Union not simply as an organization to which Ireland belongs, but as an integral part of our future. We see ourselves increasingly as Europeans' (Government White Paper 1996: 3.8).

Implications for Irish democracy

Membership in the EU presents many challenges for the operation of Irish democracy. Ireland has given up substantial sovereignty in order to participate in the shared sovereignty of the EU, although as a small state the trade-off in benefits and influence has been well worth the sacrifice. The Irish Oireachtas (parliament) plays comparatively little role in the development of foreign policy, although the establishment of the Joint Committee on Foreign Affairs provided a potential structure for involvement. In practice this committee has met with only modest success due to such problems as limited resources. As Tonra (Chapter 2) noted, the political parties play an important and largely supportive role in the foreign policy process. Differences between the parties are usually not great, especially on EU matters, but there are differences of emphasis and style (Rees 1998: 136–7). NGOs have grown in number and significance with many having substantial access to the policy process. Although this implies greater inclusiveness, it must be noted that the NGOs themselves are not heavily constrained by democratic controls. The desire of foreign policy-makers for greater public input confronts a number of challenges including the remoteness and complexity of many foreign policy issues. It is fair to say that there has been some democratisation of the foreign policy process, especially in a structural and consultative sense; yet the nature of foreign policy issues makes them appear less important to citizens who might see specific domestic issues as more relevant to their interests (Keatinge 1998: 35–6).

From a social perspective membership in the EU has helped bring benefits to sectors of Irish society that previously had much less opportunity. Women in particular have experienced increased opportunities partly due to EU mandates (Galligan 1998b). As Niamh Hardiman (Chapter 11) pointed out, however, the government's quest for DFI has probably contributed to more modest levels of redistribution through taxation and social programmes, as the overriding goal is to attract and please foreign investors. Despite the attempt in recent social partnership negotiations to include more social groups and NGOs, Irish governments have been influenced in their policy decisions mainly by electoral politics. The comparatively greater electoral clout of the more privileged members of society means that government is less likely to engage in significant schemes of redistribution. With respect to industrial democracy, Hardiman also observed that workplace participation tends to be less significant than in other European systems.

For Northern Ireland the most fundamental point regarding internationalisation and democratic control has been the great opportunity for reform and compromise created by changes in the international environment. European integration was particularly important in reducing the significance of the border between North and South, in providing a model of shared sovereignty, and in producing a cooperative attitude between the leaders of the United Kingdom and the Republic of Ireland. Despite differing viewpoints and constituencies these European partners created an environment where bitter rivals and enemies could negotiate and ultimately ratify the Good Friday Agreement, which has at least the potential over time of creating orderly and representative politics in the North.

The experience gained through international mediation efforts around the world has also contributed to a rich store of techniques and personalities that can be a positive force for conflict resolution. The success of the British and Irish governments as well as international participants from the United States, Canada, Finland and South Africa, is partly due to the experience gained in other settings. In many ways, then, international influences have been a vital part of the endeavour to bring democracy and peace to Northern Ireland.

Conclusion

A central theme of this book has been the positive contribution of Ireland's international outreach to its economic, social and political progress. From the 1960s on government policy has been geared toward encouraging direct foreign investment, joining the EEC and providing necessary support for long-term economic growth and competitiveness. The decision to dramatically reform education was especially crucial. It is clear, however, that a number of mistakes were made during the early years and that sustained positive management of the modernisation process did not come about until the late 1980s and 1990s.

The success of the Irish economy has made it a model for states seeking their own economic take-offs, particularly the former communist states of central and eastern Europe. The citizens of Ireland have enjoyed dramatically increased standards of living and employment opportunities. Yet Ireland faces a number of challenges and risks for the future. Scandals concerning financial improprieties by political and corporate figures during the past decade not only undermine domestic trust but could also contribute to a less attractive environment for international business. Effective reform in this area could have positive implications for Ireland's international economic outreach. Resentment created by differentials between the highly paid and lower-salaried workers as well as tension over the advantages enjoyed by public sector workers make pay agreements more difficult to achieve. Labour instability and more rapid growth in wages would make Ireland less competitive. The EMU also presents challenges for the control of inflation since monetary policy is now out of the hands of Irish government.

As John Bradley (Chapter 3) noted technologically based industry has a rather narrow range so that a change in technologies could threaten these firms, and much of Ireland's economy is owned primarily by foreign companies. Global competition is increasing and multinational corporations rather than the governments of small countries determine where investments will be made and facilities shut down. Ireland must also cope effectively and democratically with the problem of immigration and asylum by people who are disadvantaged or refugees. Additionally, the increasing international involvement by the Irish military will continue to challenge policy-makers who are concerned that Ireland also maintain its traditional policy of neutrality.

In sum, Ireland has benefited greatly from the changes in the international environment, largely due to imaginative and effective national policies, but there are significant challenges and potential dangers. Many of the forces determining Ireland's future are beyond its control. Nevertheless, imaginative and effective policies can help the Republic of Ireland not only maximise the economic and social opportunities of globalisation but also enable it to build upon its historic role as a contributor to the betterment of the world community.

References

Barrington, D. (1999) 'The impact of the EU on the Irish constitution', in Dooge, J. and Barrington, R. (eds), *A Vital National Interest: Ireland in Europe 1973–1998* (Dublin: Institute of Public Administration).

Brown, T. (1999) 'Defence, peace-keeping and arms control', in Dooge, J. and Barrington, R. (eds), *A Vital National Interest: Ireland in Europe 1973–1998* (Dublin: Institute of Public Administration).

Cullen, M. (2000) 'Sharing sovereignty', in O'Donnell, R. (ed.), *Europe: the Irish Experience* (Dublin: Institute of European Affairs).

Fahey, T. (1998) 'Progress or decline: demographic change in political context', in Crotty, W. and Schmitt, D. (eds), *The Politics of Change* (London: Longman).

Galligan, Y. (1998a) 'The changing role of women', in Crotty, W. and Schmitt, D. (eds), *The Politics of Change* (London: Longman).

Galligan, Y. (1998b) *Women and Contemporary Politics in Ireland: from the Margins to the Mainstream* (London: Cassell).

Garvin, T. (2000) 'The French are on the sea', in O'Donnell, R. (ed.), *Europe: the Irish Experience* (Dublin: Institute of European Affairs).

Ireland (1996) *Challenges and Opportunities Abroad: White Paper on Foreign Policy* (Dublin: Government Publications).

Keatinge, P. (1998) 'Ireland and European security: continuity and change', *Irish Studies in International Affairs*, 9, pp. 31–8.

Laffan, B. and O'Donnell, R. (1998) 'Ireland and the growth of international governance', in Crotty, W. and Schmitt, D. (eds), *The Politics of Change* (London: Longman).

O'Donnell, R. (2000) 'The new Ireland in the new Europe', in O'Donnell, R. (ed.), *Europe: the Irish Experience* (Dublin: Institute of European Affairs).

O'Higgins, T. (1999) 'The court of justice', in Dooge, J. and Barrington, R. (eds), *A Vital National Interest: Ireland in Europe 1973–1998* (Dublin: Institute of Public Administration).

O'Neill, H. (1998) 'Ireland's foreign aid in 1997', *Irish Studies in International Affairs*, 9, pp. 161–78.

Rees, N. (1998) 'Ireland's foreign relations in 1997', *Irish Studies in International Affairs*, 9, pp. 135–60.

Ryan, L. (2000) 'Strengthening Irish identity through openness', in O'Donnell, R. (ed.), *Europe: the Irish Experience* (Dublin: Institute of European Affairs).

United Kingdom (1999) *The Agreement: Agreement Reached in the Multi-party Negotiations*, updated [Good Friday Agreement]. http://www.nio.gov.uk/agr_links.htm

Index

Note: The Republic of Ireland is referred to as Ireland in the text. This is reflected in the index.